TOKYO JAPAN
TRAVEL GUIDE 2024-2025

Insider Tips, Local Insights, Must-see Spots
and Memorable Experiences.

Evelyn Blair

TABLE OF CONTENTS

INTRODUCTION

Planning a trip to Tokyo, Japan, is like opening the door to a whole new world. As one of the most captivating cities in the world, Tokyo effortlessly blends the old with the new. You will find futuristic skyscrapers towering over ancient temples, world-class dining next to bustling street food stalls, and luxury shopping just a short walk from serene gardens and parks.

Tokyo can seem overwhelming at first, especially with its sheer size and the fast-paced nature of life here. But don't worry—this guide is packed with practical advice, insider tips, and recommendations to help you navigate the city like a seasoned traveler. Whether you're interested in exploring the historic districts, getting lost in the vibrant shopping areas, or experiencing Japan's rich cultural traditions, you'll find all the information you need to plan a smooth, enjoyable, and memorable trip.

One of the best things about Tokyo is how diverse it is, not just in terms of attractions, but also in its neighborhoods. Each district offers something different: Shibuya is famous for its iconic crossing and youth culture, while Asakusa takes you back in time with its traditional atmosphere and temples. Shinjuku is the place to go for nightlife and entertainment, while Ginza offers some of the best luxury shopping in the world. Akihabara will thrill anyone interested in electronics or anime, while Ueno is known for its beautiful parks and cultural landmarks. And these are just a few of the many areas you'll discover as you make your way around the city.

Understanding how to get around is key to making the most of your time in Tokyo. The city's public transportation system is extensive and can be confusing at first, but once you get the hang of it, you'll see how efficient and convenient it is. This guide will walk you through everything you need to know about using Tokyo's trains, subways, buses, and taxis so you can travel around the city without any stress. You'll also find tips on how to get from the airport to your hotel, as well as advice on different ways to explore Tokyo on foot or by bicycle, giving you the freedom to enjoy the city at your own pace.

Choosing where to stay is another important part of planning your Tokyo trip. With so many options available—from high-end hotels and traditional ryokans to budget hostels and capsule hotels—it can be tough to decide what's best for you. This guide will help you understand the different types of accommodations in Tokyo, what to expect in terms of price and comfort, and which neighborhoods are best depending on what you want to see and do. Whether you're looking for luxury, convenience, or a unique experience, this guide will help you find the perfect place to stay during your visit.

No trip to Tokyo would be complete without diving into the food scene, which is one of the most exciting parts of visiting Japan. From Michelin-starred restaurants to tiny ramen shops tucked away in narrow alleys, Tokyo is a paradise for food lovers. In this guide, you'll find recommendations on where to get the best sushi, ramen, tempura, and more, as well as tips on how to experience the city's vibrant street food culture. We'll also cover some must-try traditional dishes, give you an overview of the city's izakayas (Japanese pubs), and suggest places to eat for those with specific dietary preferences, such as vegetarians or vegans.

Of course, Tokyo isn't just about food, shopping, and sightseeing. It's a city with deep cultural roots, and this guide will help you get a sense of local customs and etiquette that will enhance your experience and help you connect with the people and the culture on a deeper level. Whether it's learning the correct way to bow, knowing how to behave at a shrine or temple, or understanding the do's and don'ts of Japanese dining etiquette, the cultural tips in this guide will make sure you feel confident and respectful during your stay.

Another aspect of Tokyo that makes it such a fascinating destination is its ability to offer both fast-paced excitement and peaceful relaxation. You can spend the morning exploring a busy market, the afternoon taking in breathtaking views from the top of a skyscraper, and end the day with a peaceful walk through a tranquil garden. For those interested in history and tradition, there are plenty of temples, shrines, and museums to explore. For travelers looking for fun and entertainment, Tokyo offers everything from theme parks to live music venues to vibrant nightlife. And for those who want a bit of both, Tokyo is the perfect place to experience it all.

This guide also includes information on day trips you can take from Tokyo if you're looking to explore beyond the city. From the iconic Mount Fuji to the peaceful hot springs of Hakone, there are many beautiful and interesting places just a short train ride away. These trips allow you to experience the natural beauty of Japan without straying too far from Tokyo.

Finally, safety and convenience are essential when traveling, and this guide has you covered with practical advice on how to stay safe, where to find help if needed, and what to do in case of an emergency. Tokyo is one of the safest cities in the world, but it's always a good idea to be prepared, especially when visiting a new place. You'll also find tips on health services, local laws, and other important information to ensure your trip is not only fun but also worry-free.

WHY YOU SHOULD VISIT TOKYO

Tokyo is a city that offers a mix of modern innovation and deep-rooted traditions, making it one of the most unique and fascinating places to visit as a tourist. There are many reasons why you should consider visiting Tokyo, especially if you're interested in experiencing a city that blends cutting-edge technology with ancient cultural practices. The range of activities, sights, and experiences in Tokyo is truly endless, and the city has something to offer every type of traveler.

One of the first reasons why Tokyo stands out as a top destination is its ability to cater to a wide variety of interests. Whether you're a history enthusiast, a foodie, a shopping fanatic, or someone who simply enjoys exploring new places, Tokyo has it all. For those who love history and culture, Tokyo is home to some of Japan's most significant temples and shrines, such as Senso-ji in Asakusa, Meiji Shrine in Harajuku, and Zojoji Temple near Tokyo Tower. Visiting these sites gives you a glimpse into Japan's rich cultural heritage, where you can learn about the country's deep respect for tradition, spirituality, and nature. The mix of ancient structures nestled within a modern urban environment is one of the many contrasts that make Tokyo so intriguing.

Food is another major reason to visit Tokyo. The city has one of the most diverse and exciting food scenes in the world. It's not just about sushi (though Tokyo is famous for having some of the best sushi restaurants on the planet); you can find a vast range of Japanese cuisine and international dishes here. From ramen and tempura to izakayas and high-end kaiseki meals, there's something for every budget and taste. Street food is also a big part of the Tokyo experience. You can enjoy snacks like takoyaki (octopus balls), taiyaki (fish-shaped cakes), and yakitori (grilled chicken skewers) from vendors scattered around the city. Beyond the traditional food, Tokyo is also home to many Michelin-starred restaurants, offering fine dining experiences that attract food lovers from around the world.

Another reason to visit Tokyo is the city's unique neighborhoods, each with its own personality and attractions. You could spend days just exploring the different districts, and each one would feel like a completely new adventure. For example, Shibuya is known for its lively atmosphere and iconic crossing, which is one of the busiest pedestrian intersections in the world. Shinjuku is a great place to experience Tokyo's nightlife, with countless bars, clubs, and entertainment options to choose from. If you're interested in fashion and youth culture, Harajuku is a must-see, where you'll find everything from trendy boutiques to quirky shops selling colorful clothing and accessories. Ginza is the luxury shopping district, offering high-end stores and world-class restaurants. Then there's Akihabara, the go-to place for fans of anime, manga, and electronics. Each neighborhood offers a different slice of Tokyo life, and exploring them will give you a well-rounded experience of the city.

The sheer scale and energy of Tokyo is another aspect that draws tourists from all over the world. The city is massive, and while that can feel overwhelming at first, it also means there's always something new to discover. From towering skyscrapers to peaceful parks, Tokyo offers an incredible variety of landscapes and experiences. You can walk through bustling shopping districts filled with neon lights and high-tech gadgets one minute, and then step into a quiet, tranquil garden like Shinjuku Gyoen or the Imperial Palace grounds the next. The contrast between the city's fast-paced energy and its calm, reflective spaces is part of what makes it such an interesting place to visit.

Tokyo is also a fantastic destination for anyone who enjoys shopping. Whether you're looking for the latest in fashion, cutting-edge technology, or traditional Japanese crafts, you'll find it in Tokyo. Major shopping areas like Shibuya, Shinjuku, and Ginza offer a mix of department stores, boutique shops, and specialty stores where you can find everything from high-end luxury goods to one-of-a-kind souvenirs. For a more traditional shopping experience, you can visit markets like Tsukiji Outer Market, where vendors sell fresh seafood, produce, and Japanese food items, or Ameya-Yokocho, a busy shopping street in Ueno where you can find a variety of products at bargain prices.

Tokyo's public transportation system is another reason why the city is such a great place to visit. The city is known for having one of the most efficient, clean, and punctual public transportation networks in the world. The trains and subways are easy to navigate, even for tourists, and they connect all the major parts of the city, making it convenient to get around.

Whether you're trying to get from the airport to your hotel, visit a major tourist attraction, or simply explore a new neighborhood, the public transportation system makes it easy and affordable. The Japan Rail (JR) lines, including the popular Yamanote Line, make it simple to travel between Tokyo's major districts, while the subway system provides access to even more parts of the city. Additionally, Tokyo is a very safe city, and many tourists feel comfortable traveling around on their own at any time of day or night.

In addition to the city itself, Tokyo is a gateway to many other fascinating destinations in Japan. You can take easy day trips from Tokyo to places like Mount Fuji, Hakone, Nikko, or Kamakura, where you can explore nature, hot springs, or even more temples and shrines. This makes Tokyo an ideal base for exploring both the modern and traditional sides of Japan. If you're looking for a more relaxed experience, you can escape the city's hustle and bustle by heading to nearby towns and countryside areas, where you can enjoy Japan's natural beauty and slower pace of life.

Tokyo also stands out because of its attention to detail in everything it offers. From the design of its buildings and public spaces to the presentation of its food and the quality of its service, Tokyo is a city that takes pride in doing things well. The hospitality here is exceptional, and you'll find that people go out of their way to be helpful, even if there's a language barrier. Whether you're staying in a hotel, eating in a restaurant, or simply asking for directions, you'll be impressed by the politeness, kindness, and professionalism of the people you meet.

All of these reasons, and many more, make Tokyo an incredibly rewarding destination for tourists. The city offers an endless variety of things to see, do, and experience, and it's easy to tailor your trip to your personal interests. Whether you're visiting for a week or a month, you'll find that there's always something new to explore, and each day will bring a different side of Tokyo to life. The combination of modernity, tradition, culture, and hospitality is what makes Tokyo such a special place, and it's why many people choose to visit the city again and again. For anyone looking for a travel experience that's exciting, diverse, and enriching, Tokyo is a destination that should be at the top of the list.

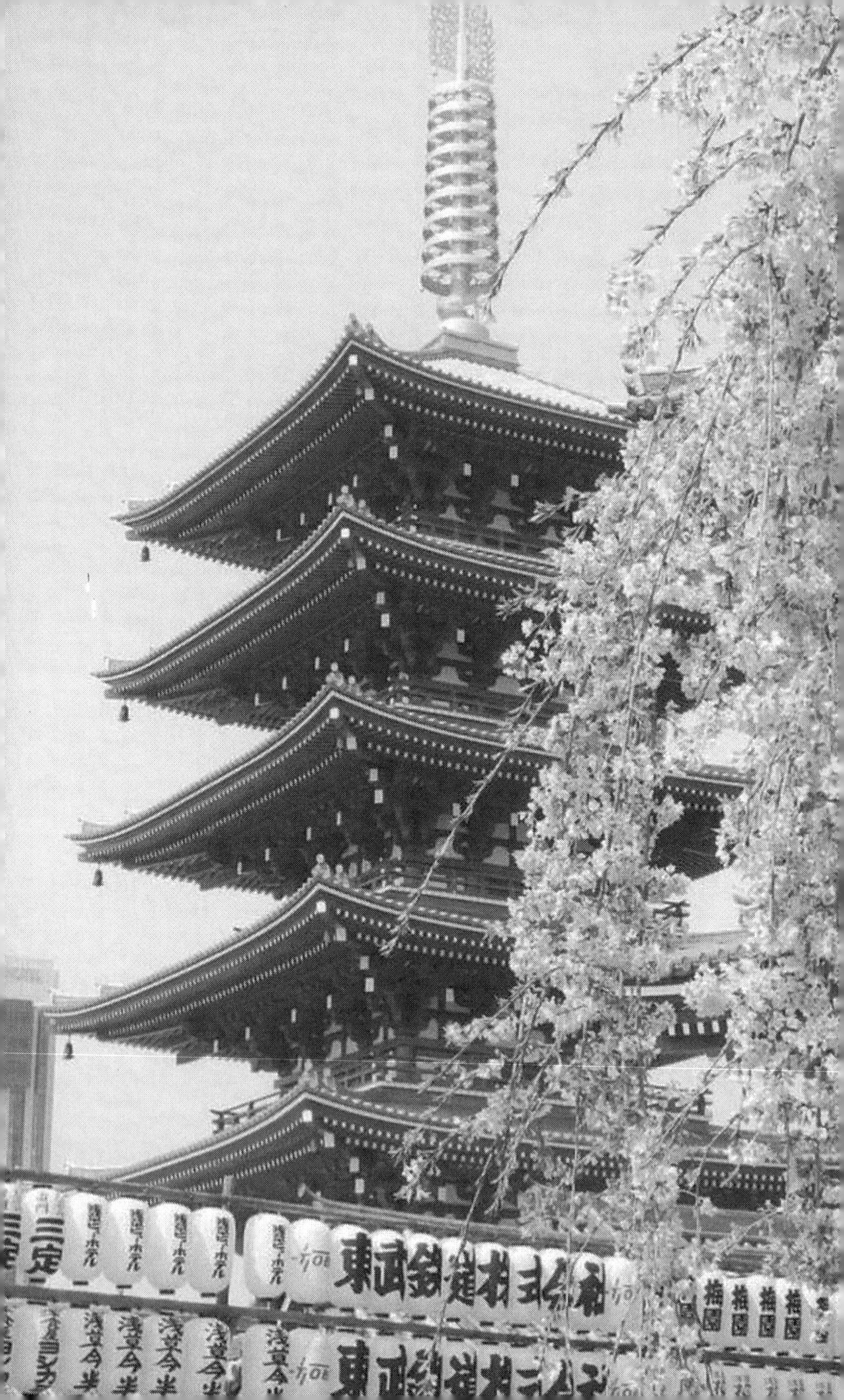
三定
東武鉄道株式会社
梅園
浅草今半

THE HISTORY OF TOKYO

Tokyo, the bustling capital of Japan, has a rich and fascinating history that spans hundreds of years. The story of Tokyo, which was once a small fishing village, is one of transformation, growth, and resilience.

The origins of Tokyo date back to the 12th century when it was known as Edo. Edo was originally a small settlement near what is now Tokyo Bay, and it did not hold any major political or cultural significance at the time. The village of Edo was founded in 1180 by a member of the Taira clan, one of Japan's most powerful samurai families. However, it wasn't until the early 17th century that Edo's fortunes changed dramatically.

The turning point for Edo came in 1603, when Tokugawa Ieyasu, a powerful warlord, established the Tokugawa Shogunate, a military government that would rule Japan for over 250 years. Tokugawa Ieyasu chose Edo as the seat of his government, which marked the beginning of Edo's transformation into a major city. Under the Tokugawa Shogunate, Edo grew rapidly as it became the political, economic, and cultural center of Japan. During this period, known as the Edo period, the city's population soared, and it became one of the largest cities in the world, with over a million residents by the 18th century.

The Edo period was a time of relative peace and stability in Japan, thanks to the strict policies of the Tokugawa Shogunate. Japan was largely isolated from the rest of the world during this time, with very limited contact with foreign nations. This isolation allowed Edo to develop its own distinct culture, free from outside influence. The city became known for its art, literature, and theater, particularly the development of ukiyo-e woodblock prints and kabuki theater. The city's streets were filled with merchants, craftsmen, and samurai, creating a vibrant urban society.

While Edo grew in size and importance, the city also faced many challenges, including fires and natural disasters. Edo was prone to devastating fires, earning the nickname "the city of fires." The wooden structures that made up much of the city were particularly vulnerable, and fires would often destroy large portions of the city. Despite these setbacks, the people of Edo were able to rebuild time and time again, and the city continued to thrive.

The end of the Edo period came in the mid-19th century when Japan was forced to open its doors to the outside world after more than two centuries of isolation. In 1853, U.S. Commodore Matthew Perry arrived in Japan with a fleet of ships, demanding that Japan open its ports to trade. This event marked the beginning of the end for the Tokugawa Shogunate, as Japan faced increasing pressure from foreign powers. In 1868, the Meiji Restoration took place, a pivotal event that saw the collapse of the Tokugawa Shogunate and the restoration of power to the emperor.

With the Meiji Restoration, Edo was renamed Tokyo, which means "Eastern Capital," as the imperial capital was moved from Kyoto to Tokyo. The Meiji period, which followed, was a time of rapid modernization and industrialization in Japan. The new government sought to transform Japan into a modern nation-state, and Tokyo became the center of this transformation. The city underwent significant changes as Western technology, ideas, and infrastructure were introduced. Railroads, telegraph lines, and modern buildings began to appear in Tokyo, and the city's population continued to grow.

During the late 19th and early 20th centuries, Tokyo emerged as a modern city, but it still retained many of its traditional elements. The juxtaposition of old and new became a defining characteristic of Tokyo as the city balanced modernization with its historical and cultural heritage. However, Tokyo would face even greater challenges in the 20th century.

The Great Kanto Earthquake of 1923 was one of the most devastating events in Tokyo's history. The earthquake, which struck on September 1, 1923, caused widespread destruction across the city, and the resulting fires compounded the damage. Over 100,000 people were killed, and much of Tokyo was left in ruins. Despite the massive destruction, Tokyo was rebuilt in the years that followed, with an emphasis on modernizing the city and making it more resilient to future disasters.

Just as Tokyo was recovering from the Great Kanto Earthquake, the city faced another catastrophe during World War II. In 1945, Tokyo was heavily bombed by Allied forces, and large parts of the city were once again destroyed. The firebombing of Tokyo in March 1945 was particularly devastating, killing tens of thousands of people and flattening entire neighborhoods. At the end of the war, Japan was left in ruins, and Tokyo, along with the rest of the country, faced the daunting task of rebuilding.

After the war, Tokyo became the focal point of Japan's post-war recovery. The 1950s and 1960s saw rapid economic growth, and Tokyo was at the heart of Japan's transformation into a global economic power. The city hosted the 1964 Summer Olympics, which was a symbolic moment in Japan's recovery, showcasing Tokyo as a modern, forward-looking city. The Olympics also spurred further development in the city, leading to the construction of new infrastructure such as highways, subways, and modern buildings.

In the decades that followed, Tokyo continued to grow both in size and influence. The city became a major financial and cultural hub, attracting people from all over the world. By the 1980s, Tokyo was known as one of the world's leading cities in terms of business, technology, and culture. However, Tokyo's rapid growth also brought challenges, such as overcrowding, high real estate prices, and environmental issues.

Despite these challenges, Tokyo has remained resilient, continuing to evolve and adapt to the changing times. The city has also maintained a balance between modernity and tradition. Today, visitors to Tokyo can experience the latest technological innovations, while also enjoying centuries-old cultural practices. From the neon-lit streets of Shibuya to the peaceful grounds of the Meiji Shrine, Tokyo offers a unique blend of the old and the new.

Tokyo's history is a testament to the city's ability to overcome adversity and reinvent itself. From its humble beginnings as a small fishing village to its current status as one of the world's most dynamic cities, Tokyo has undergone incredible transformations. Its history is filled with moments of great triumph as well as moments of hardship, but through it all, Tokyo has remained a city that embodies the spirit of resilience and progress. Today, Tokyo stands as a symbol of Japan's rich history, cultural heritage, and its future-facing approach to innovation and development.

CHAPTER 1

WHEN TO VISIT TOKYO

Best Times of the Year to Travel

Tokyo is a city that can be enjoyed at any time of the year, but the experience can vary greatly depending on when you visit. The city goes through distinct seasons, each with its own appeal, weather patterns, and cultural events, so choosing the best time to visit Tokyo often depends on your personal preferences and the kind of trip you want to have.

One of the most popular times to visit Tokyo is during the spring, especially in late March and early April. This period is when the cherry blossoms, or sakura, are in full bloom, creating breathtaking landscapes across the city. Visiting Tokyo during cherry blossom season is considered by many to be a magical experience, as the city's parks, rivers, and temples are draped in delicate pink and white flowers. One of the best places to see the cherry blossoms is Ueno Park, where hundreds of cherry trees bloom, attracting locals and tourists alike. Another popular spot is Shinjuku Gyoen, a large park in the heart of the city, where visitors can enjoy a peaceful walk surrounded by blossoms. The sight of cherry blossoms in full bloom is so iconic in Japan that it even has its own tradition, called hanami, which involves picnicking under the blooming trees. However, because cherry blossom season is so short, typically lasting only about a week or two, this time of year is also one of the busiest in terms of tourism. Hotels tend to book up quickly, and popular sightseeing spots can be crowded, so planning ahead is essential if you want to experience Tokyo during this beautiful season.

Spring in Tokyo also offers mild and pleasant weather. Temperatures during this time are generally comfortable, ranging from around 10°C (50°F) in the early spring to 20°C (68°F) by the end of May. The days are usually sunny, with occasional rain, but the weather is ideal for outdoor activities like walking tours, visiting parks, and exploring Tokyo's neighborhoods on foot. If you're interested in avoiding the cherry blossom crowds but still want to enjoy the fresh air and pleasant temperatures, visiting Tokyo in late April or May is a good option. During this time, the flowers of spring are still in bloom, and the weather remains mild before the heat and humidity of summer set in.

Summer in Tokyo, which runs from June to August, brings hot and humid weather, with temperatures often rising above 30°C (86°F). The heat can feel intense, especially during the peak of summer in July and August, when the humidity levels are at their highest. This period also coincides with the rainy season, known as tsuyu, which typically lasts from early June to mid-July. During the rainy season, you can expect frequent, though often light, rainfall, with cloudy skies and damp conditions. While the rain is not usually heavy enough to disrupt travel plans entirely, it's a good idea to pack an umbrella and prepare for some wet weather if you plan to visit Tokyo in early summer.

Despite the heat and rain, summer is a great time to visit Tokyo if you want to experience some of the city's most exciting festivals and cultural events. One of the most famous summer events is the Sumida River Fireworks Festival, held in late July, which features a spectacular display of fireworks over the Sumida River. This event attracts massive crowds, but it's a great way to experience a traditional Japanese festival atmosphere, with street food stalls, festive decorations, and people wearing colorful yukata (summer kimono). Another highlight of summer in Tokyo is the Obon festival, a Buddhist event in mid-August that honors the spirits of ancestors. During this time, you'll see lanterns, dancing, and other traditional ceremonies throughout the city.

Summer in Tokyo is also the season for matsuri, or local festivals, which take place in various neighborhoods. These festivals often include parades, performances, and food stalls, giving visitors a chance to experience traditional Japanese culture in a lively and festive setting. However, if you're sensitive to heat or humidity, it's important to plan your activities accordingly. It's best to do outdoor sightseeing early in the morning or in the evening when it's cooler, and take advantage of Tokyo's many indoor attractions, such as museums, shopping malls, and cafes, during the hottest parts of the day.

Autumn, from September to November, is another fantastic time to visit Tokyo. After the heat of summer subsides, the temperatures cool down, and the humidity drops, making it one of the most comfortable seasons for outdoor activities. In autumn, the average temperatures range from 15°C to 25°C (59°F to 77°F), providing pleasant weather for exploring the city's parks, gardens, and neighborhoods. One of the most beautiful aspects of autumn in Tokyo is the changing of the leaves. The city's parks and tree-lined streets burst into brilliant shades of red, orange, and yellow as the autumn foliage reaches its peak, usually in late November. Just like in spring, Shinjuku Gyoen and Ueno Park are popular spots to admire the changing leaves, but there are also less crowded areas like the gardens of the Imperial Palace and the Meiji Shrine forest.

Autumn is also a season for traditional festivals and harvest celebrations. One of the major events is the Tokyo International Film Festival, which takes place in October and showcases films from around the world. The autumn months are also ideal for food lovers, as this is when many seasonal ingredients are at their best. You'll find fresh seafood, mushrooms, and chestnuts featured in dishes across the city's restaurants, and the cooler weather makes it the perfect time to enjoy a warm bowl of ramen or hot pot.

Winter in Tokyo, from December to February, is much colder, but it can still be a wonderful time to visit, especially if you prefer fewer crowds and are interested in experiencing the city's winter charm. Temperatures during the winter months generally range from around 2°C to 10°C (36°F to 50°F), with occasional cold snaps, but Tokyo rarely sees heavy snowfall. When it does snow, the city looks magical, with snow-dusted temples, parks, and rooftops creating a serene atmosphere.

Winter is also the season for illumination displays, where various parts of the city are decorated with stunning light installations. From mid-November through early January, you can find impressive illuminations in areas like Roppongi Hills, Omotesando, and Marunouchi, where the trees and buildings are adorned with sparkling lights. Visiting Tokyo during the winter holidays can be especially enchanting, as the city celebrates Christmas and New Year with festive decorations, special events, and seasonal foods. For those interested in traditional Japanese celebrations, New Year's in Tokyo is a special time, marked by visits to temples and shrines for the first prayer of the year, called hatsumode.

While winter may not be as popular as spring or autumn, it's a great time to experience a quieter side of Tokyo, with fewer tourists and shorter lines at major attractions. It's also a good time to take advantage of Tokyo's indoor attractions, such as museums, galleries, and shopping centers. And if you're interested in skiing or snowboarding, you can easily take a day trip or overnight trip from Tokyo to nearby mountains, where you can enjoy winter sports in areas like Nagano or Niigata.

Ultimately, the best time to visit Tokyo depends on what you want to experience. Spring offers beautiful cherry blossoms and mild weather, summer brings exciting festivals and lively streets, autumn showcases stunning foliage and comfortable temperatures, and winter offers festive lights and a peaceful atmosphere. Each season has its own unique charm, and no matter when you choose to visit, Tokyo promises an unforgettable experience filled with culture, history, and endless opportunities to explore.

Tokyo's Four Seasons: What to Expect

Tokyo experiences four distinct seasons, and each one brings its own unique character to the city. Understanding what to expect in each season is important for anyone planning to visit, as the weather, activities, and atmosphere can change significantly throughout the year. Tokyo's seasons are well-defined, and the city offers something different depending on whether you visit in the mild spring, the humid summer, the crisp autumn, or the chilly winter. Each season has its own charm, and the way the city transforms can make it feel like a completely new place each time you visit.

Spring in Tokyo, typically from March to May, is one of the most popular times to visit. The highlight of spring is undoubtedly the cherry blossom season, which usually takes place in late March or early April. During this time, cherry trees all over the city burst into bloom, creating beautiful landscapes that attract both locals and tourists. The cherry blossoms, or sakura, can be seen in parks, along rivers, and even on some streets, turning Tokyo into a sea of soft pink and white. This is also the season for hanami, or flower-viewing parties, where people gather in parks like Ueno Park, Shinjuku Gyoen, and along the Meguro River to enjoy picnics under the blooming trees. These gatherings are festive, often involving food, drinks, and a lot of socializing, as everyone comes together to appreciate the fleeting beauty of the blossoms.

However, cherry blossom season is short, typically lasting only about a week or two, depending on the weather.

Aside from the cherry blossoms, spring is a wonderful time to explore Tokyo because of the mild weather. Temperatures usually range from 10°C to 20°C (50°F to 68°F), making it comfortable to walk around the city and visit outdoor attractions. You'll find flower festivals and gardens in full bloom, and the city feels alive with fresh energy after the colder winter months. Spring is also a time when many traditional Japanese festivals take place, giving visitors the chance to experience local culture. However, it's worth noting that this is a popular travel season, so Tokyo can be quite crowded, especially around the peak of the cherry blossom season.

Summer in Tokyo, which runs from June to August, is a time of both heat and excitement. The weather during summer is hot and humid, with temperatures often reaching 30°C (86°F) or higher, especially in July and August. Humidity levels are also quite high, which can make the heat feel more intense. Summer also brings the rainy season, known as tsuyu, which typically lasts from early June to mid-July. During this period, you can expect frequent rain showers, though they are usually light and not enough to disrupt most plans. The weather can be unpredictable during the rainy season, with cloudy days and occasional downpours, but it doesn't usually rain all day, so there are still plenty of opportunities to get out and explore the city.

Despite the heat and rain, summer in Tokyo is full of energy and activity. One of the highlights of summer is the many matsuri, or festivals, that take place throughout the city. These festivals often feature parades, traditional music, food stalls, and fireworks. One of the most famous summer events is the Sumida River Fireworks Festival, held in late July, which draws large crowds to watch a spectacular fireworks display over the river. Other popular festivals include the Asakusa Samba Carnival and the Koenji Awa Odori Dance Festival, both of which bring the streets of Tokyo to life with vibrant performances and colorful costumes. Summer is also a great time to experience traditional summer foods like kakigori (shaved ice) and cold soba noodles, which are perfect for cooling down on a hot day.

In August, Japan celebrates the Obon festival, a time when people honor their ancestors. While this is more of a cultural and religious event, there are often traditional dances, lanterns, and other events that you can see around the city. Despite the heat, summer can be a rewarding time to visit Tokyo if you're interested in experiencing the lively festival atmosphere. However, it's important to stay hydrated, wear light clothing, and take breaks in air-conditioned spaces to avoid feeling overwhelmed by the weather.

Autumn in Tokyo, from September to November, is considered by many to be the best time to visit the city. After the hot and humid summer, the weather in autumn is cooler and more comfortable, with temperatures ranging from 15°C to 25°C (59°F to 77°F). The humidity levels drop, and the days are often sunny and clear, making it perfect for outdoor activities like sightseeing, hiking, and exploring Tokyo's parks and gardens. One of the most beautiful aspects of autumn is the changing of the leaves. Just as cherry blossoms define the spring, the vibrant reds, oranges, and yellows of autumn foliage bring a special beauty to the city in the fall. The peak of the autumn foliage season usually occurs in November, and popular places to see the leaves include Shinjuku Gyoen, Yoyogi Park, and the Imperial Palace East Gardens.

Autumn is also a time when many cultural events and festivals take place, such as the Tokyo International Film Festival in October. The cooler weather also makes it a great time for food lovers, as many seasonal ingredients, like mushrooms, sweet potatoes, and chestnuts, become available. Restaurants often offer special autumn menus, and street food stalls pop up at local festivals, offering a chance to try fresh, seasonal flavors. Autumn is a relatively quiet season in terms of tourism compared to spring, so it's a good time to visit if you prefer to avoid the larger crowds while still enjoying comfortable weather and beautiful scenery.

Winter in Tokyo, from December to February, is much colder, but it offers a completely different experience from the other seasons. Temperatures during winter typically range from 2°C to 10°C (36°F to 50°F), so you'll need to pack warm clothing, especially if you plan to spend a lot of time outdoors. Although Tokyo doesn't experience heavy snowfall, there may be occasional light snowfalls that give the city a soft, wintry atmosphere. Even when there is no snow, winter in Tokyo can be charming, with many parts of the city decorated with illuminations and lights for the holiday season. From mid-November through January, areas like Omotesando, Roppongi, and Marunouchi feature stunning light displays that brighten the long winter nights.

Winter in Tokyo also offers several unique experiences. New Year's is one of the most important holidays in Japan, and many people visit temples and shrines for hatsumode, the first prayer of the year. If you're in Tokyo during this time, visiting a shrine like Meiji Shrine or Senso-ji can give you a glimpse into Japanese traditions and celebrations. Another winter highlight is the chance to enjoy warm comfort foods like nabe (hot pot), ramen, and oden (a stew-like dish), which are perfect for warming up on a cold day.

While winter is a quieter time in terms of tourism, it's also a good time to explore Tokyo's indoor attractions, such as museums, galleries, and shopping centers. The city's indoor attractions are numerous, and you'll have plenty of options to choose from when the weather is chilly. And if you're interested in winter sports, Tokyo is conveniently located near several mountain areas where you can enjoy skiing, snowboarding, or simply relaxing in a hot spring.

Each season in Tokyo offers a different experience, and knowing what to expect can help you plan the best time for your visit. Whether you're looking for the beauty of cherry blossoms in spring, the excitement of summer festivals, the colorful leaves of autumn, or the peaceful charm of winter, Tokyo's seasons add an extra layer of richness to any trip. By understanding how the city changes throughout the year, you can choose the time that best matches your interests and enjoy all that Tokyo has to offer, no matter when you decide to visit.

Popular Festivals and Events Throughout the Year

Tokyo is a city that never sleeps, and one of the best ways to experience its vibrant culture is by attending the many festivals and events that take place throughout the year. These festivals reflect Japan's rich traditions, seasonal changes, and the unique character of each neighborhood in the city. Some festivals are centuries old, with deep cultural and historical significance, while others are more modern, celebrating contemporary interests and global cultures. No matter what time of year you visit, there is always something happening in Tokyo, and these events offer an unforgettable glimpse into the heart of Japanese culture.

The year in Tokyo begins with New Year celebrations, which are among the most important and widely observed events in Japan. The Japanese New Year, or Shogatsu, is marked by a variety of customs and traditions, and while it is often a time for family gatherings, there are also public celebrations that visitors can enjoy. In the days leading up to the New Year, many people visit shrines and temples for a ritual known as hatsumode, the first prayer of the year. The Meiji Shrine in Tokyo is one of the most popular spots for this, and it draws huge crowds from midnight on December 31 through the first days of January. Visitors come to pray for good fortune in the coming year and to purchase traditional good luck charms. During this time, Tokyo is also decorated with festive lights and decorations, and the city's parks and temples host New Year's markets selling food, drinks, and souvenirs. It's a time of reflection, renewal, and hope for the future, and it gives visitors a chance to experience Japanese spiritual practices firsthand.

As the year progresses, spring brings one of Tokyo's most famous and beloved festivals: the cherry blossom season. While not a festival in the traditional sense, hanami, or flower viewing, is an important cultural event that draws large crowds to Tokyo's parks, gardens, and riversides. Cherry blossoms, or sakura, typically bloom in late March or early April, depending on the weather, and for a few short weeks, the entire city is transformed by the delicate pink and white flowers. People gather with friends and family to picnic under the blooming trees, enjoying food, drinks, and music in a celebratory atmosphere. The most popular places for hanami in Tokyo include Ueno Park, Shinjuku Gyoen, and the banks of the Meguro River, where cherry blossoms line the water in an unforgettable display. During this time, many cafes, restaurants, and shops offer seasonal sakura-themed treats and products, making the entire city feel immersed in the spirit of spring.

After the beauty of spring, summer in Tokyo is a season of festivals and fireworks, with events happening almost every weekend. One of the most famous summer festivals is the Sumida River Fireworks Festival, which takes place in late July. This event, known as hanabi taikai, draws millions of spectators who come to watch spectacular fireworks light up the night sky over the Sumida River. Fireworks festivals are a beloved tradition in Japan, and the Sumida River Fireworks Festival is one of the biggest and oldest, dating back to the Edo period. Visitors flock to the riverbanks early in the day to secure a good spot for viewing the display, and the streets nearby are filled with food stalls selling classic Japanese festival snacks like yakitori (grilled chicken skewers), takoyaki (octopus balls), and taiyaki (fish-shaped cakes filled with sweet red bean paste). The atmosphere is lively and fun, with many people dressing in colorful summer yukata (light kimono) and enjoying the festive vibe.

Another highlight of summer in Tokyo is the Asakusa Samba Carnival, which takes place in late August. This event brings a touch of Brazil to Tokyo's historic Asakusa district, as teams of dancers and musicians parade through the streets, performing samba in elaborate costumes. The carnival is a joyful and energetic celebration, drawing crowds from all over Japan to enjoy the music, dancing, and colorful displays. Asakusa, home to the famous Senso-ji Temple, provides a striking backdrop for this event, with its mix of traditional Japanese architecture and vibrant carnival festivities.

In addition to fireworks and samba, summer is also the season for matsuri, or traditional Japanese festivals. These events are often centered around local shrines, and they feature parades of portable shrines known as mikoshi, along with traditional music, dancing, and food stalls. One of the most famous matsuri in Tokyo is the Kanda Matsuri, which is held every two years in mid-May. This festival, associated with the Kanda Myojin Shrine, celebrates prosperity and good fortune, and it features a grand procession of mikoshi through the streets of central Tokyo. Another popular festival is the Sanno Matsuri, also held every two years, alternating with the Kanda Matsuri, and it features a similar procession that winds its way through the streets of Tokyo over several days.

As summer transitions into autumn, Tokyo's festival calendar continues with a focus on culture, food, and the arts. One of the key events of the autumn season is the Tokyo International Film Festival, which takes place in late October. This event attracts filmmakers and movie lovers from around the world, showcasing a wide variety of films, from Japanese cinema to international blockbusters and independent films. The festival offers screenings, discussions, and special events at theaters around the city, making it a great opportunity for visitors to experience Tokyo's vibrant film culture.

Autumn in Tokyo is also the season for harvest festivals and food events. As the weather cools down and the leaves begin to change color, Tokyoites celebrate the bounty of the harvest with festivals that highlight seasonal ingredients like chestnuts, sweet potatoes, and mushrooms. Many neighborhoods host food festivals where visitors can sample local dishes and seasonal specialties. These events often take place in parks or open-air markets, providing a relaxed and festive atmosphere for enjoying autumn's flavors.

Winter in Tokyo is marked by a quieter, more reflective mood, but it's also a time for spectacular light displays and New Year's celebrations. Starting in mid-November and continuing through the New Year, many parts of Tokyo are illuminated with stunning winter light displays. Areas like Roppongi Hills, Omotesando, and Marunouchi are famous for their elaborate illuminations, which transform the city's streets into glowing winter wonderlands. These light displays attract both locals and tourists, and they add a festive atmosphere to the city during the holiday season.

As the year comes to a close, Tokyo celebrates the New Year with traditional events and ceremonies. One of the most important traditions is the New Year's Eve joya no kane, a Buddhist ritual where temples across the city ring their bells 108 times to purify the soul and bring good luck for the coming year. Visitors can experience this solemn and spiritual tradition at major temples like Zojoji and Senso-ji. Following the New Year's Eve celebrations, the first few days of January are marked by visits to shrines and temples for hatsumode, the first prayer of the year. It's a time of hope and renewal, and many people visit Meiji Shrine or other major religious sites to pray for health, happiness, and success in the coming year.

Tokyo's festivals and events are as diverse as the city itself, offering a mix of ancient traditions, modern celebrations, and cultural exchanges. No matter when you visit, you'll find that the city's festivals provide a window into the soul of Tokyo, allowing you to connect with its history, people, and traditions in a meaningful way.

Weather Patterns and Their Impact on Your Trip

Tokyo's weather patterns can greatly influence your trip, determining what you'll be able to see, do, and experience while in the city. As a traveler, understanding how the weather changes throughout the year can help you make informed decisions about when to visit, what to pack, and how to plan your daily activities. Tokyo experiences four distinct seasons: spring, summer, autumn, and winter, each with its own set of weather conditions that can enhance or challenge your travel plans.

Spring, which generally runs from March to May, is one of the most popular times to visit Tokyo due to its mild weather and the iconic cherry blossom season. During these months, temperatures typically range from 10°C (50°F) in early spring to around 20°C (68°F) by May. The weather is generally pleasant, with cool mornings and evenings and warmer afternoons. This makes spring an ideal time for outdoor activities like walking tours, park visits, and exploring Tokyo's neighborhoods. The clear, sunny days are perfect for sightseeing, and the cool breeze ensures that you won't feel too hot while spending hours outdoors.

However, spring is also known for occasional rain showers, particularly in late March and early April. These rains can be unpredictable, but they are usually light and short-lived. Packing a light raincoat or an umbrella is advisable, especially if you're visiting during the peak of cherry blossom season, when outdoor picnics and walks through parks are popular. The rain can sometimes bring out the beauty of the cherry blossoms even more, as the wet ground and fresh air create a peaceful atmosphere for viewing the blooms. Nonetheless, it's important to be prepared for the possibility of sudden rain, especially if your plans involve a lot of time outdoors.

As spring gives way to summer, the weather in Tokyo begins to heat up. Summer in Tokyo, which lasts from June to August, is characterized by hot, humid conditions. Temperatures during these months often exceed 30°C (86°F), with humidity levels making it feel even warmer. The early part of summer, particularly June, is also marked by the rainy season, known as tsuyu. This rainy season usually lasts for several weeks, bringing frequent rain showers and cloudy skies. While the rain during tsuyu is not usually torrential, it can still affect your plans if you're hoping for sunny days to explore the city.

The high humidity during summer can be uncomfortable for some travelers, especially those not used to hot and sticky weather. Walking around the city can feel tiring, and staying hydrated is essential to avoid feeling overheated. Fortunately, Tokyo's efficient public transportation system means you can quickly move between air-conditioned trains and buses to escape the heat. Many attractions, such as shopping malls, museums, and restaurants, are also air-conditioned, providing a cool break from the outdoors. Summer in Tokyo is a time when it's best to plan outdoor activities for early in the morning or later in the evening when the temperatures are a bit cooler.

Despite the heat and humidity, summer is a vibrant time to visit Tokyo. It's festival season, and many traditional Japanese festivals, or matsuri, take place during the summer months. These festivals often feature fireworks, food stalls, and lively parades, creating a fun and energetic atmosphere that can make the hot weather more bearable. The Sumida River Fireworks Festival, for example, is a major summer event, and while the crowds and heat can be intense, it's a quintessential Tokyo experience. If you're visiting Tokyo in summer, be sure to dress in light, breathable clothing, wear a hat, and apply sunscreen to protect yourself from the sun.

As the summer heat subsides, autumn arrives in Tokyo, typically from September to November. Autumn is considered by many to be one of the best times to visit Tokyo, as the weather becomes much more comfortable. Temperatures in early autumn remain warm, averaging around 25°C (77°F), but by November, the temperatures drop to a more comfortable range of 10°C to 15°C (50°F to 59°F). The humidity of summer disappears, and the crisp, cool air makes outdoor exploration a pleasure.

One of the most beautiful aspects of autumn in Tokyo is the changing of the leaves. The city's parks and gardens, such as

Shinjuku Gyoen and Yoyogi Park, are filled with trees that turn vibrant shades of red, orange, and yellow. The autumn foliage usually reaches its peak in late November, drawing both locals and tourists to admire the colors. This is a great time for taking scenic walks through the city's many green spaces or enjoying the natural beauty of Tokyo's outskirts, such as Mount Takao, which offers hiking trails with stunning autumn views.

Autumn also brings fewer tourists compared to the busy spring season, making it a more peaceful time to visit Tokyo's major attractions. You can enjoy popular sites like the Tokyo Skytree, Senso-ji Temple, and the Imperial Palace without the heavy crowds of peak travel months. The pleasant weather also means that autumn is an excellent time for outdoor activities, from exploring local markets to taking boat rides along the Sumida River.

As the year progresses, winter arrives in Tokyo, lasting from December to February. Winter in Tokyo is generally cool but not as harsh as in other parts of Japan, such as the northern regions. Temperatures typically range from 2°C to 10°C (36°F to 50°F), with occasional cold snaps. Snow is rare in Tokyo, but it can happen, particularly in January and February. When it does snow, it usually melts quickly and doesn't cause major disruptions to travel or daily life in the city.

Winter in Tokyo offers a different kind of beauty, with clear, crisp skies and a calm atmosphere. The colder weather makes it an ideal time to enjoy warm comfort foods like ramen, hot pot, and oden, which are widely available throughout the city. Winter is also the season for illuminations, where various parts of Tokyo are decorated with elaborate light displays. These illuminations, which start in mid-November and continue through early January, create a festive and magical atmosphere in neighborhoods like Roppongi, Shibuya, and Marunouchi.

Winter is a quieter time for tourism in Tokyo, and many attractions are less crowded, making it easier to visit popular spots without long lines. It's also a good time for indoor activities, such as exploring Tokyo's many museums, galleries, and shopping centers. For those interested in traditional Japanese culture, winter offers the chance to experience New Year's rituals and customs, such as visiting temples for hatsumode, the first prayer of the year.

CHAPTER 2

PREPARING FOR YOUR TRIP

Visa Requirements for Tourists

When planning a trip to Tokyo, Japan, understanding the visa requirements is one of the first steps you need to take. Whether you need a visa to enter Japan as a tourist depends largely on your nationality, the length of your stay, and the purpose of your visit. Japan has agreements with many countries that allow travelers to enter the country without a visa for short stays, while other nationalities are required to apply for a visa in advance.

For citizens of many countries, including the United States, Canada, Australia, the United Kingdom, and most countries in the European Union, Japan offers visa-free entry for short-term stays, typically up to 90 days. This means that travelers from these countries do not need to apply for a visa in advance if they are visiting Japan for tourism, business meetings, or short-term visits to family or friends. However, it's important to note that this visa-free entry is only valid for tourism or business purposes, and travelers are not permitted to engage in paid work or long-term activities without a proper visa.

To enter Japan under the visa waiver program, you will need to present a valid passport when you arrive at immigration. Your passport must be valid for the entire duration of your stay, and it is generally recommended to have at least six months of validity remaining on your passport at the time of entry, although Japan does not have an official six-month passport rule. However, it's always a good idea to check your passport's expiration date before traveling to avoid any issues. In addition to your passport, you may also be asked to provide proof of onward travel, such as a return flight ticket or a ticket for onward travel to another destination. Immigration officials may also ask for proof of accommodation, such as a hotel booking, as well as evidence that you have enough funds to support yourself during your stay.

While many nationalities can enjoy visa-free travel to Japan, travelers from other countries are required to apply for a visa in advance. If you are from a country that does not have a visa exemption agreement with Japan, you will need to apply for a temporary visitor visa before your trip. This is typically a single-entry visa that allows you to stay in Japan for up to 90 days for tourism, visiting family or friends, or other short-term purposes. To apply for a tourist visa, you will need to submit an application to the Japanese embassy or consulate in your home country. The visa application process usually involves filling out an application form, providing a valid passport, a passport-sized photo, and supporting documents such as proof of accommodation, a detailed itinerary of your trip, and proof of sufficient funds.

For those who need to apply for a visa, it is important to allow plenty of time for the processing of your application. Visa processing times can vary depending on the country and the specific consulate, but it typically takes anywhere from a few days to a few weeks. In some cases, you may be asked to attend an interview or provide additional documents, so it is a good idea to start the visa application process well in advance of your planned travel dates. If you are planning to visit Tokyo during peak travel periods, such as during the cherry blossom season or major holidays, processing times may be longer due to the increased number of visa applications, so it's best to plan accordingly.

In addition to the standard tourist visa, Japan also offers other types of visas for specific purposes. For example, if you are visiting Japan for business, you may need to apply for a business visa, which allows you to attend meetings, conferences, or business-related events. If you are planning to study or work in Japan, you will need to apply for the appropriate long-term visa, such as a student visa or a work visa, which requires additional documentation and approvals. Each type of visa has its own requirements, so it's important to check with the Japanese embassy or consulate to determine which visa is right for your specific situation.

Once you arrive in Japan, immigration officials will review your passport and visa (if applicable) before granting you entry into the country. If you are traveling under the visa waiver program or with a temporary visitor visa, you will typically be allowed to stay for up to 90 days. Upon entry, you will receive a landing permission stamp in your passport, which indicates the date of entry and the length of time you are allowed to stay in Japan. It is crucial to keep track of this date and ensure that you do not overstay your visa, as overstaying can lead to penalties, fines, and potential difficulties with future travel to Japan.

Japan takes its immigration rules seriously, and overstaying a visa can result in deportation or a ban on re-entering the country in the future. If you find that you need to extend your stay for any reason, it is possible to apply for an extension at a regional immigration office in Japan, but you must do so before your authorized stay expires. Extensions are not guaranteed and are usually only granted in exceptional circumstances, so it's important to plan your trip carefully to avoid overstaying.

In recent years, Japan has introduced a new electronic system for foreign visitors called the "Japan eVisa," which allows eligible travelers to apply for a visa online. This system was introduced as part of Japan's efforts to simplify the visa application process and attract more tourists to the country. However, the Japan eVisa is currently available only for certain nationalities and under specific conditions, so it's important to check whether you are eligible to apply for an eVisa before your trip.

It is also worth noting that Japan has strict entry requirements for travelers who have certain medical conditions or who are carrying prohibited items. For example, certain medications that are commonly used in other countries may be restricted or banned in Japan, so if you are taking prescription medication, it is important to check whether your medication is allowed in

Japan before traveling. You may need to obtain prior approval from the Japanese authorities or carry documentation from your doctor to bring certain medications into the country. Additionally, Japan has strict rules regarding the importation of goods such as food, plants, and animals, so it's a good idea to familiarize yourself with these regulations before your trip.

Language and Communication Tips

When visiting Tokyo, one of the most important aspects of your experience will be how you communicate with the locals. Tokyo is a global city, and while many people speak or understand basic English, Japanese remains the primary language spoken by the vast majority of residents. Understanding some basic language and communication tips can make a big difference in how easily you navigate the city, interact with people, and get the most out of your trip.

First, it's helpful to know that many Japanese people study English in school, but not all of them feel comfortable speaking it. In large international areas such as airports, hotels, and tourist-heavy parts of the city like Shibuya or Asakusa, you are more likely to encounter people who speak English, especially those working in the service industry. However, once you step outside the central tourist zones or venture into smaller restaurants, shops, or local neighborhoods, English may not be as commonly understood. While some signage in Tokyo, especially at train stations and major landmarks, is often written in both Japanese and English, there will still be many instances where only Japanese is used. Learning a few basic phrases in Japanese can go a long way in helping you interact with locals and get what you need during your trip.

A good starting point for communication is simple greetings and polite phrases. Japanese society places a high value on politeness, and using basic greetings like "hello" (konnichiwa), "goodbye" (sayonara), "thank you" (arigatou gozaimasu), and "excuse me" (sumimasen) can help you make a positive impression. When entering a store or restaurant, it's customary to say "sumimasen" to get the attention of the staff. Saying "arigatou gozaimasu" when receiving something, whether it's food, help, or directions, is always appreciated. Even if your pronunciation isn't perfect, locals will generally appreciate your effort to speak Japanese, and it often makes interactions smoother and friendlier.

When asking for help or directions, you can use simple phrases like "doko desu ka?" which means "Where is…?" For example, if you're looking for a specific place, you could say "Eki wa doko desu ka?" (Where is the train station?) or "Toire wa doko desu ka?" (Where is the restroom?). This basic question format can be very useful when you're trying to navigate the city. It's also helpful to have key destinations written down in Japanese, especially if the name of the place is complex or hard to pronounce. Showing the written name to someone will often be more effective than trying to pronounce it yourself.

One of the key things to understand about communication in Japan is that non-verbal cues are just as important as spoken language. Japanese people tend to be more reserved in their communication style compared to some other cultures, so body language, facial expressions, and gestures can play a big role in interactions. Bowing is a common form of greeting and a sign of respect, and it's something you'll see often in Tokyo. While tourists aren't expected to bow in the same formal way that locals do, offering a small nod when greeting or thanking someone is a polite gesture that shows respect for the local culture.

Another important aspect of communication in Japan is the use of indirect language. In Japan, it's often considered impolite to say "no" directly, especially in customer service settings. Instead, people may use more subtle ways to indicate that something isn't possible. For example, if you ask a shopkeeper or hotel staff for something and they respond with a hesitant "chotto…" or a long pause, this may be their way of politely saying that they cannot fulfill your request. Understanding these indirect signals can help you avoid misunderstandings and make your interactions more pleasant.

If you find yourself in a situation where language becomes a barrier, there are several strategies you can use to overcome it. One of the most useful tools for travelers is a translation app. Many apps, such as Google Translate, can help you quickly translate between English and Japanese, either by typing or speaking into the app. Some apps even allow you to point your phone's camera at written Japanese text, such as signs or menus, and translate it in real time. This can be incredibly helpful when navigating places where English is not widely used, such as small restaurants or rural areas.

Speaking of restaurants, one of the most common concerns for tourists in Tokyo is ordering food when menus are only in Japanese. In many restaurants, especially in tourist-friendly areas, menus are often available in English, or there may be pictures of the dishes, which makes it easier to order. However, in more traditional or local places, you might encounter menus with only Japanese text. In these cases, don't be afraid to ask for help. You can simply point to an item on the menu and say "kore o kudasai," which means "this, please." Many restaurants also have plastic food models (known as shokuhin sampuru) displayed in their windows, and you can point to these models if you're unsure of what to order.

It's also worth noting that Tokyo is a highly organized city, and many public services are designed with foreign visitors in mind. For example, the Tokyo Metro and JR train lines provide announcements and signs in both Japanese and English, making it easier for tourists to use public transportation. When traveling by train, you'll often hear station announcements in English, and major stations like Shinjuku, Tokyo Station, and Shibuya have English-speaking staff who can assist you with tickets, directions, and other travel needs.

While many people in Tokyo may not speak English fluently, you'll often find that people are eager to help. Japanese people are known for their hospitality and politeness, and even if there's a language barrier, locals will often go out of their way to assist you. Whether it's giving directions, helping you order food, or guiding you through the train system, the willingness of locals to help tourists can make a big difference in how smoothly your trip goes. Being patient and open to these kinds of interactions will help you enjoy your time in Tokyo and make the most of your experiences.

For travelers who want to learn more than just a few basic phrases, it can be helpful to study some key words and expressions before arriving in Tokyo. While you don't need to be fluent in Japanese to have a great time, knowing a few more common phrases can enhance your trip. For example, learning how to say "how much does this cost?" (Ikura desu ka?), or "check, please" (Okanjo o onegai shimasu) can make shopping and dining out much easier. You can also learn simple ways to express gratitude, such as saying "thank you very much" (doumo arigatou gozaimasu), which is a more polite version of "thank you."

In addition to spoken language, written Japanese can be helpful to learn if you're planning to explore Tokyo in more depth. Japanese uses three writing systems: kanji (Chinese characters), hiragana, and katakana. While kanji is often the most difficult for beginners to learn, hiragana and katakana are phonetic alphabets that can be useful for reading basic signs, menus, and place names. Many foreign words, including the names of some foods and products, are written in katakana, so learning to recognize a few key characters can make it easier to navigate menus or identify items in stores.

Finally, while English is becoming more common in Tokyo, especially among younger generations and in international settings, it's still important to approach communication with flexibility and a sense of humor. Misunderstandings may happen, but they can also lead to fun and memorable moments during your trip. The key to enjoying your time in Tokyo is to be open to new experiences, patient when things don't go as planned, and respectful of the local culture.

Budgeting for Your Tokyo Trip

When planning a trip to Tokyo, one of the most important aspects to consider is how to budget for your visit. Tokyo is known for being one of the most modern and exciting cities in the world, and while it has a reputation for being expensive, it's possible to visit the city on almost any budget if you plan carefully.

The first thing to consider when budgeting for a trip to Tokyo is your accommodation. The cost of hotels and other lodging in Tokyo can vary widely depending on the type of accommodation you choose and its location within the city. Tokyo is divided into several distinct neighborhoods, each offering different price points for accommodation. Luxury hotels, particularly those in upscale areas like Ginza, Roppongi, and Shinjuku, can be quite expensive, with nightly rates often starting at $200 or more. These hotels typically offer high-end amenities, such as spacious rooms, restaurants, gyms, and breathtaking city views. If you prefer a more luxurious stay and are willing to pay for it, Tokyo has some of the world's best hotels that will provide top-notch service and comfort.

For travelers on a more moderate budget, mid-range hotels, business hotels, and boutique accommodations are excellent options. Business hotels, which are common throughout Tokyo, offer clean, comfortable rooms that are smaller in size but come with essential amenities like free Wi-Fi, en suite bathrooms, and sometimes breakfast. These hotels are typically located near train stations and can range in price from $70 to $150 per night, depending on the location and time of year. Staying in a business hotel is a great way to balance comfort with affordability.

If you're traveling on a tighter budget, hostels, capsule hotels, and budget inns offer more affordable accommodation options. Hostels in Tokyo are generally well-maintained, and many offer private rooms as well as dormitory-style accommodation. Prices for hostels typically range from $20 to $60 per night, making them a great choice for solo travelers or backpackers looking to save money. Capsule hotels, another unique accommodation option in Tokyo, provide small, individual sleeping pods at prices ranging from $30 to $60 per night. While these pods are compact and don't offer much space, they are clean and convenient, often located near major train stations. Staying in a capsule hotel can also be an interesting experience for travelers looking to try something new.

Another significant factor to include in your budget is food. Tokyo is a city that offers a wide variety of dining options, ranging from inexpensive street food and casual eateries to high-end Michelin-starred restaurants. For budget-conscious travelers, Tokyo's convenience stores, also known as konbini, are a fantastic resource. These stores, such as 7-Eleven, FamilyMart, and Lawson, offer a wide range of affordable, fresh, and tasty meals, including bento boxes, sandwiches, onigiri (rice balls), and instant noodles. A meal from a convenience store can cost as little as $5, making it an excellent option for breakfast, lunch, or even a quick snack.

In addition to convenience stores, Tokyo is home to countless casual restaurants and street food vendors where you can enjoy a satisfying meal without breaking the bank. Noodle shops serving ramen, udon, or soba can be found throughout the city, with meals typically costing between $6 and $12. Fast-food chains and gyudon (beef bowl) restaurants like Yoshinoya and Sukiya offer filling meals for under $10. Tokyo's street food scene, particularly in areas like Asakusa or near Shibuya's busy intersections, is another affordable option, with snacks like takoyaki (octopus balls), taiyaki (fish-shaped pastries), and yakitori (grilled chicken skewers) available for just a few dollars each.

If you're interested in experiencing Tokyo's more upscale dining options, there are plenty of mid-range and high-end restaurants to explore. Dining at a sushi restaurant, for example, can range from inexpensive conveyor belt sushi (kaiten-zushi) where plates typically cost around $1 to $3, to high-end sushi experiences where meals can cost over $100 per person. Izakayas, or Japanese-style pubs, offer a great middle ground, with a wide selection of small dishes, drinks, and a lively atmosphere. A meal at an izakaya can range from $20 to $50 per person, depending on what you order.

When budgeting for your trip, it's also important to factor in the cost of transportation. Tokyo has one of the most efficient and comprehensive public transportation systems in the world, and it's the best way to get around the city. The primary mode of transportation in Tokyo is the train and subway system, which connects all major neighborhoods and attractions. Fares for single rides on the Tokyo Metro or JR train lines typically range from $1.50 to $3, depending on the distance traveled. If you plan to use public transportation frequently, it may be worth purchasing a prepaid IC card, such as a Suica or Pasmo card, which can be loaded with money and used on trains, buses, and even at some convenience stores and vending machines. These cards save time and make traveling more convenient, as you simply tap the card at the gate without having to buy individual tickets.

Another option for tourists is to purchase a Tokyo Subway Ticket, which provides unlimited access to the Tokyo Metro and Toei Subway lines for a set number of days. These passes come in 24-hour, 48-hour, and 72-hour versions, with prices ranging from around $7 to $15. These passes can be a great value if you plan to explore many parts of the city in a short amount of time.

While Tokyo's public transportation system is affordable, taxis are more expensive. Fares typically start at around $5 for the first kilometer, with additional charges based on distance and time. Taxis are generally not recommended for budget travelers unless you are traveling late at night when the trains have stopped running or if you have heavy luggage that makes public transportation difficult. However, for shorter distances or if you're traveling with a group, taking a taxi can sometimes be a convenient option.

Sightseeing is another important aspect of your trip that you'll need to budget for. Fortunately, many of Tokyo's most popular attractions, such as temples, parks, and museums, have low or no entry fees. For example, entry to the famous Senso-ji Temple in Asakusa is free, as is access to many of the city's parks and gardens, like Yoyogi Park or the Imperial Palace East Gardens. Visiting these sites can be an excellent way to enjoy Tokyo's rich culture and history without spending much money.

However, some attractions, particularly observatories and theme parks, do have admission fees. For example, tickets to the Tokyo Skytree, one of the city's tallest towers, cost around $20 to $30, depending on how high you want to go. Tokyo Disneyland and Tokyo DisneySea, two of Japan's most popular theme parks, have daily admission prices that range from $60 to $80 for adults. If you're planning to visit multiple paid attractions, it's a good idea to research ticket prices in advance and include these costs in your budget.

Beyond the basics of accommodation, food, transportation, and sightseeing, you should also consider budgeting for extras like shopping and souvenirs. Tokyo is a shopper's paradise, with everything from luxury fashion brands in Ginza to quirky shops selling anime merchandise in Akihabara. Whether you're interested in clothing, electronics, or traditional Japanese crafts, it's easy to spend more than expected if you're not careful. Setting aside a specific amount of money for shopping will help you manage your expenses while still enjoying the unique items that Tokyo has to offer.

It's also a good idea to plan for miscellaneous expenses, such as travel insurance, tips (though tipping is not common in Japan), and any unexpected costs that may arise during your trip. Having a small buffer in your budget will give you peace of mind and ensure that you're prepared for any surprises.

Travel Apps You Should Download

When planning a trip to Tokyo, having the right travel apps on your phone can make a huge difference in how smoothly your trip goes. Tokyo is a large, bustling city, and navigating its streets, public transportation, and various attractions can sometimes feel overwhelming, especially if you're visiting for the first time. Fortunately, there are several apps that can help you with everything from finding your way around, understanding the language, booking activities, and even ordering food. Downloading and familiarizing yourself with these apps before you go can save you a lot of time and stress once you're in the city. Whether you're looking for directions, recommendations, or communication tools, these apps can turn your phone into a helpful guide during your trip.

One of the most useful apps you can have for getting around Tokyo is a navigation app that works well with public transportation. Tokyo has one of the most extensive and efficient train and subway systems in the world, but it can also be quite complex, especially for first-time visitors. Google Maps is an essential tool for navigating the city's streets and transit networks. In addition to providing walking directions, Google Maps also gives detailed information about Tokyo's train and subway lines, including which platform to use, train schedules, and the fastest routes between stations. It can even calculate the cost of your trip based on the route you choose. Having Google Maps at your fingertips means you can confidently explore Tokyo without worrying about getting lost or missing a train.

Another popular navigation app for public transportation is Japan Transit Planner (Jorudan). This app is specifically designed for navigating Japan's complex train systems and is highly recommended for travelers who want detailed, real-time information about train routes, schedules, and fares. Japan Transit Planner allows you to input your starting location and destination, and it will provide the best route options, including transfers, travel times, and costs. The app also gives updates on delays or service disruptions, which is especially useful when traveling during busy periods or bad weather. While Google Maps is a great all-around app, Japan Transit Planner is tailored specifically to Japan's train networks, making it a valuable resource for navigating Tokyo's subway and JR train lines.

For communication, language, and translation needs, Google Translate is one of the most essential apps for any traveler visiting Tokyo. Although English is spoken and understood in many tourist areas, there will still be times when you'll encounter signs, menus, or people who communicate primarily in Japanese. Google Translate offers a simple way to bridge the language gap. One of its most useful features is the ability to translate text by pointing your phone's camera at Japanese signs, menus, or other written materials. The app can quickly translate the Japanese characters into English (or another language of your choice), making it easier to understand what's around you, even if you don't know any Japanese. Additionally, Google Translate allows you to type or speak a phrase in English and have it translated into Japanese, which can be incredibly helpful when asking for directions, ordering food, or making basic conversation with locals. While it's always a good idea to learn a few basic Japanese phrases before your trip, having Google Translate can give you peace of mind when language barriers arise.

Another valuable app for communication is LINE, which is the most popular messaging app in Japan. While tourists may not use LINE as frequently as locals, it's worth downloading if you plan to communicate with friends, family, or contacts in Japan. Many businesses, restaurants, and hotels also use LINE to communicate with customers, so having the app can be handy for making reservations or contacting service providers while you're in Tokyo. LINE also offers stickers and emojis that reflect Japanese culture, making it a fun way to communicate while you're abroad.

For travelers who want to stay connected with free Wi-Fi, Japan Connected-Free Wi-Fi is a great app to have on your phone. While Tokyo is known for being technologically advanced, free public Wi-Fi is not as widely available as it might be in some other major cities. Japan Connected-Free Wi-Fi helps you find free Wi-Fi hotspots throughout the city, including in train stations, cafes, shopping centers, and tourist attractions. Once you've registered with the app, it allows you to automatically connect to available Wi-Fi networks without having to log in every time. This can be especially helpful for travelers who don't have an international data plan or want to avoid high roaming charges. With this app, you can stay online, check maps, and use other apps without worrying about finding a reliable internet connection.

For food lovers, there are also apps designed to help you discover the best dining options in Tokyo. Tabelog is a popular app in Japan for finding restaurant reviews and recommendations. Similar to Yelp, Tabelog features user-generated reviews and rankings for a wide variety of restaurants across Tokyo, from high-end sushi establishments to casual ramen shops. The app is available in English and allows you to search for restaurants by cuisine, location, and price range. It's especially useful for finding hidden gems that might not appear in typical tourist guides. With Tabelog, you can explore Tokyo's diverse food scene with confidence, knowing you're choosing places that are highly rated by locals and visitors alike.

For those who enjoy exploring cities by foot, the Tokyo Metro app is another useful tool. This app provides a detailed map of Tokyo's subway system, making it easy to find your way around the city's many stations and transfer points. The app also includes information on train times, platform numbers, and the most convenient exits for popular tourist attractions. While Google Maps and Japan Transit Planner are excellent for overall navigation, the Tokyo Metro app is specifically designed to help you navigate the subway system, providing offline access to subway maps and route information even when you don't have an internet connection.

If you're planning to visit specific attractions or events during your trip, TripAdvisor's app is an excellent resource for checking reviews, photos, and recommendations for things to do in Tokyo. Whether you're looking for popular tourist spots like Tokyo Skytree or hidden local attractions, TripAdvisor offers user-generated reviews that can help you decide what's worth visiting. The app also provides information on tours, tickets, and activities, allowing you to book directly from your phone. This is especially useful for planning day trips or excursions outside the city, such as visits to Mount Fuji or Nikko.

For travelers who enjoy booking activities and experiences ahead of time, Klook is a must-have app. Klook allows you to browse and book a variety of experiences, tours, and attraction tickets in Tokyo, often at discounted prices. From cultural experiences like tea ceremonies and kimono rentals to tickets for theme parks like Tokyo Disneyland, Klook offers a wide range of options to suit every traveler's interests. The app provides detailed descriptions of each activity, along with user reviews and photos, so you can make informed decisions about what to book. Booking through Klook can also save you time by allowing you to skip ticket lines at busy attractions.

For those interested in the convenience of ride-hailing services, Uber is available in Tokyo, though it's not as widely used as in some other cities. Taxi apps like JapanTaxi are more commonly used by locals, and they offer a convenient way to book a taxi in advance or on-demand. JapanTaxi allows you to input your pickup and drop-off locations, estimate fares, and pay through the app. While taxis are more expensive than public transportation, they can be a convenient option if you're traveling with luggage or if you're out late at night when trains are no longer running.

Additionally, if you're planning to explore Tokyo's many temples, shrines, and historic landmarks, having an app like Google Arts & Culture can enrich your experience. This app offers virtual tours, detailed descriptions, and background information on many of Tokyo's cultural sites, allowing you to learn more about the history and significance of each location. Whether you're visiting the Meiji Shrine, Senso-ji Temple, or the Tokyo National Museum, Google Arts & Culture can provide context and insights that enhance your understanding of Tokyo's rich cultural heritage.

Packing Guide: What to Bring

When preparing for a trip to Tokyo, Japan, packing wisely can make a huge difference in how comfortable and enjoyable your experience will be. Tokyo is a city that offers a blend of tradition and modernity, with bustling urban areas, serene parks, and cultural sites all coexisting. As a traveler, you'll want to be prepared for the diverse range of activities and situations you might encounter. Understanding the climate, cultural norms, and practical needs you'll have while in Tokyo will help guide what you should pack to ensure that your trip is as smooth as possible.

First and foremost, consider the time of year you'll be visiting Tokyo, as the weather can vary significantly depending on the season. Tokyo experiences four distinct seasons: a mild spring, a hot and humid summer, a cool autumn, and a cold winter. Each season requires different types of clothing and preparation, so it's essential to pack accordingly.

If you're visiting during the spring, which typically runs from March to May, you'll need to prepare for mild but changeable weather. Spring in Tokyo is generally cool, with average temperatures ranging from 10°C to 20°C (50°F to 68°F), but it can also be rainy at times, particularly in late March and early April. A lightweight, waterproof jacket or a compact umbrella will be useful for staying dry during the occasional spring showers. Layering is key during this season, as mornings and evenings can be cool, while afternoons can be warm and sunny. Bringing long-sleeved shirts or light sweaters that you can easily remove or add as the temperature changes will help you stay comfortable throughout the day.

During summer, which lasts from June to August, the weather in Tokyo is hot and humid, with temperatures often exceeding 30°C (86°F) and high levels of humidity making it feel even warmer. The rainy season, or tsuyu, usually occurs from early June to mid-July, so you should be prepared for frequent rain showers. Lightweight, breathable clothing is essential to help you stay cool in the heat, but you'll also want to bring a compact umbrella or rain jacket to keep dry during the rainy days. Loose-fitting clothes made from natural fibers like cotton or linen are great for staying comfortable in the heat, and don't forget to pack a hat, sunglasses, and sunscreen to protect yourself from the sun.

If you're visiting Tokyo during the autumn months (September to November), you can expect cooler, more comfortable weather. Temperatures in autumn range from around 15°C to 25°C (59°F to 77°F), making it an ideal time for outdoor activities like exploring parks, walking tours, or visiting temples and shrines. The weather is generally dry, and the humidity of summer disappears, so packing light layers like sweaters or long-sleeved shirts, along with comfortable walking shoes, will be perfect for this season. Since autumn in Tokyo is known for its beautiful fall foliage, you'll likely spend a lot of time outdoors, so wearing comfortable and durable shoes for walking long distances is a good idea.

Winter in Tokyo (December to February) is cold, but generally not as extreme as in other parts of Japan. Temperatures usually range from 2°C to 10°C (36°F to 50°F), so packing warm clothing is essential. A good winter coat, along with scarves, gloves, and a hat, will keep you warm while you explore the city during the cooler months. While Tokyo doesn't get heavy snowfall, it can occasionally snow in January and February, so be prepared for cold mornings and evenings, especially if you plan to visit outdoor attractions like temples or gardens. Wearing thermal layers under your clothing can help keep you warm without having to pack too many bulky items. Comfortable, insulated shoes are also important for staying warm, especially if you'll be walking a lot or visiting outdoor areas.

Regardless of the season, there are a few essential items you should always bring when visiting Tokyo. Comfortable footwear is a must, as you'll likely be walking long distances throughout the city, whether you're exploring neighborhoods, shopping districts, or parks. Tokyo is a pedestrian-friendly city, and many of its most interesting areas are best explored on foot. Sneakers or walking shoes with good support are ideal for getting around without discomfort.

Since Japan has a reputation for being very clean and hygienic, it's a good idea to pack a small bottle of hand sanitizer and tissues. Public restrooms in Tokyo are generally clean and widely available, but many of them do not provide paper towels, so carrying tissues or a handkerchief with you can be useful for drying your hands or other purposes. Additionally, many restaurants and shops offer wet towels or wipes before meals, but having your own hand sanitizer is always a good idea, especially when traveling on public transportation.

For those interested in technology or who plan to stay connected during their trip, packing the right electronics is important. Tokyo is a tech-savvy city, but you'll still need to bring an international power adapter to charge your devices, as Japan uses a 100-volt electrical system with Type A and Type B plugs, which are the same as those used in the United States. If you're coming from a country that uses different plug types, make sure to bring the appropriate adapter. It's also worth considering bringing a portable charger, as you may be out exploring all day and want to ensure your phone or camera stays charged. Having a fully charged phone is crucial for using maps, translation apps, and taking photos of the many sights you'll encounter.

Speaking of photos, if you're someone who enjoys documenting your travels, bringing a camera or smartphone with plenty of storage is essential. Tokyo is a visually stunning city, with countless photo-worthy spots, from the neon-lit streets of Shibuya to the peaceful gardens surrounding temples. If you plan to take a lot of pictures, consider packing an extra memory card or a backup storage option like a portable hard drive or cloud storage to avoid running out of space. A small tripod can also be useful if you're taking photos at night or want to capture group shots without asking for help.

For those who want to stay healthy and comfortable during their trip, packing any necessary medications or health-related items is important. While Tokyo has pharmacies (known as kusuriya) where you can find basic over-the-counter medicines, it's always better to bring any specific medications or supplements you might need. Japan has strict rules regarding certain medications, so if you're bringing prescription drugs, it's a good idea to check the regulations in advance to ensure they're allowed into the country. Carrying a copy of your prescription or a letter from your doctor can also be helpful, especially for medications that require special approval.

In terms of personal items, a small daypack or travel bag is a convenient way to carry your essentials while exploring Tokyo. A lightweight, foldable backpack or shoulder bag is perfect for holding your wallet, phone, water bottle, camera, and any purchases you make during the day. Since Tokyo's public transportation is very efficient, you'll likely be out and about for long periods of time, so having a bag that can comfortably carry your necessities is key. You may also want to bring a reusable water bottle, as Tokyo's tap water is safe to drink, and staying hydrated is important, especially during the warmer months.

If you plan to visit temples, shrines, or other cultural sites, it's also worth considering the local customs regarding dress. While there is no formal dress code for most places, it's a good idea to dress modestly when visiting religious or historical sites. For example, wearing clothing that covers your shoulders and knees is a respectful gesture when entering temples or shrines. Bringing a lightweight scarf or shawl can also be helpful if you want to cover up more in these settings.

Don't forget to bring copies of important travel documents. In addition to your passport, it's a good idea to carry a photocopy of your passport and keep it in a separate place from the original, just in case. You should also have copies of any travel insurance documents, hotel reservations, flight information, and any other important details related to your trip. Having both physical copies and digital backups of these documents stored on your phone or in the cloud can provide peace of mind in case anything goes wrong.

CHAPTER 3

GETTING TO TOKYO

When planning a trip to Tokyo, one of the first things you'll need to think about is which international airport to fly into. Tokyo is served by two major international airports: Narita International Airport (NRT) and Haneda Airport (HND). Each of these airports has its own advantages, and understanding their locations, facilities, and transport options can help you make the best choice depending on your travel needs. Both airports are modern, well-equipped, and handle millions of passengers each year, making them key gateways to Japan and, in particular, to the Tokyo metropolitan area.

Narita International Airport is located about 60 kilometers (37 miles) east of central Tokyo, in Chiba Prefecture. It has long been the main international gateway to Japan and handles the majority of international long-haul flights coming into the Tokyo area. Narita is a large, sprawling airport with three terminals that serve a wide range of airlines from around the world. Many international carriers, particularly those flying from Europe, North America, and other long-distance destinations, use Narita as their primary entry point into Japan. The airport itself is modern and well-equipped, with a wide variety of shops, restaurants, and services designed to make the travel experience as smooth as possible. You'll find duty-free stores, lounges, currency exchange services, and even showers for freshening up after a long flight.

While Narita is further from central Tokyo than Haneda, it is well-connected to the city via several transportation options. One of the most popular ways to travel between Narita and Tokyo is by train. The Narita Express (N'EX) is a direct train service that connects Narita Airport with major stations in Tokyo, including Tokyo Station, Shinjuku, Shibuya, and Yokohama. The journey takes approximately 60 to 90 minutes, depending on your destination, and the trains are comfortable, spacious, and equipped with luggage racks for your convenience. The Narita Express is a convenient option for travelers who want a fast and direct connection to central Tokyo. Tickets for the Narita Express can be purchased at the airport, and there are also special discounted round-trip tickets available for foreign tourists.

Another popular train option is the Keisei Skyliner, which connects Narita Airport to Ueno Station and Nippori Station in northeastern Tokyo. The Skyliner is known for its speed and efficiency, with a travel time of around 40 minutes to Ueno, making it one of the fastest ways to reach the city from the airport. This train service is particularly convenient for travelers staying in the Ueno or Asakusa areas, and it also connects to other train lines at Nippori Station, making it easy to transfer to other parts of Tokyo. Like the Narita Express, tickets for the Keisei Skyliner can be purchased at the airport or online in advance.

In addition to the trains, there are also bus services that run between Narita Airport and various parts of Tokyo. Limousine buses offer direct routes to many major hotels and key destinations within the city, including popular neighborhoods like Shibuya, Shinjuku, and Roppongi. The bus services are a good option if you have a lot of luggage or if you prefer to be dropped off directly at your hotel rather than navigating Tokyo's train stations. The travel time by bus can vary depending on traffic, but it typically takes around 90 minutes to reach central Tokyo. Buses are comfortable and come equipped with Wi-Fi and plenty of space for luggage.

If you prefer a more private form of transportation, taxis are also available from Narita Airport, though they are significantly more expensive than public transport options. A taxi ride from Narita to central Tokyo can take anywhere from 60 to 90 minutes, depending on traffic, and costs around ¥20,000 to ¥30,000 (approximately $180 to $270), making it a more costly option unless you're traveling with a group or have specific needs that make taking a taxi more convenient.

Haneda Airport, on the other hand, is located much closer to central Tokyo, just about 14 kilometers (9 miles) south of the city center. Historically, Haneda was used primarily for domestic flights, but in recent years, it has expanded its international operations and now handles a growing number of international flights, particularly from nearby countries in Asia, as well as long-haul destinations like the United States and Europe. Haneda is a modern airport with three terminals: one for international flights and two for domestic flights. The international terminal, in particular, is well-designed, with a wide range of amenities, shops, and dining options, as well as excellent transportation links to Tokyo.

One of the biggest advantages of flying into Haneda Airport is its proximity to central Tokyo. Because it's so close to the city, getting from Haneda to your hotel or other destinations in Tokyo is much quicker and more convenient than from Narita. The most popular way to travel from Haneda to the city is by train, and there are two main train lines that serve the airport: the Tokyo Monorail and the Keikyu Line.

The Tokyo Monorail connects Haneda Airport to Hamamatsucho Station, which is located in central Tokyo and provides easy access to the JR Yamanote Line, a loop line that connects many of Tokyo's major neighborhoods. The monorail ride to Hamamatsucho takes about 15 to 20 minutes, making it a quick and efficient option for travelers who want to get into the city center as quickly as possible. The monorail is modern and comfortable, with plenty of space for luggage, and it offers great views of Tokyo Bay as you travel into the city.

The Keikyu Line is another popular option for getting from Haneda Airport to central Tokyo. It provides direct train service to Shinagawa Station, which is a major transportation hub and connects to the JR Yamanote Line as well as the Tokaido Shinkansen (bullet train) that runs to cities like Kyoto and Osaka. The Keikyu Line also offers connections to other parts of Tokyo and can take you directly to Asakusa, Shinjuku, and other popular areas without needing to transfer. The travel time from Haneda to Shinagawa is about 15 minutes, making it a very convenient choice for travelers staying in that area.

Like Narita, Haneda Airport also offers limousine bus services that run to various parts of Tokyo. These buses provide direct service to many major hotels and attractions, making them a good choice if you want to avoid navigating Tokyo's train system with heavy luggage. The travel time by bus from Haneda to central Tokyo is usually around 30 to 45 minutes, depending on your destination and the traffic conditions.

Because of its closer location to central Tokyo, taxis from Haneda are also a more affordable option compared to those from Narita. A taxi ride from Haneda to most central Tokyo destinations typically costs between ¥5,000 and ¥10,000 (about $45 to $90), and the journey takes around 20 to 40 minutes, depending on traffic. This makes Haneda a good choice for travelers who want the convenience of a taxi without the high cost associated with the longer journey from Narita.

Direct Flights from Major Cities

When planning a trip to Tokyo, one of the most important considerations is how to get there. As one of the busiest cities in the world, Tokyo is well-connected to major cities across the globe, and many airlines offer direct flights to both Narita International Airport (NRT) and Haneda Airport (HND), the two primary airports serving the Tokyo metropolitan area. Having a direct flight means you won't need to worry about layovers or connecting flights, which can make your journey much easier and more convenient, especially for long-haul trips.

Tokyo's major airports receive direct flights from numerous cities in North America, Europe, Asia, and Oceania, making it accessible to travelers from all over the world. If you're flying from the United States, there are several cities that offer direct flights to Tokyo. For example, you can fly directly to Tokyo from cities like New York, Los Angeles, San Francisco, Chicago, Seattle, and Dallas. Airlines such as Japan Airlines (JAL), All Nippon Airways (ANA), Delta, American Airlines, and United operate direct flights from these major U.S. hubs to Tokyo. The flight time from most cities in the United States to Tokyo ranges from about 10 to 14 hours, depending on where you're departing from.

Flights from Los Angeles and San Francisco to Tokyo are particularly popular due to the large number of flights that depart daily and the relatively short distance compared to other parts of the United States. The Pacific coast's proximity to Japan means that flights from cities like Los Angeles, San Francisco, and Seattle are often shorter and more frequent, making these locations convenient departure points for travelers heading to Tokyo. Los Angeles International Airport (LAX), in particular, serves as a major gateway for flights to Tokyo, with both Japanese and U.S. carriers offering multiple direct flights each day. For those on the East Coast of the U.S., cities like New York and Washington, D.C., also offer direct flights, though the travel time is typically longer, often around 14 hours due to the greater distance.

For travelers from Canada, direct flights to Tokyo are available from cities such as Toronto and Vancouver. Airlines like Air Canada, ANA, and JAL operate flights from these major Canadian cities, with Vancouver being one of the most frequent departure points for flights to Tokyo due to its location on the west coast. A direct flight from Vancouver to Tokyo typically takes about 9 to 11 hours, while flights from Toronto usually take around 13 to 14 hours. Canadian travelers can also find flights from other cities, but these may require a layover in Vancouver, Seattle, or other connecting airports.

If you're traveling to Tokyo from Europe, many major cities also offer direct flights. London, Paris, Frankfurt, Amsterdam, and Zurich are some of the key European hubs with direct flights to Tokyo. Airlines such as British Airways, Air France, Lufthansa, KLM, and Swiss International Airlines operate direct flights from these cities, along with Japan Airlines and ANA. The flight time from Europe to Tokyo typically ranges from 11 to 14 hours, depending on the city of departure. London Heathrow (LHR) is one of the busiest airports for flights to Tokyo, with several airlines offering daily flights between the two cities. Travelers from Paris can also fly directly to Tokyo's Narita or Haneda airports with Air France or JAL, while those flying from Germany often have the option of flying with Lufthansa or ANA from Frankfurt or Munich.

For those traveling from Asia, Tokyo is extremely well-connected to most major cities in the region. Direct flights to Tokyo are available from cities such as Beijing, Shanghai, Hong Kong, Seoul, Bangkok, Singapore, Kuala Lumpur, and Jakarta, among many others. Asian airlines such as ANA, JAL, Cathay Pacific, Korean Air, China Eastern Airlines, Singapore Airlines, and Thai Airways operate frequent direct flights to Tokyo. Given the relatively short flight times between Tokyo and other Asian cities, these routes are highly convenient for both business and leisure travelers. For example, a direct flight from Seoul to Tokyo takes about 2 to 3 hours, while flights from Hong Kong or Bangkok usually take around 4 to 6 hours.

Travelers from Australia and New Zealand also have the option of flying directly to Tokyo from cities like Sydney, Melbourne, Brisbane, and Auckland. Qantas, ANA, JAL, and Air New Zealand are some of the airlines that operate direct flights from these cities to Tokyo. The flight time from Sydney to Tokyo is typically around 9 to 10 hours, while flights from Melbourne and Brisbane take slightly longer. Direct flights from Auckland to Tokyo usually take around 10 to 11 hours.

Tokyo's status as a global hub for business, tourism, and culture means that airlines from all over the world compete to offer direct flights, making it easier than ever to reach the city from almost anywhere. Whether you're traveling from North America, Europe, Asia, or Oceania, you'll find a wide range of options for direct flights, allowing you to choose the airline, schedule, and airport that best suits your travel plans.

In addition to the convenience of flying directly to Tokyo, it's worth considering which airport you prefer to arrive at—Narita or Haneda. As mentioned earlier, Narita International Airport is located about 60 kilometers outside central Tokyo, and it handles the majority of long-haul international flights. While it's a bit further from the city center, Narita offers a wide range of transportation options, including the Narita Express train, the Keisei Skyliner, and limousine buses, making it easy to reach central Tokyo within about an hour.

Haneda Airport, on the other hand, is located much closer to central Tokyo, just about 14 kilometers south of the city center. Haneda is becoming increasingly popular for international flights, especially for travelers coming from nearby Asian countries, as well as some long-haul destinations. Haneda's proximity to Tokyo means that getting from the airport to your hotel or other destinations within the city is faster and more convenient. Both airports are modern, efficient, and well-equipped, but your choice may depend on which flights are available from your home city and how quickly you want to reach central Tokyo.

Airport Transfers: From Airport to Central Tokyo

Getting from the airport to central Tokyo is an important part of planning your trip, as it sets the tone for the rest of your visit. Tokyo is served by two major airports, Narita International Airport and Haneda Airport, both of which offer a variety of transportation options to help you reach your destination in central Tokyo efficiently and comfortably. The choice of transport depends on several factors, including your budget, the amount of luggage you have, and how quickly you want to get to your destination.

If you are arriving at Narita International Airport, which is located about 60 kilometers (37 miles) east of central Tokyo, you will have several options for getting into the city. One of the most popular and efficient ways to travel from Narita to Tokyo is by train. The Narita Express (N'EX) is a direct train service operated by Japan Railways (JR) that connects Narita Airport to major stations in Tokyo, including Tokyo Station, Shibuya, Shinjuku, and Yokohama. The Narita Express is known for its speed and convenience, with a travel time of around 60 to 90 minutes depending on your final destination. The trains are comfortable, with spacious seating, luggage racks, and free Wi-Fi, making them a great option for travelers who want a quick and hassle-free journey into the city. Tickets for the Narita Express can be purchased at the airport, and for foreign tourists, there are special discounted round-trip tickets available, which offer excellent value if you are planning to return to the airport within two weeks.

Another train option from Narita is the Keisei Skyliner, which is known for being one of the fastest ways to get from the airport to central Tokyo. The Skyliner connects Narita Airport to Ueno Station and Nippori Station in the northeastern part of Tokyo, with a travel time of around 40 minutes to Ueno, making it one of the quickest options for reaching the city. The Skyliner is particularly convenient for travelers who are staying in the Ueno, Asakusa, or Akihabara areas, and it also connects to other train lines at Nippori Station, allowing for easy transfers to other parts of Tokyo. Like the Narita Express, the Skyliner offers comfortable seating, ample space for luggage, and a smooth ride, making it a top choice for travelers who value speed and efficiency. Tickets for the Skyliner can be purchased at the airport or online in advance, and there are often discounted fares available for foreign tourists.

In addition to the express trains, there are also regular train services available from Narita Airport to Tokyo. The Keisei Main Line, for example, offers a slower but more affordable option for travelers on a tighter budget. While it takes longer to reach central Tokyo—around 70 to 80 minutes to Ueno— the Keisei Main Line is a good choice for budget-conscious travelers who don't mind a slightly slower journey. Similarly, the JR Sobu Line offers a direct train from Narita to Tokyo Station, but it is slower than the Narita Express, with a travel time of around 90 minutes.

For travelers who prefer a more direct form of transportation, airport limousine buses offer a convenient alternative to the trains. Limousine buses operate from both Narita and Haneda airports and provide direct service to many of Tokyo's major hotels and neighborhoods, including Shibuya, Shinjuku, Roppongi, and Ginza. The advantage of taking a bus is that it often drops you off directly at your hotel or very close to your destination, which can be especially helpful if you have a lot of luggage or are unfamiliar with Tokyo's train system. The travel time by bus from Narita to central Tokyo is typically around 90 minutes to two hours, depending on traffic, and the buses are equipped with comfortable seats, air conditioning, and Wi-Fi. Limousine bus tickets can be purchased at the airport, and there is usually staff available to assist foreign travelers with finding the right bus for their destination.

Another option for travelers arriving at Narita is the Airport Shuttle, which offers shared ride services to specific areas of Tokyo. The shuttle service is more affordable than a private taxi but offers the convenience of door-to-door service, making it a good middle-ground option for those who want the comfort of a direct transfer without the high cost of a private taxi. The Airport Shuttle operates on a reservation basis, so it's important to book your ride in advance, especially if you are arriving during peak travel times.

For those who prioritize comfort and convenience over cost, taxis and private car services are available from Narita Airport to central Tokyo. A taxi ride from Narita to central Tokyo can take around 60 to 90 minutes depending on traffic and costs between ¥20,000 and ¥30,000 (approximately $180 to $270). While this is a more expensive option compared to public transportation, it is ideal for travelers with a lot of luggage, those traveling in groups, or anyone who wants to avoid the hassle of navigating trains or buses. Private car services can also be booked in advance, offering a similar level of convenience but with the added benefit of personalized service, such as English-speaking drivers or luxury vehicles.

If you are arriving at Haneda Airport, which is located much closer to central Tokyo—about 14 kilometers (9 miles) south of the city center—your transportation options are similar, but the journey is generally shorter and more affordable due to the airport's proximity to the city. One of the most popular ways to travel from Haneda to central Tokyo is by train. The Tokyo Monorail connects Haneda Airport to Hamamatsucho Station, which is located on the JR Yamanote Line, a loop line that connects many of Tokyo's major neighborhoods. The monorail ride to Hamamatsucho takes about 15 to 20 minutes, making it one of the quickest ways to get into the city. From Hamamatsucho, you can easily transfer to the Yamanote Line to reach areas like Shibuya, Shinjuku, and Tokyo Station. The monorail is a popular choice for travelers because it's fast, reliable, and provides scenic views of Tokyo Bay as you approach the city.

Another train option from Haneda is the Keikyu Line, which offers direct service to Shinagawa Station, a major transportation hub in Tokyo. The Keikyu Line is a convenient option for travelers staying in the Shinagawa area or for those who need to connect to the Shinkansen (bullet train) for onward travel to other parts of Japan. The travel time from Haneda to Shinagawa is about 15 minutes, making it a quick and efficient choice. The Keikyu Line also connects to other train lines that can take you directly to destinations like Asakusa and Shinjuku without the need for a transfer.

Like Narita, Haneda also offers limousine bus services that provide direct transfers to major hotels and key areas within Tokyo. The buses are a great option if you prefer to avoid navigating the train system, especially if you have heavy luggage or are unfamiliar with the city. The travel time by bus from Haneda to central Tokyo is usually around 30 to 45 minutes, depending on traffic. Limousine buses from Haneda are slightly cheaper than those from Narita, given the shorter distance.

For travelers who prefer the convenience of a taxi, the cost of taking a taxi from Haneda to central Tokyo is significantly lower than from Narita, with fares ranging from ¥5,000 to ¥10,000 (about $45 to $90). The journey takes around 20 to 40 minutes, depending on traffic. This makes taking a taxi from Haneda a more feasible option for travelers who want a direct, door-to-door transfer without spending too much money.

CHAPTER 4

WHERE TO STAY: CHOOSING THE PERFECT ACCOMMODATION

Tokyo's Main Districts: Where to Stay and Why

Tokyo is an enormous city, made up of several distinct districts, each with its own unique atmosphere, attractions, and accommodations. Where you choose to stay in Tokyo can have a big impact on your experience, as different districts cater to different interests and offer various conveniences depending on what you want to see and do.

One of the most popular districts for visitors to stay in is Shinjuku. Shinjuku is a bustling, high-energy area located in the western part of central Tokyo. It's known for its towering skyscrapers, endless shopping options, and vibrant nightlife. Shinjuku Station is one of the busiest train stations in the world, making it an ideal place to stay for easy access to the rest of Tokyo. The area around the station is filled with department stores, restaurants, and entertainment venues, offering plenty to see and do within walking distance of your hotel. Shinjuku is also home to some of Tokyo's most famous nightlife spots, particularly in the Kabukicho area, where you'll find bars, clubs, and karaoke lounges. Despite its urban hustle, Shinjuku also offers moments of peace with places like Shinjuku Gyoen, a large and beautifully landscaped park where you can relax amidst nature. Staying in Shinjuku is ideal if you want to be in the heart of the action, with a wide range of accommodations from luxury hotels to more affordable business hotels and hostels.

If you prefer a more upscale and polished atmosphere, Ginza might be the perfect district for your stay. Located closer to the eastern part of central Tokyo, Ginza is synonymous with luxury shopping, fine dining, and elegant architecture. This area is home to many high-end international and Japanese brands, making it a shopping paradise for those interested in fashion and luxury goods. Ginza's wide, tree-lined streets are filled with designer boutiques, flagship stores, and upscale department stores like Mitsukoshi and Wako. It's also a center for gourmet dining, with numerous Michelin-starred restaurants and top-tier sushi bars. Despite its reputation for luxury, Ginza also offers a variety of mid-range accommodation options. The district's proximity to attractions like the Imperial Palace and Tokyo Station also makes it a convenient location for travelers who want to explore other parts of the city. If you enjoy shopping, art galleries, and fine dining, staying in Ginza will put you at the center of Tokyo's chic and refined side.

For travelers looking to experience Tokyo's pop culture, youth fashion, and vibrant street scenes, Shibuya is a fantastic choice. Shibuya is one of Tokyo's most iconic neighborhoods, famous for its scramble crossing, which is one of the busiest intersections in the world. The area around Shibuya Station is packed with shopping centers, trendy boutiques, and entertainment venues that cater to a younger crowd. Streets like Takeshita Street and Cat Street are lined with shops selling unique clothing, accessories, and pop culture items, making Shibuya a hotspot for youth fashion and street culture. It's also a great place to experience Tokyo's food scene, with countless cafes, casual eateries, and late-night restaurants. Shibuya comes alive at night, with its neon lights and bustling nightlife, offering everything from live music venues to casual bars and clubs. Accommodations in Shibuya range from luxury hotels to more affordable options, making it accessible for different budgets. If you're interested in Tokyo's modern, youthful energy and want to be in the middle of its fast-paced action, Shibuya is an ideal place to stay.

For those who want to explore Tokyo's traditional side, Asakusa is a district that offers a glimpse into Japan's past. Located in the northeastern part of Tokyo, Asakusa is famous for its historic temples and traditional shopping streets. The most notable attraction in Asakusa is Senso-ji, Tokyo's oldest and most visited temple. The streets leading to the temple are lined with traditional shops selling souvenirs, snacks, and local crafts, making it a popular destination for tourists looking to experience a more traditional Tokyo. Asakusa also retains much of its old-world charm, with rickshaws still ferrying visitors around the streets and many old-style inns, called ryokan, offering a more authentic Japanese lodging experience. Staying in Asakusa is perfect for travelers who want to immerse themselves in Japanese culture and history, while still being close to modern conveniences and attractions. While it's slightly quieter than other major districts, Asakusa is well-connected by public transport, making it easy to reach other parts of Tokyo.

Akihabara, also known as "Electric Town," is the perfect district for those interested in electronics, anime, and manga. Located just a short distance from Tokyo Station, Akihabara is famous for its vast array of electronics stores, from large department-style shops to small specialty stores selling the latest gadgets, cameras, and computers. In recent years, Akihabara has also become a hub for fans of anime, manga, and video games. You'll find countless stores selling merchandise, collectibles, and games, as well as themed cafes where you can immerse yourself in Japan's otaku (geek) culture. If you're a fan of Japanese pop culture or are looking for the latest electronics, staying in Akihabara will put you right in the middle of this vibrant and colorful district. Accommodation options in Akihabara tend to be more affordable, with plenty of business hotels and hostels catering to travelers who want to experience the neighborhood's unique energy.

Tokyo Station, located in the Marunouchi district, is another excellent area to consider for your stay, especially if you're planning to take day trips or travel around Japan via the Shinkansen (bullet train). Tokyo Station is a major transportation hub, offering access to numerous train lines, including the Shinkansen that connects Tokyo to other major cities like Kyoto, Osaka, and Hiroshima. Staying near Tokyo Station provides the ultimate convenience for transportation, but the area itself also has much to offer. The Marunouchi district is home to sleek office buildings, upscale shopping malls, and fine dining restaurants. The nearby Imperial Palace and its surrounding gardens offer a peaceful contrast to the modernity of the area, making it a great spot for leisurely walks. Tokyo Station's central location means that you're just a short train ride away from many of Tokyo's other districts, making it a strategic place to stay for those who want easy access to everything the city has to offer.

Roppongi is another popular district, known for its nightlife, international community, and art scene. Roppongi has a reputation for being one of Tokyo's top nightlife spots, with countless bars, clubs, and restaurants that cater to both locals and expatriates. It's also home to several high-end shopping and entertainment complexes, such as Roppongi Hills and Tokyo Midtown, which offer a mix of luxury stores, art galleries, and restaurants. The area has become a hub for contemporary art, with attractions like the Mori Art Museum drawing visitors interested in modern exhibitions and installations. Roppongi's cosmopolitan atmosphere makes it a great place for travelers who want to enjoy both Tokyo's nightlife and cultural attractions. The district offers a range of accommodations, from luxury hotels to more budget-friendly options, making it a versatile place to stay.

For travelers seeking a more relaxed and residential vibe, the district of Ebisu is a great option. Located just a short distance from Shibuya, Ebisu offers a quieter and more laid-back atmosphere while still being close to Tokyo's major attractions. The area is known for its sophisticated dining scene, with numerous restaurants, cafes, and izakayas offering a range of international and Japanese cuisine. Ebisu is also home to Yebisu Garden Place, a stylish complex with shops, restaurants, and an art museum. Staying in Ebisu provides a nice balance between the excitement of Tokyo's central districts and the tranquility of a more residential neighborhood. It's an excellent choice for travelers who want to experience local life while still having easy access to the rest of the city.

Luxury Hotels

When visiting Tokyo, luxury hotels provide an exceptional level of service, comfort, and style, catering to tourists looking for a refined and memorable experience. Tokyo is home to some of the finest luxury hotels in the world, each offering its own unique atmosphere, world-class amenities, and convenient locations. These hotels cater to discerning travelers who want to enjoy the best that Tokyo has to offer, from impeccable service and breathtaking views to gourmet dining and proximity to the city's top attractions.

One of the most iconic luxury hotels in Tokyo is The Ritz-Carlton, located in the upscale Roppongi district. The hotel occupies the top floors of the Tokyo Midtown Tower, one of the tallest buildings in the city, offering sweeping views of Tokyo's skyline, including Tokyo Tower and, on clear days, Mount Fuji. The Ritz-Carlton Tokyo is known for its luxurious accommodations, with spacious rooms and suites that feature modern design and traditional Japanese touches. The hotel offers world-class amenities such as an indoor swimming pool, a full-service spa, and several fine dining options, including a Michelin-starred restaurant. Guests can also enjoy the hotel's stylish bar and lounge, which provides a perfect setting for evening drinks with panoramic views of the city.

The Ritz-Carlton's location in Roppongi makes it a convenient base for exploring both modern and traditional Tokyo. The Roppongi district is known for its vibrant nightlife, high-end shopping, and art galleries, including the nearby Mori Art Museum. From Narita International Airport, you can reach The Ritz-Carlton Tokyo by taking the Narita Express train to Tokyo Station, followed by a short taxi ride or a transfer to the Hibiya subway line to Roppongi Station, which is just a short walk from the hotel. Alternatively, Haneda Airport is even closer, with direct access to Roppongi via the Keikyu Line and Tokyo Metro. The Ritz-Carlton's room rates typically range from $700 to over $2,000 per night, depending on the type of room or suite you choose.

Another highly acclaimed luxury hotel is Aman Tokyo, located in the Otemachi district, close to the Imperial Palace. Aman Tokyo is part of the exclusive Aman hotel group, known for its minimalist aesthetic, serene atmosphere, and personalized service. The hotel's design combines modern urban style with traditional Japanese influences, featuring large rooms with natural materials such as stone, wood, and washi paper. Aman Tokyo offers a range of top-tier amenities, including a 30-meter indoor pool with panoramic city views, a tranquil spa with traditional Japanese treatments, and an elegant restaurant that serves both Japanese and international cuisine.

Aman Tokyo is ideally located for those who want to be close to Tokyo's historical and cultural sites. The Imperial Palace is within walking distance, and the nearby Otemachi and Tokyo stations provide easy access to other parts of the city. From Narita International Airport, you can take the Narita Express to Tokyo Station and then either walk or take a short taxi ride to the hotel. Haneda Airport is also conveniently connected to Tokyo Station via the Tokyo Monorail and JR Yamanote Line. Room rates at Aman Tokyo typically range from $900 to over $3,000 per night, with higher rates for suites and rooms offering expansive views of the city.

The Four Seasons Hotel Tokyo at Marunouchi offers a more intimate luxury experience, with a boutique hotel atmosphere located in the heart of Tokyo's business district. Despite its smaller size compared to other luxury hotels, the Four Seasons Marunouchi provides personalized service and spacious, elegantly designed rooms. The hotel features a full-service spa, a Michelin-starred French restaurant, and easy access to the upscale shopping and dining options of the Marunouchi and Ginza districts. The hotel's location near Tokyo Station makes it incredibly convenient for travelers arriving by train or those planning to take the Shinkansen (bullet train) to other parts of Japan.

Travelers arriving at Narita can easily reach the Four Seasons Hotel Tokyo at Marunouchi by taking the Narita Express to

Tokyo Station, which is just a few minutes' walk from the hotel. Haneda Airport is similarly well-connected to Tokyo Station via the Tokyo Monorail or the Keikyu Line. Room rates at the Four Seasons Marunouchi generally range from $600 to $1,500 per night, depending on the room category and time of year.

The Peninsula Tokyo, located in the upscale Marunouchi district near the Imperial Palace and Ginza, is another top choice for luxury accommodation in Tokyo. The Peninsula brand is known for its commitment to exceptional service, and the Tokyo property is no exception. The hotel's spacious rooms feature contemporary design with Japanese influences, and many offer views of the Imperial Palace gardens or the city skyline. Guests can enjoy a range of world-class amenities, including an indoor swimming pool, a luxurious spa, and several fine dining options, including a renowned Cantonese restaurant and a rooftop bar with spectacular views.

The Peninsula Tokyo is perfectly located for exploring both the cultural landmarks and luxury shopping areas of central Tokyo. It's within walking distance of the Imperial Palace and the high-end shops of Ginza, making it a great base for tourists who want to combine sightseeing with shopping. From Narita Airport, you can take the Narita Express to Tokyo Station and either walk or take a short taxi ride to the hotel. Haneda Airport is even more accessible, with direct trains to nearby Yurakucho Station. Room rates at The Peninsula Tokyo generally range from $700 to over $2,500 per night, depending on the type of room or suite.

Park Hyatt Tokyo is another renowned luxury hotel, located in the bustling district of Shinjuku. The Park Hyatt Tokyo gained international fame after being featured in the movie Lost in Translation, and it continues to be one of the city's most iconic luxury hotels. Perched on the top floors of the Shinjuku Park Tower, the hotel offers stunning views of Tokyo, including Mount Fuji on clear days. The Park Hyatt Tokyo is known for its understated elegance, with spacious rooms featuring floor-to-ceiling windows, modern amenities, and luxurious furnishings. The hotel's amenities include an indoor swimming pool, a full-service spa, and several dining options, including the New York Grill, which offers panoramic views of the city.

Shinjuku is one of Tokyo's most vibrant neighborhoods, known for its shopping, entertainment, and nightlife. The Park Hyatt Tokyo's location makes it ideal for visitors who want to be close to the action while still enjoying a peaceful and luxurious retreat. From Narita Airport, you can take the Narita Express to Shinjuku Station and either walk or take a short taxi ride to the hotel. From Haneda, you can take the Keikyu Line to Shinagawa Station and transfer to the JR Yamanote Line to reach Shinjuku. Room rates at the Park Hyatt Tokyo typically range from $800 to over $2,000 per night, depending on the room type and season.

When booking luxury hotels in Tokyo, there are several ways to go about it. You can book directly through the hotel's website, which often offers special packages, loyalty programs, or exclusive deals. Another option is to use online travel agencies such as Booking.com, Expedia, or Agoda, which allow you to compare prices, read reviews, and book rooms easily. Additionally, if you have a membership with luxury hotel programs or travel companies, such as American Express Fine Hotels & Resorts or Virtuoso, you may be able to access special benefits like room upgrades, early check-in, or complimentary breakfast.

Budget Hotels

For travelers visiting Tokyo on a budget, the city offers a wide range of affordable accommodation options that provide comfort, convenience, and good value for money. Tokyo may have a reputation for being expensive, but you can still find budget hotels that cater to tourists who want to save on lodging while exploring everything the city has to offer. These budget hotels often provide clean, functional rooms with essential amenities, making them ideal for those who plan to spend most of their time out and about but still want a comfortable place to rest at the end of the day.

One of the most popular budget hotel chains in Tokyo is Toyoko Inn, known for offering clean, no-frills accommodations at affordable prices. Toyoko Inn has multiple locations throughout the city, including near major transportation hubs like Shinjuku, Ikebukuro, and Ueno, making it a convenient choice for travelers who want easy access to Tokyo's train and subway lines. Rooms at Toyoko Inn are simple but comfortable, equipped with all the basics such as free Wi-Fi, air conditioning, a small refrigerator, and a flat-screen TV. Some locations also offer free breakfast, usually consisting of a light Japanese or Western-style meal. Toyoko Inn is particularly appealing to budget-conscious travelers because of its loyalty program, which offers discounts for repeat guests. Room rates typically range from ¥6,000 to ¥10,000 (approximately $50 to $90) per night, depending on the location and time of year.

If you're arriving at Narita International Airport, you can reach the Toyoko Inn near Shinjuku by taking the Narita Express to Shinjuku Station, followed by a short walk to the hotel. From Haneda Airport, you can take the Keikyu Line to Shinagawa Station and transfer to the JR Yamanote Line, which will take you to Shinjuku. Toyoko Inn is a popular choice for business travelers and tourists alike, and you can book a room directly through the hotel's website or via online booking platforms like Agoda, Booking.com, or Expedia.

Another excellent option for budget accommodation in Tokyo is Hotel Mystays, which offers a variety of properties across the city, ranging from standard business hotels to more affordable options geared toward tourists. Hotel Mystays is known for its clean, modern rooms and reasonable prices, making it a popular choice for travelers looking for comfort on a budget. The rooms are typically compact but come with essential amenities like free Wi-Fi, air conditioning, a small refrigerator, and a flat-screen TV. Some locations also have laundry facilities, which can be helpful for longer stays. One of the most affordable Hotel Mystays locations is in Asakusa, a charming neighborhood known for its traditional atmosphere and iconic Senso-ji Temple. Staying in Asakusa provides a more relaxed experience while still being close to central Tokyo.

To get to Hotel Mystays Asakusa from Narita Airport, you can take the Keisei Skyliner to Ueno Station and then transfer to a local subway line to reach Asakusa Station. From Haneda Airport, the easiest way to get there is by taking the Keikyu Line to Asakusa directly. Room rates at Hotel Mystays typically range from ¥5,000 to ¥12,000 (about $45 to $100) per night, depending on the location and room size. Booking can be done directly through the Hotel Mystays website or through major travel websites like Booking.com or Expedia.

Capsule hotels are another unique and affordable accommodation option in Tokyo, offering a minimalist and space-saving solution for budget travelers. Capsule hotels provide small, individual sleeping pods that offer privacy and basic amenities in a shared space. One of the most well-known capsule hotels in Tokyo is Nine Hours, which has locations in various parts of the city, including Shinjuku, Shibuya, and Narita Airport itself. Nine Hours is a futuristic, minimalist-style capsule hotel that provides clean, modern sleeping pods equipped with comfortable bedding, air conditioning, and a small shelf for personal items. The hotel also offers shared bathroom facilities, lockers for luggage storage, and free Wi-Fi throughout the property.

Capsule hotels like Nine Hours are ideal for solo travelers or those who don't need a lot of space and are looking for a unique and affordable place to sleep. The Narita Airport location is especially convenient for travelers with early flights or late arrivals, as it allows you to stay right at the airport. The cost of staying at Nine Hours typically ranges from ¥3,500 to ¥6,500 per night (about $30 to $60), making it one of the most affordable options in Tokyo. You can book a capsule directly through the Nine Hours website or via popular booking platforms like Agoda, Hostelworld, or Booking.com.

For travelers who prefer the feel of a traditional Japanese inn but still want to keep costs down, K's House Tokyo offers a budget-friendly option with a welcoming atmosphere. Located in the Asakusa neighborhood, K's House is a hostel that features both dormitory-style rooms and private rooms, making it a great option for both solo travelers and those traveling in groups. The hostel is known for its clean facilities, friendly staff, and comfortable common areas where guests can relax and meet other travelers. K's House offers free Wi-Fi, a shared kitchen, laundry facilities, and even free tea and coffee, which adds to its appeal for budget travelers. The hostel's location in Asakusa provides easy access to the Senso-ji Temple, Nakamise Shopping Street, and the Tokyo Skytree.

To get to K's House from Narita Airport, you can take the Keisei Skyliner to Ueno Station and transfer to the Ginza subway line to reach Asakusa Station. From Haneda, you can take the Keikyu Line to Asakusa directly. Room rates at K's House Tokyo range from ¥3,000 to ¥10,000 (about $25 to $90) per night, depending on whether you choose a dormitory bed or a private room. You can book a stay at K's House through the hostel's website or via Hostelworld, Booking.com, or Agoda.

Sakura Hotel, another popular budget hotel chain, offers affordable accommodations with a homey, welcoming atmosphere. With several locations in Tokyo, including one in Jimbocho, Sakura Hotel provides budget-friendly rooms with basic amenities like free Wi-Fi, air conditioning, and shared or private bathrooms, depending on the room type. The hotel also has a 24-hour café that serves a variety of international dishes, as well as a communal kitchen where guests can prepare their own meals. Sakura Hotel is known for its international atmosphere, with staff and guests from all over the world, making it a great place for travelers who want to meet other people during their stay.

Jimbocho is a lively neighborhood known for its bookstores, cafes, and proximity to the Imperial Palace and Tokyo Dome, making it a convenient place to stay for sightseeing. To get to Sakura Hotel from Narita Airport, you can take the Narita Express to Tokyo Station and transfer to the Tokyo Metro Hanzomon Line to reach Jimbocho Station. From Haneda Airport, the easiest route is to take the Keikyu Line to Mita Station and transfer to the Hanzomon Line. Room rates at Sakura Hotel typically range from ¥4,000 to ¥10,000 per night (about $35 to $90), and you can book a room directly on the hotel's website or through major booking platforms like Booking.com, Expedia, or Hostelworld.

Hostels

Tokyo is an exciting city to visit, and for travelers on a budget, hostels provide an excellent accommodation option. Hostels in Tokyo offer affordable lodging without sacrificing comfort, and they cater to a wide range of travelers, from solo backpackers to groups of friends. Many hostels also provide opportunities to meet other travelers, which can make your stay more enjoyable. Hostels in Tokyo are generally clean, modern, and well-located, offering easy access to public transportation and the city's top attractions.

One of the most well-known hostels in Tokyo is Khaosan Tokyo Origami, located in the historic Asakusa neighborhood. Asakusa is famous for its traditional atmosphere and cultural landmarks, including the iconic Senso-ji Temple and the lively Nakamise shopping street. Khaosan Tokyo Origami is just a short walk from Senso-ji, making it an ideal location for travelers who want to explore this traditional area. The hostel offers a mix of dormitory-style rooms and private rooms, catering to both solo travelers and groups. The dorms have capsule-style beds with privacy curtains, individual reading lights, and personal lockers, while private rooms offer a bit more space for couples or small groups. Amenities at Khaosan Tokyo Origami include free Wi-Fi, a shared kitchen, a common lounge area with views of the Tokyo Skytree, and laundry facilities. Prices for dormitory beds typically range from ¥2,500 to ¥4,500 per night (about $20 to $40), while private rooms can cost between ¥7,000 and ¥12,000 (approximately $60 to $100) per night, depending on the room size and season.

To get to Khaosan Tokyo Origami from Narita International Airport, you can take the Keisei Skyliner to Ueno Station and transfer to the Tokyo Metro Ginza Line, which will take you to Asakusa Station. From there, the hostel is just a short walk away. From Haneda Airport, you can take the Keikyu Line to Asakusa directly. Booking can be done through the hostel's website or via popular online platforms like Hostelworld, Booking.com, or Agoda.

Another popular hostel option is Nui. Hostel & Bar Lounge, which is also located in the Asakusa area. Nui. Hostel is known for its stylish, industrial-chic design and welcoming atmosphere. The ground floor of the hostel features a bar and lounge that is open to both guests and locals, creating a lively social environment where travelers can meet new people and enjoy drinks and light meals. The hostel offers a range of accommodation options, including dormitory beds and private rooms, all of which are designed with a minimalist aesthetic. Dormitory beds are equipped with privacy curtains, reading lights, and personal lockers, while private rooms are comfortable and cozy. Nui. Hostel also provides free Wi-Fi, a shared kitchen, and a common area where guests can relax.

Prices at Nui. Hostel & Bar Lounge typically range from ¥3,000 to ¥4,500 (about $25 to $40) per night for dormitory beds, while private rooms can range from ¥8,000 to ¥12,000 (approximately $70 to $100) per night. To get to Nui. Hostel from Narita Airport, you can take the Keisei Skyliner to Ueno Station, then transfer to the Tokyo Metro Ginza Line to Asakusa Station. From Haneda, the easiest route is to take the

Keikyu Line directly to Asakusa. Booking is available through the Nui. Hostel website, as well as through booking platforms like Hostelworld, Booking.com, and Expedia.

Hostel Chapter Two Tokyo is another excellent option for budget travelers looking for a friendly, social atmosphere. This hostel is located along the Sumida River in Asakusa, offering beautiful views of the Tokyo Skytree from its common areas. The location is perfect for travelers who want to experience the traditional side of Tokyo while still being close to modern attractions. Hostel Chapter Two Tokyo has a variety of room options, including mixed and female-only dormitories, as well as private rooms. The dormitory beds come with privacy curtains, reading lights, and personal storage, while private rooms are great for couples or small groups. The hostel has a shared kitchen, free Wi-Fi, and a rooftop terrace with views of the river and Skytree, making it a relaxing place to unwind after a day of sightseeing.

Dormitory beds at Hostel Chapter Two Tokyo typically cost between ¥3,000 and ¥5,000 (about $25 to $45) per night, while private rooms range from ¥8,000 to ¥12,000 (approximately $70 to $100) per night. To get to the hostel from Narita Airport, you can take the Keisei Skyliner to Ueno Station and transfer to the Ginza Line to Asakusa Station. From Haneda, you can take the Keikyu Line directly to Asakusa. Reservations can be made directly on the hostel's website or through platforms like Hostelworld and Booking.com.

For travelers looking for a hostel with a more contemporary design, Citan Hostel in the Nihonbashi area is a fantastic choice. Citan Hostel is located in a central part of Tokyo, providing easy access to major neighborhoods like Ginza, Akihabara, and Shinjuku. The hostel's modern design and friendly atmosphere make it a favorite among younger travelers and backpackers. Citan offers mixed and female-only dormitory rooms, as well as private rooms for those who want more privacy. The dormitory beds are capsule-style, offering privacy curtains, personal lights, and storage space. The hostel also has a stylish café and bar on the ground floor, where guests can enjoy coffee, meals, and drinks while socializing with other travelers. Additional amenities include free Wi-Fi, a shared kitchen, and laundry facilities.

Dormitory beds at Citan Hostel generally range from ¥3,500 to ¥5,000 (about $30 to $45) per night, while private rooms can cost between ¥9,000 and ¥13,000 (approximately $80 to $115) per night. To reach Citan Hostel from Narita Airport, you can take the Narita Express to Tokyo Station, followed by a short subway ride to Bakuroyokoyama Station, which is a few minutes' walk from the hostel. From Haneda, you can take the Keikyu Line to Shinagawa and transfer to the JR Yamanote Line to reach Bakurocho Station. Bookings can be made through Citan's website or popular platforms like Hostelworld, Agoda, or Booking.com.

For those seeking a hostel with a community-oriented vibe, K's House Tokyo Oasis is a great option. Located in the lively Asakusa district, K's House Tokyo Oasis offers a warm, welcoming atmosphere with a focus on providing travelers with a comfortable and budget-friendly stay. The hostel features both dormitory-style rooms and private rooms, catering to solo travelers, couples, and small groups. Dormitory beds are equipped with privacy curtains, reading lights, and personal lockers, while private rooms are simple and functional. K's House also has a shared kitchen, common lounge area, free Wi-Fi, and laundry facilities. The staff at K's House are known for being helpful and friendly, providing guests with tips on sightseeing and local dining options.

Dormitory beds at K's House Tokyo Oasis range from ¥2,500 to ¥4,000 (about $20 to $35) per night, while private rooms cost between ¥6,000 and ¥10,000 (approximately $50 to $90) per night. To reach K's House from Narita Airport, take the Keisei Skyliner to Ueno Station and transfer to the Ginza Line to reach Asakusa. From Haneda, the Keikyu Line offers direct access to Asakusa. Reservations can be made through the K's House website or through Hostelworld, Booking.com, or Agoda.

These hostel options offer budget-friendly accommodations without sacrificing comfort, and they provide a great way to experience Tokyo while meeting other travelers. Whether you're staying in the traditional Asakusa area or closer to the city center, Tokyo's hostels cater to all kinds of travelers, offering clean facilities, friendly atmospheres, and convenient access to public transportation. Booking can be done directly through the hostels' websites or through major travel platforms like Hostelworld, Booking.com, or Expedia, ensuring you find the perfect place to stay during your Tokyo adventure.

Ryokan Experience: Traditional Japanese Inns

Experiencing a stay in a ryokan, or traditional Japanese inn, offers a unique and memorable way to immerse yourself in Japan's culture. Unlike standard hotels, ryokan stays focus on traditional hospitality, often involving Japanese-style rooms with tatami mats, futons, sliding paper doors, and hot spring baths (onsen). A ryokan experience is more than just a place to sleep; it's an opportunity to experience Japanese customs, relax in serene surroundings, and enjoy carefully prepared meals that highlight regional ingredients. While ryokan are often found in rural or mountainous areas, there are several excellent options in Tokyo for travelers who want to enjoy this traditional form of accommodation without leaving the city.

HOSHINOYA Tokyo is one of the most luxurious ryokan experiences in the city, offering a blend of modern comfort and traditional Japanese aesthetics. Located in the heart of the city, near the Imperial Palace in the Otemachi district, HOSHINOYA Tokyo is an urban ryokan that provides a peaceful escape from the hustle and bustle of Tokyo's fast-paced streets. The rooms are designed with traditional tatami floors and sliding doors, while also offering modern amenities like Wi-Fi, air conditioning, and spacious bathrooms. The hotel features a stunning rooftop hot spring bath (onsen) that is fed by natural mineral waters, providing guests with a serene bathing experience under the open sky. Guests can also enjoy traditional kaiseki meals, a multi-course dining experience that showcases seasonal ingredients and meticulous preparation.

HOSHINOYA Tokyo is located conveniently near Tokyo Station, which makes it easily accessible from both Narita International Airport and Haneda Airport. From Narita, you can take the Narita Express to Tokyo Station, followed by a short walk or taxi ride to the ryokan. From Haneda, you can take the Tokyo Monorail to Hamamatsucho Station and transfer to the JR Yamanote Line to Tokyo Station. HOSHINOYA Tokyo is a luxury ryokan, and prices reflect this level of exclusivity, with room rates typically ranging from ¥100,000 to ¥150,000 (approximately $900 to $1,400) per night, depending on the season and room type. You can book your stay directly through the HOSHINOYA website or via luxury travel platforms like Virtuoso or Expedia.

For those seeking a more intimate and traditional experience, Homeikan is a charming ryokan located in the Bunkyo area of Tokyo, near the University of Tokyo. Homeikan consists of three separate buildings, each of which retains the atmosphere of a classic ryokan, with tatami rooms, futons, and traditional sliding paper doors. The rooms are simple but charming, offering a quiet retreat in the heart of Tokyo. Unlike more modern hotels, Homeikan emphasizes a true ryokan experience, meaning there are no Western-style beds or modern conveniences like televisions in the rooms. Instead, the focus is on simplicity, relaxation, and immersion in traditional Japanese hospitality. While Homeikan does not have an onsen, it does offer traditional bathing facilities, and the staff are known for their warm and friendly service.

To reach Homeikan from Narita Airport, you can take the Narita Express to Tokyo Station and then transfer to the Tokyo Metro Marunouchi Line, followed by a short taxi ride or walk. From Haneda, you can take the Keikyu Line to Shinagawa Station and transfer to the JR Yamanote Line to reach the nearest station, Hongo-sanchome. Room rates at Homeikan are much more affordable than luxury ryokan like HOSHINOYA, with prices typically ranging from ¥7,000 to ¥15,000 per night (about $60 to $130). Bookings can be made through Homeikan's website or via platforms like Booking.com or Japanican.

Another great option for travelers wanting to experience a traditional ryokan stay in Tokyo is Sawanoya Ryokan, located in the Yanaka neighborhood. Yanaka is known for its old Tokyo charm, with narrow streets, traditional shops, and a slower pace of life compared to the rest of the city. Sawanoya Ryokan offers a warm and welcoming atmosphere, with simple, traditional rooms featuring tatami floors and futons. What sets Sawanoya apart is its focus on providing a friendly, family-run experience, with staff who are happy to assist with sightseeing recommendations and make your stay comfortable. The ryokan also features two private baths that guests can reserve for a relaxing soak after a day of exploring the city.

To get to Sawanoya Ryokan from Narita, take the Keisei Skyliner to Nippori Station, which is just a short walk from Yanaka. From Haneda, you can take the Keikyu Line to Nippori Station as well. Room rates at Sawanoya Ryokan are quite affordable, with prices ranging from ¥6,500 to ¥9,500 per night (approximately $55 to $85). This makes Sawanoya a great option for travelers on a budget who still want to experience traditional Japanese accommodation. You can book directly through the ryokan's website or through popular booking sites like Booking.com or Agoda.

For travelers looking for a blend of modern convenience and traditional charm, Andon Ryokan offers a contemporary twist on the ryokan experience. Located in the Taito ward, not far from Ueno and Asakusa, Andon Ryokan is known for its stylish, minimalist design that combines traditional Japanese elements with modern touches. The rooms are small but cozy, featuring tatami floors and futons, while the common areas are decorated with contemporary art and furniture. One of the highlights of Andon Ryokan is its private Jacuzzi, which guests can reserve for a relaxing soak. The ryokan also offers free bicycle rentals, allowing you to explore the surrounding neighborhoods at your own pace.

To reach Andon Ryokan from Narita, you can take the Keisei Skyliner to Ueno Station and then transfer to the Hibiya Line to Minowa Station, which is just a short walk from the ryokan. From Haneda, the Keikyu Line connects to the Hibiya Line at Higashi-Ginza Station, making it easy to get to Minowa. Room rates at Andon Ryokan typically range from ¥6,000 to ¥10,000 per night (approximately $50 to $90), making it an affordable option for travelers looking for a modern twist on the traditional ryokan experience. You can book your stay through Andon Ryokan's website or on platforms like Booking.com or Hostelworld.

Lastly, Ryokan Kamogawa Asakusa is an excellent choice for travelers who want to stay in the heart of Tokyo's most historic neighborhood. Located just steps from Senso-ji Temple and the Nakamise shopping street, Ryokan Kamogawa Asakusa provides a peaceful retreat in one of Tokyo's most vibrant areas. The rooms are designed in the traditional Japanese style, with tatami floors, futons, and sliding doors. The ryokan also offers a traditional Japanese breakfast, featuring seasonal ingredients and carefully prepared dishes that reflect Japan's culinary heritage. The location makes it perfect for tourists who want to explore Asakusa's temples, shops, and nearby attractions like the Tokyo Skytree.

From Narita Airport, you can take the Keisei Skyliner to Ueno Station and transfer to the Ginza Line to Asakusa. From Haneda, you can take the Keikyu Line directly to Asakusa Station. Room rates at Ryokan Kamogawa Asakusa are quite reasonable, with prices ranging from ¥10,000 to ¥18,000 per night (about $90 to $160). You can make a reservation through the ryokan's website or on popular booking platforms like Agoda, Expedia, or Booking.com.

Capsule Hotels: A Unique Tokyo Experience

When visiting Tokyo, one of the most unique and affordable accommodation experiences available to tourists is staying in a capsule hotel. Capsule hotels, a concept that originated in Japan, offer small, individual sleeping pods that provide a minimalist, space-efficient solution for travelers looking for convenience at a low price. These hotels are particularly popular among solo travelers and those who don't require the full amenities of a traditional hotel but still want comfort and privacy. While the space in each capsule is limited, these hotels are often equipped with modern features, including communal lounges, shared bathrooms, and high-tech facilities that create a futuristic, yet functional atmosphere.

One of the most popular capsule hotel chains in Tokyo is Nine Hours, which has several locations throughout the city, including Shinjuku, Akasaka, and Narita Airport. Nine Hours is known for its sleek, minimalist design, with capsules that provide just the right amount of space for sleeping. Each capsule is equipped with a mattress, bedding, a personal reading light, and a small shelf for personal belongings. Although the capsules are compact, the hotel emphasizes cleanliness and comfort, ensuring that each guest has a quiet, relaxing stay. The hotel also offers modern communal facilities, including clean showers, lockers for luggage storage, and free Wi-Fi throughout the property.

Nine Hours Narita Airport is particularly convenient for travelers with early morning flights or late arrivals, as it is located right inside the airport terminal. To reach the Nine

Hours Shinjuku location, travelers can take the Narita Express or Keisei Skyliner from Narita Airport to Shinjuku Station, followed by a short walk to the hotel. From Haneda Airport, the Keikyu Line connects to the JR Yamanote Line, which will take you to Shinjuku Station. Room rates at Nine Hours typically range from ¥3,500 to ¥6,500 (approximately $30 to $60) per night, depending on the location and season. Bookings can be made directly through the Nine Hours website or via popular booking platforms like Booking.com, Hostelworld, and Agoda.

Another top option for capsule hotels in Tokyo is First Cabin Tsukiji, located near the famous Tsukiji Fish Market. While technically not a traditional capsule hotel, First Cabin offers a more spacious alternative, with cabin-style rooms that provide more room to stretch out while still maintaining the capsule hotel concept. The hotel is inspired by the design of airplane cabins, and guests can choose between "First Class" and "Business Class" cabins, depending on their preference for space. First Cabin Tsukiji offers clean, modern facilities, including shared bathrooms, a lounge area, and free Wi-Fi. The hotel's proximity to Tsukiji makes it an excellent choice for early risers who want to explore the market and its surrounding attractions.

From Narita Airport, you can take the Narita Express to Tokyo Station, followed by a transfer to the Tokyo Metro Hibiya Line to Tsukiji Station, which is just a short walk from the hotel. From Haneda, the Keikyu Line also connects to the Hibiya Line, providing easy access to Tsukiji. Room rates at First

Cabin Tsukiji range from ¥4,500 to ¥7,500 (about $40 to $70) per night, depending on the cabin type. Bookings can be made directly on the First Cabin website or through online travel platforms like Booking.com or Expedia.

For travelers looking for a capsule hotel that offers a bit more comfort and luxury, The Millennials Shibuya is a standout choice. Located in the trendy Shibuya district, this capsule hotel combines the minimalist design of traditional capsule hotels with modern amenities aimed at making your stay more enjoyable. The Millennials features spacious, high-tech capsules equipped with reclining beds, storage spaces, personal lighting, and individual climate controls. The hotel is designed with a futuristic and youthful vibe, attracting a younger crowd. It also features a communal kitchen, shared workspaces, and a cozy lounge area where guests can socialize or relax after a day of exploring Tokyo.

Shibuya is one of Tokyo's most popular neighborhoods, known for its shopping, nightlife, and famous Shibuya Crossing. To get to The Millennials from Narita Airport, you can take the Narita Express to Shibuya Station, followed by a short walk to the hotel. From Haneda, the Keikyu Line connects to the JR Yamanote Line, which will take you directly to Shibuya Station. Room rates at The Millennials typically range from ¥5,000 to ¥9,000 per night (about $45 to $80), depending on the time of year and availability. You can book your stay through The Millennials website or through major booking platforms like Agoda, Booking.com, or Expedia.

Capsule Hotel Anshin Oyado Premier in Shinjuku is another excellent capsule hotel that offers a more upscale experience. This hotel focuses on providing a relaxing environment with thoughtful amenities, including large public baths (similar to an onsen), saunas, massage chairs, and free beverages in the lounge. The capsules at Anshin Oyado are a bit larger than typical capsules, and they come equipped with comfortable bedding, a TV, free Wi-Fi, and individual climate controls. This capsule hotel is also known for its cleanliness and attention to detail, ensuring that guests have a pleasant stay. The communal areas are quiet and well-maintained, making it a great choice for those looking for relaxation after a busy day.

To reach Capsule Hotel Anshin Oyado Premier from Narita Airport, you can take the Narita Express to Shinjuku Station, which is just a short walk from the hotel. From Haneda Airport, the Keikyu Line connects to the JR Yamanote Line, providing direct access to Shinjuku. Room rates at Anshin Oyado Premier range from ¥4,500 to ¥7,000 per night (approximately $40 to $65). Bookings can be made directly on the hotel's website or through booking platforms like Agoda, Expedia, or Booking.com.

Finally, Book and Bed Tokyo is a capsule hotel that offers a unique twist on the traditional capsule experience. Located in the Ikebukuro and Shinjuku neighborhoods, this capsule hotel combines the concept of a hostel with a library, allowing guests to sleep surrounded by bookshelves filled with a wide variety of reading materials. Each capsule is built into the bookshelf, providing a cozy, quiet environment for book lovers. The hotel offers basic amenities such as free Wi-Fi, shared bathrooms, and a lounge area where guests can relax with a book. Book and Bed is designed for travelers who want a quirky, creative stay in Tokyo, with an emphasis on relaxation and reading.

To get to the Book and Bed Ikebukuro location from Narita Airport, you can take the Narita Express to Ikebukuro Station, followed by a short walk to the hotel. From Haneda, the Keikyu Line connects to the JR Yamanote Line, which will take you to Ikebukuro Station. Room rates at Book and Bed generally range from ¥3,500 to ¥6,500 (about $30 to $60) per night, depending on the location and room type. You can book your stay through the Book and Bed website or through booking platforms like Booking.com or Hostelworld.

Vacation Rentals and Airbnb Options

When planning a trip to Tokyo, many travelers are now turning to vacation rentals and Airbnb options as a flexible and comfortable alternative to traditional hotels. Vacation rentals offer a unique way to experience life in Tokyo, providing you with more space, privacy, and often a more local feel than staying in a hotel. These rentals come in a variety of styles and sizes, from cozy apartments in the heart of the city to entire homes tucked away in quiet residential neighborhoods. Renting a vacation home or an apartment allows you to enjoy amenities such as full kitchens, living areas, and laundry facilities, which can be especially useful for families or those planning an extended stay. Whether you're looking for a modern apartment in Shibuya or a traditional machiya

(Japanese townhouse) in Asakusa, Tokyo's vacation rental options provide something for every type of traveler.

One of the most popular Airbnb options in Tokyo is a modern one-bedroom apartment located in Shinjuku, one of the city's busiest and most vibrant districts. Shinjuku is known for its nightlife, shopping, and entertainment, making it an ideal location for travelers who want to be in the center of the action. This Airbnb offers a clean, comfortable living space with modern furnishings, including a fully equipped kitchen, a living room with a flat-screen TV, and a cozy bedroom with a queen-sized bed. The apartment also includes high-speed Wi-Fi, air conditioning, and a washing machine, making it perfect for both short and long stays. The location is just a 10-minute walk from Shinjuku Station, providing easy access to the rest of the city via the JR Yamanote Line and Tokyo Metro.

To reach this Airbnb from Narita International Airport, you can take the Narita Express to Shinjuku Station, followed by a short walk to the apartment. From Haneda Airport, the Keikyu Line connects to the JR Yamanote Line at Shinagawa Station, allowing you to reach Shinjuku in about 30 minutes. Prices for this one-bedroom apartment typically range from ¥12,000 to ¥18,000 (about $100 to $150) per night, depending on the time of year and availability. You can book this rental directly through Airbnb's platform, where you can also check reviews and communicate with the host for any special requests or questions.

For those looking for a more traditional Japanese experience, a beautifully restored machiya townhouse in Asakusa is another excellent vacation rental option. This charming, historic home has been carefully renovated to retain its original wooden beams, tatami floors, and sliding paper doors, while also offering modern conveniences such as a fully equipped kitchen, a modern bathroom, and free Wi-Fi. The house can comfortably accommodate up to five guests, making it a great option for families or small groups traveling together. Staying in a traditional machiya gives you a unique chance to experience the architecture and atmosphere of old Japan, all while being close to popular attractions like Senso-ji Temple and the Nakamise shopping street.

To reach this machiya from Narita Airport, you can take the Keisei Skyliner to Ueno Station and then transfer to the Ginza Line, which will take you to Asakusa Station. From Haneda, the Keikyu Line provides direct access to Asakusa. Prices for this machiya rental typically range from ¥20,000 to ¥30,000 per night (approximately $180 to $270), depending on the season and availability. You can book this property on Airbnb, where the host provides detailed instructions for check-in and tips for exploring the local area.

For travelers seeking a sleek, modern apartment in one of Tokyo's trendiest neighborhoods, there is a stylish studio apartment available in Shibuya. This Airbnb features a minimalist design, with a bright, open living space, a comfortable double bed, a small kitchen, and a modern bathroom. The apartment is ideal for solo travelers or couples who want to stay in a lively area known for its shopping, dining, and nightlife. Shibuya Crossing, one of the most famous landmarks in Tokyo, is just a short walk away, as are numerous cafes, bars, and fashion boutiques. The apartment also offers free Wi-Fi, air conditioning, and a washing machine, making it a convenient and comfortable option for longer stays.

To get to this Shibuya apartment from Narita Airport, you can take the Narita Express to Shibuya Station, which is just a 10-minute walk from the rental. From Haneda, the Keikyu Line connects to the JR Yamanote Line, which will take you directly to Shibuya. Prices for this Shibuya studio apartment range from ¥10,000 to ¥15,000 per night (about $90 to $130), making it a relatively affordable option in one of Tokyo's most sought-after neighborhoods. You can book this apartment through Airbnb, where you'll find additional details about the property and the host's recommendations for things to do in the area.

If you're traveling with a larger group or prefer more space, a spacious two-bedroom apartment in the quiet residential district of Nakameguro offers the perfect balance between comfort and location. Nakameguro is known for its charming canals lined with cherry trees, trendy cafes, and laid-back atmosphere, making it a great choice for travelers who want to experience a more local side of Tokyo. This two-bedroom apartment can comfortably accommodate up to six guests, with two large beds, a sofa bed, a fully equipped kitchen, and a spacious living area. The apartment also features a private balcony, free Wi-Fi, and air conditioning, making it ideal for families or groups of friends looking for a home-away-from-home experience in Tokyo.

To reach this Nakameguro apartment from Narita Airport, you can take the Narita Express to Shibuya Station and then transfer to the Tokyu Toyoko Line, which will take you to Nakameguro Station in just a few minutes. From Haneda, the Keikyu Line connects to the Tokyu Toyoko Line at Shinagawa Station, providing a direct route to Nakameguro. Prices for this two-bedroom apartment typically range from ¥18,000 to ¥25,000 per night (about $160 to $220), depending on availability. You can book this rental through Airbnb or other vacation rental platforms like Vrbo or HomeAway.

For a truly luxurious vacation rental experience, a penthouse apartment in the upscale Roppongi district offers sweeping views of Tokyo's skyline, including Tokyo Tower. This spacious, modern apartment features floor-to-ceiling windows, high-end furnishings, and a fully equipped kitchen, making it a great choice for travelers who want to experience Tokyo in style. The penthouse can accommodate up to four guests, with two bedrooms, a large living and dining area, and a private rooftop terrace where you can relax and take in the city's lights. Roppongi is known for its nightlife, art galleries, and international dining options, making it a prime location for tourists who want to explore Tokyo's more cosmopolitan side.

From Narita Airport, you can reach the Roppongi penthouse by taking the Narita Express to Tokyo Station and transferring to the Tokyo Metro Hibiya Line, which will take you to Roppongi Station. From Haneda, the Keikyu Line connects directly to the Hibiya Line, providing easy access to Roppongi. Prices for this luxury penthouse typically range from ¥35,000 to ¥50,000 per night (about $300 to $450), depending on the season. This penthouse can be booked on Airbnb, where the host offers detailed information about check-in procedures and recommendations for nearby attractions and restaurants.

CHAPTER 5

GETTING AROUND TOKYO

Tokyo's Public Transportation System

Tokyo's public transportation system is one of the most advanced, efficient, and reliable in the world. It plays a key role in connecting this sprawling metropolis of more than 37 million people. Whether you are a local resident or a tourist, navigating Tokyo using its public transportation is the best way to get around. The system covers every corner of the city, ensuring that even the most remote areas are easily accessible. Tokyo's transportation is a complex network made up of trains, subways, buses, and taxis, all of which are designed to work together seamlessly. While it might seem overwhelming at first glance due to its size and complexity, once you get familiar with it, you'll find that it's incredibly user-friendly, well-signposted, and convenient.

The backbone of Tokyo's public transportation system is its extensive train network, which is primarily operated by Japan Railways (JR) and several private railway companies. The most famous and widely used train line is the JR Yamanote Line, a circular route that connects many of Tokyo's major districts, such as Shibuya, Shinjuku, Ikebukuro, Ueno, and Tokyo Station. The Yamanote Line is a key part of the city's public transit, and it's one of the best options for tourists, as it stops at many of the most important sightseeing spots and commercial areas. Trains on the Yamanote Line are frequent, running every few minutes, and they operate from early morning until midnight.

Another essential part of Tokyo's transportation network is its subway system. Tokyo has two main subway operators: Tokyo Metro and Toei Subway. Together, they operate 13 subway lines that run across the city and into surrounding areas. The subway is known for its punctuality, cleanliness, and ease of use, with trains arriving every few minutes during peak hours. It's especially useful for getting to places that are not as easily accessible by the JR lines. For instance, popular tourist destinations like Asakusa, Ginza, and Roppongi are best reached via subway. Each subway line is color-coded and given a letter and number, making it easier for passengers to identify which line they are on and which station they are approaching. Stations and trains have signs in both Japanese and English, which is helpful for foreign visitors.

In addition to the Yamanote Line and the subway, there are also many private railway lines that extend further into the suburbs and surrounding areas. Companies like Keio, Odakyu, and Tokyu operate these lines, which serve both local commuters and travelers heading to areas outside central Tokyo. For example, if you're planning a trip to the scenic areas around Mount Takao or Hakone, you'll likely be using one of these private rail lines. These trains are just as clean and reliable as the JR and subway systems, and they offer easy connections with the rest of Tokyo's transit network.

One thing that makes traveling around Tokyo even easier is the IC card system. IC cards are prepaid transportation cards that can be used on almost all trains, subways, and buses across Tokyo (and even other parts of Japan). The most commonly used IC cards are Suica and Pasmo, which can be purchased and recharged at ticket machines located in every station. Once you have a Suica or Pasmo card, you can simply tap it on the card readers at the gates, and the fare will be deducted automatically, eliminating the need to buy individual tickets each time you travel. The cards can also be used at many convenience stores, vending machines, and some restaurants, making them incredibly convenient for both transportation and small purchases.

Tokyo's bus system, while less popular with tourists compared to trains and subways, is another important part of the city's public transportation. Buses are especially useful for reaching areas that are not well served by trains or subways, such as certain residential neighborhoods or sightseeing spots that are a bit off the beaten path. Buses in Tokyo are well-maintained, punctual, and equipped with electronic signboards that display stops in both Japanese and English. While they may not be as fast as the trains, they are a good option for shorter trips or for reaching destinations that are too far to walk to from the nearest station. The fare for most buses is a flat rate, and you can use your Suica or Pasmo card to pay when you board.

For those staying in Tokyo for an extended period or planning to travel extensively within the city, there are also various types of transportation passes that can save you money. One popular option is the Tokyo Subway Ticket, which offers unlimited rides on all Tokyo Metro and Toei Subway lines for 24, 48, or 72 hours, depending on the type of ticket you purchase. These passes are available at major subway stations, as well as at Narita and Haneda airports, and are a great option for tourists who plan to use the subway frequently during their stay. There are also JR passes, such as the JR Tokyo Wide Pass, which is designed for tourists and allows unlimited travel on JR lines in the Tokyo area and beyond for a set number of days. This pass is particularly useful for travelers planning day trips to areas outside of central Tokyo.

In terms of connectivity, Tokyo's public transportation system is incredibly efficient. Many stations serve as major transfer hubs, where passengers can easily switch between JR lines, subway lines, and private railways. For example, Shinjuku Station is one of the busiest train stations in the world, with multiple train and subway lines converging in one place. While the station can feel overwhelming due to its size and the sheer number of people passing through it, it's well-organized, with plenty of signs and information to help guide passengers. Similarly, Tokyo Station is another key hub for transfers between JR lines, including the Shinkansen (bullet trains), which connect Tokyo to other major cities like Kyoto, Osaka, and Hiroshima.

For international travelers, getting to and from Tokyo's airports is also made easy by the city's public transportation system. From Narita International Airport, the Narita Express (N'EX) offers a direct train service to major stations in central

Tokyo, such as Tokyo Station, Shibuya, and Shinjuku. The journey from Narita to central Tokyo takes about an hour and is a comfortable, convenient option for those arriving in Japan. There are also limousine buses that provide service from Narita to many major hotels and districts in Tokyo, which can be a good option if you're carrying a lot of luggage. From Haneda Airport, which is closer to central Tokyo, you can take the Tokyo Monorail to Hamamatsucho Station, where you can easily transfer to the JR Yamanote Line or other subway lines. Alternatively, the Keikyu Line connects Haneda to Shinagawa Station, offering another easy way to get into the city.

Despite the size and complexity of Tokyo's public transportation system, it's designed with the passenger in mind, making it surprisingly easy to navigate once you understand the basics. Stations are equipped with clear signage, maps, and information in multiple languages, including English. Many stations also have staff on hand who can help with directions or answer questions. In addition, there are a variety of apps and online tools that can help you plan your journey. Google Maps is widely used in Tokyo and provides accurate public transit directions, including which trains or buses to take, where to transfer, and how long your trip will take. There are also Japanese apps like Japan Transit Planner (Jorudan) and Navitime that offer detailed train schedules and route planning, which can be particularly useful for navigating more complex journeys.

How to Use the JR Yamanote Line

The JR Yamanote Line is one of the most important and widely used train lines in Tokyo. It's a circular line that connects many of Tokyo's major neighborhoods, business districts, and tourist attractions, making it essential for both locals and visitors alike. If you're planning to explore Tokyo, getting familiar with the Yamanote Line will make your travels much easier and more efficient. The line loops around central Tokyo, and with 30 stations along its route, it connects areas such as Shibuya, Shinjuku, Ikebukuro, Ueno, and Tokyo Station. What makes the Yamanote Line particularly convenient for tourists is that it stops at some of the city's most popular spots, so knowing how to use it can save you time and confusion.

The first thing to understand about the Yamanote Line is that it's operated by Japan Railways (JR), which means it is part of the larger JR East network. The Yamanote Line is unique in that it runs in both directions — clockwise and counterclockwise — and it takes about an hour to complete a full loop. Trains run frequently, with one arriving every few minutes, so you'll rarely have to wait long. Trains start running early in the morning, around 5:00 AM, and continue until around midnight. This makes it a reliable way to get around the city at almost any time of the day.

To begin using the Yamanote Line, the first step is to get a ticket or use an IC card, such as a Suica or Pasmo card, to pay for your trip. If you don't have an IC card, you can buy a single-use paper ticket from the ticket machines located in every station. The machines are easy to use, with English language options, and they allow you to choose your destination by selecting the fare that corresponds to the distance you'll be traveling. However, most visitors prefer to use an IC card, which can be purchased and recharged at the same machines. With an IC card, you simply tap the card on the reader at the ticket gate when entering and exiting the station, and the correct fare is automatically deducted from your balance.

Once you have your ticket or IC card, you'll head to the ticket gates. You'll find clear signage indicating the entrance to the Yamanote Line, with its distinctive green color and logo. Pay attention to whether you're taking a train in the clockwise or counterclockwise direction, as this will determine which side of the platform you need to be on. Stations typically have overhead signs that show which direction each platform serves. For example, if you're at Shibuya Station and you want to head toward Shinjuku, you'll take the train that's going in a clockwise direction. If you're going to Ebisu or Shinagawa from Shibuya, you'll take the train in the counterclockwise direction.

The Yamanote Line is well-marked in both Japanese and English, so even if you don't speak the language, it's easy to navigate. Inside the trains, there are digital displays and audio announcements in both languages, so you'll always know which station is coming up next. The stations themselves are also clearly marked, with maps and signs that make it simple to identify where you are and where you need to go next. Each train car also features route maps that show all 30 stations on the Yamanote Line, making it easy to follow along during your journey.

One of the major benefits of using the Yamanote Line is that it connects directly to many other train lines, subways, and bus routes. This makes transferring between different forms of transportation seamless. For example, Tokyo Station is a key transfer point for the Shinkansen bullet trains, which travel to other cities like Kyoto, Osaka, and Hiroshima. Shibuya, Shinjuku, and Ikebukuro stations also offer connections to various subway lines, such as the Tokyo Metro and Toei Subway, allowing you to reach areas that aren't directly on the Yamanote Line. If you're traveling to or from the airports, the Yamanote Line connects with the Narita Express at Tokyo Station and the Keikyu Line to Haneda Airport at Shinagawa Station.

When using the Yamanote Line, it's important to pay attention to rush hour times, especially if you're traveling on weekdays. During the morning and evening rush hours, which typically occur between 7:30 AM to 9:30 AM and 5:00 PM to 7:00 PM, the trains can become extremely crowded with commuters. If possible, try to avoid traveling during these times, especially if you have large luggage or prefer a more comfortable ride. However, even during peak hours, the trains are very efficient and continue to run on time.

One of the great advantages of the Yamanote Line is that it gives you easy access to many of Tokyo's top tourist attractions. For example, if you're heading to the popular shopping and nightlife district of Shibuya, the Yamanote Line will drop you off right near the famous Shibuya Crossing. For those wanting to explore the vibrant nightlife and entertainment in Shinjuku, you can easily get off at Shinjuku Station, which is one of the busiest train stations in the world. Ikebukuro is another major hub along the Yamanote Line, known for its department stores, shopping centers, and Sunshine City, a large commercial complex that includes an aquarium and observatory.

If you're interested in Tokyo's rich history and traditional culture, the Yamanote Line also stops near important cultural sites. For example, Ueno Station is just a short walk from Ueno Park, where you can visit the Tokyo National Museum, Ueno Zoo, and several art galleries. Ueno Park is also one of the best spots in the city for cherry blossom viewing during the spring. Akihabara, known for its electronics stores and anime culture, is another popular stop on the Yamanote Line. This area is a must-visit for fans of Japanese pop culture, offering a variety of shops selling manga, video games, and anime merchandise.

Tokyo Station, which is another key stop on the Yamanote Line, offers access to the Imperial Palace, one of Tokyo's most important historical landmarks. The palace grounds and surrounding gardens are a peaceful escape from the busy city, and you can explore them for free. Tokyo Station itself is also known for its beautiful red-brick architecture and underground shopping and dining areas, where you can find everything from luxury boutiques to affordable ramen shops.

When you're using the Yamanote Line, it's also worth noting that there is no need to worry about which train to take, as all the trains on the line stop at every station along the route. This makes the Yamanote Line very simple to use, as you don't have to worry about express or local trains that skip stations, which is common on other train lines. Each train follows the same loop, so it's just a matter of choosing the direction and boarding the next available train.

The Yamanote Line is well-equipped to accommodate passengers with disabilities. Most stations have elevators, escalators, and accessible restrooms, and there are priority seating areas in each train car. If you have specific needs, station staff are usually available to assist and provide guidance.

Understanding the Subway and Bus Networks

Understanding Tokyo's subway and bus networks is essential for getting around the city efficiently, especially if you want to explore areas that are not directly served by the JR train system or if you're heading to specific spots in the city that the trains don't reach. Tokyo's public transportation system is vast and interconnected, and while it can seem intimidating at first due to its size and complexity, it is one of the most convenient ways to travel in the city once you understand how it works. Both the subway and bus systems are known for their punctuality, cleanliness, and frequency, making them reliable options for getting around.

Tokyo's subway system is divided between two operators: Tokyo Metro and Toei Subway. Together, these two networks form a comprehensive system of 13 subway lines that crisscross the city and connect almost every major neighborhood. Tokyo Metro operates nine of these lines, and Toei operates the remaining four. While these two companies are separate, the subway lines are well-integrated, and passengers can transfer between them without much hassle. The lines are color-coded, and each line has a letter and a number, making it easier to identify where you are and where you need to go. For example, the Ginza Line, which is one of the most popular lines for tourists, is represented by the letter "G" and the color orange. Stations on this line are numbered G1, G2, G3, and so on.

Using the subway is straightforward once you understand the basics. To board a subway, you'll need either a single-use ticket or an IC card, such as Suica or Pasmo, which is also used on JR trains. Tickets can be purchased from machines located in every station, and there are English language options to help make the process easier for non-Japanese speakers. If you're only taking one or two trips, you can buy a ticket for a specific fare based on your destination. However, if you plan to use the subway frequently during your stay, it's much more convenient to use a Suica or Pasmo card. With an IC card, you simply tap the card at the gates, and the fare is automatically deducted when you tap out at your destination.

The subway system covers many of Tokyo's most famous areas, and it is particularly useful for reaching neighborhoods that aren't directly accessible by JR trains. For example, if you're visiting Asakusa, home to the famous Senso-ji Temple, you'll need to take the Tokyo Metro Ginza Line or the Toei Asakusa Line. Similarly, if you're heading to Roppongi, known for its nightlife and art galleries, you'll likely use the Tokyo Metro Hibiya Line or the Toei Oedo Line. Ginza, one of Tokyo's most upscale shopping districts, is also primarily served by the subway system, with the Tokyo Metro Ginza Line, Marunouchi Line, and Hibiya Line all passing through the area.

One of the most convenient aspects of Tokyo's subway system is that it operates on a frequent schedule, with trains arriving every few minutes during peak hours and slightly less frequently during off-peak times. Subways run from around 5:00 AM until midnight, so it's easy to rely on them for most of the day. Stations are well-marked, with signs in both Japanese and English, and each train car has electronic displays showing the next stop in multiple languages. This makes it easy to follow your journey and know when to get off. In the stations, maps are available that show the full subway network, which is helpful for planning your route and figuring out transfers.

Transfers between subway lines or between the subway and JR lines are common in Tokyo, and these connections are generally well-organized. Transfer points are clearly marked within stations, so even if you need to switch between a Tokyo Metro line and a JR line, you'll find signage that helps guide you to the correct platform. It's important to note that while

JR trains are included in the JR Pass, the subway system is not. Therefore, even if you have a JR Pass, you'll need to purchase a separate ticket or use an IC card to access the subway.

The bus network in Tokyo is less frequently used by tourists compared to the trains and subways, but it's still a vital part of the city's public transportation system, especially for reaching areas that aren't well-served by train lines. Tokyo's buses are operated by multiple companies, with Toei Buses being the largest operator. While the buses are extremely reliable and clean, they can be a little more challenging to use for visitors, as the routes are more complex and there's less English signage than in the train and subway systems. However, for certain destinations, taking a bus can be the most convenient option.

Buses are particularly useful for traveling short distances or reaching destinations that are not near train stations. For example, if you're staying in a residential area that's a bit farther from the main train stations or if you're visiting specific locations like parks or museums that don't have nearby subway access, taking a bus can save you time and walking. The buses in Tokyo operate on a flat fare system, which means that no matter how far you travel, the fare remains the same. You can pay the fare with cash or by using your Suica or Pasmo card, which makes it easier since you don't need to worry about exact change.

Most buses in Tokyo have a clear electronic display that shows the next stop in both Japanese and English, so even if you don't speak the language, you'll be able to follow along with your route. It's important to remember that buses tend to run less frequently than trains, especially during off-peak hours, so it's a good idea to check the bus schedules in advance. The major bus stops usually have signs showing the routes and departure times, and there are several apps available that can help you plan your journey, including Google Maps, which provides real-time transit information, including bus routes.

When boarding a bus, the procedure can vary depending on the type of bus. In most cases, you'll board at the front of the bus and either pay the driver or tap your IC card on the reader. When getting off, you can simply press one of the stop buttons located throughout the bus to indicate that you want to get off at the next stop. Before disembarking, you can tap your IC card again or, if you paid in cash, just exit through the front door.

Another aspect of Tokyo's public transportation network that's worth mentioning is how well-integrated the different modes of transport are. Whether you're using the subway, the JR trains, or the buses, it's easy to transfer between them and continue your journey. The IC card system makes this especially simple, as you can use the same card across all forms of transportation, which streamlines your travels and avoids the need to buy multiple tickets.

Taxis, Ride-sharing Apps, and Other Transport Options

When traveling around Tokyo, public transportation like trains and subways is usually the most efficient way to get around. However, there are times when you might prefer more flexible transportation options, such as taxis, ride-sharing services, or other forms of private transport. Tokyo is a massive city, and while public transportation can take you almost anywhere, using a taxi or a ride-sharing app can sometimes be more convenient, especially if you have heavy luggage, are traveling late at night, or want to get somewhere specific without transferring between train lines.

Taxis are a common and reliable form of transportation in Tokyo, and you'll see them everywhere, especially in busy areas like Shinjuku, Ginza, and Roppongi. Taxis in Tokyo are known for being clean, safe, and efficient. The drivers are usually professional and polite, and many taxis now accept credit cards, although it's always a good idea to carry some cash just in case. Taxi drivers in Tokyo may not always speak English, but most taxis are equipped with navigation systems, and many drivers can use translation apps to communicate with foreign passengers if needed. You can also show the driver the address of your destination written in Japanese, which helps to avoid confusion.

Hailing a taxi in Tokyo is easy. You can flag one down on the street by simply raising your hand. Taxis that are available will have a red light in the lower corner of the front windshield, indicating they are open for passengers. If the light is green, the taxi is occupied. In busy areas like train stations, shopping districts, or major tourist spots, you'll often find designated taxi stands where you can line up and wait for the next available cab. It's usually faster and more organized to use these stands rather than trying to hail a taxi in the street, especially during peak times or in crowded areas.

The cost of taking a taxi in Tokyo can vary depending on the distance you're traveling. Taxi fares start at around ¥420 to ¥500 for the first kilometer, with additional charges for each kilometer after that. There may also be surcharges for late-night rides (usually between 10 PM and 5 AM), and tolls for using expressways are added to the fare if applicable. Taxis in Tokyo are more expensive than public transportation, so they are generally better for short trips or when convenience is more important than cost. For example, if you're heading to a restaurant or hotel from a nearby train station, or if you have a lot of luggage and want to avoid crowded trains, a taxi can be a good option.

Ride-sharing apps are another way to get around Tokyo, though they work a bit differently here compared to other countries. Ride-sharing services like Uber are available, but they are not as widely used in Tokyo as they are in cities like New York or London. In Japan, Uber functions more like a premium taxi service, and its availability is somewhat limited. The fares for Uber rides tend to be higher than for regular taxis, particularly for Uber Black, the premium service. However, Uber can be convenient if you prefer to use an app to arrange your transportation, especially if you don't speak Japanese, since the app handles all the communication with the driver for you. You can enter your destination, track your driver's arrival, and pay through the app, which eliminates the need for cash or card payments.

In addition to Uber, Japan has its own ride-hailing app called JapanTaxi. This app works similarly to Uber and allows you to book taxis from your smartphone. JapanTaxi is widely used in Tokyo and across Japan, and it connects you with local taxi companies rather than private ride-sharing vehicles. The app is available in English, and you can use it to book a taxi in advance, track your ride, and pay through the app. This is a good alternative if you want the convenience of booking a ride from your phone but prefer to use a traditional taxi rather than a ride-share vehicle.

For those who are staying in Tokyo for an extended period or who want the ultimate convenience, private car hire services are another option. These services, sometimes referred to as chauffeur services, allow you to book a private vehicle with a driver for a set amount of time. This can be useful if you have a busy schedule of meetings or events or if you're planning a day of sightseeing and don't want to worry about using public transportation. Companies like Blacklane, Limousine Tokyo, and other luxury car services operate in Tokyo, offering vehicles ranging from standard sedans to high-end luxury cars. These services tend to be much more expensive than taxis or ride-sharing apps, but they offer a high level of comfort, privacy, and flexibility.

If you're traveling to or from one of Tokyo's airports, there are also specialized transport options designed to make your journey easier. Airport limousine buses are a popular choice for getting to and from Narita or Haneda airports. These buses operate on a fixed schedule and have designated stops at major hotels and transportation hubs around Tokyo, including Shibuya, Shinjuku, and Tokyo Station. The buses are spacious, comfortable, and equipped with luggage storage, making them a good option if you're carrying a lot of bags. The fare for a limousine bus from Narita Airport to central Tokyo is typically around ¥3,000, while buses from Haneda to central Tokyo cost about ¥1,000 to ¥1,500.

For a faster and more direct transfer from the airport, you can also take an airport taxi or arrange for a private car service. Airport taxis are available at both Narita and Haneda airports, and while they are more expensive than public transportation, they offer the convenience of door-to-door service. From Narita, a taxi ride to central Tokyo can cost anywhere from ¥20,000 to ¥30,000 depending on traffic and tolls, while taxis from Haneda are generally much cheaper, usually ranging from ¥5,000 to ¥8,000. If you prefer to have a car waiting for you upon arrival, you can book a private transfer in advance through a car service or ride-sharing app.

Another option for getting around Tokyo, particularly for tourists, is renting a bicycle. Tokyo is becoming more bike-friendly, with dedicated bike lanes and cycle paths in certain areas. Bike rental services are available in many parts of the city, and this can be a fun and eco-friendly way to explore neighborhoods like Ueno, Asakusa, or along the Sumida River. Many hotels also offer bicycle rentals, or you can use rental services like Docomo's Community Cycle, which allows you to rent bikes at various stations around the city and drop them off at another location. Renting a bike is typically very affordable, with rates starting at around ¥200 to ¥300 per hour.

While taxis and ride-sharing apps provide the most convenient and direct ways to travel, they can also be affected by Tokyo's notorious traffic, especially during rush hour or in busy areas like Shibuya or Shinjuku. If you're in a hurry or need to travel a long distance, taking the train or subway may be faster, as they operate independently of road traffic. However, for shorter trips or when traveling late at night when trains aren't running, taxis, ride-sharing services, and other transport options become invaluable.

Renting a Bicycle in Tokyo

Renting a bicycle in Tokyo is a fantastic way to explore the city at your own pace. Although Tokyo is well-known for its excellent public transportation system, cycling allows you to experience the city from a different perspective, giving you access to areas that are less reachable by train or bus and offering the freedom to stop and explore whenever you like. Tokyo is increasingly becoming more bike-friendly, with designated bike lanes, cycling paths in parks, and improved infrastructure aimed at encouraging more people to use bicycles as a means of transportation. For tourists, renting a bike can be a convenient and enjoyable way to get around, especially in neighborhoods where distances are short but too far to walk comfortably.

One of the best reasons to rent a bicycle in Tokyo is that it allows you to experience the city's many parks, riversides, and neighborhoods up close. Popular areas like Asakusa, Ueno, and Yanaka are ideal for cycling because of their historic streets, smaller roads, and proximity to cultural sites. Instead of navigating crowded trains or buses, you can leisurely ride through these charming districts, stopping at temples, museums, local markets, or small cafés along the way. In addition, places like the Imperial Palace, Sumida River, and Tokyo Bay offer scenic cycling routes where you can enjoy the views and get a sense of Tokyo's mix of modern and traditional landscapes.

Renting a bicycle in Tokyo is easy, and there are several options depending on your location and needs. Many bike rental shops are spread across the city, particularly in popular tourist areas, and some hotels also offer bicycle rentals for their guests. These rentals are typically available on an hourly or daily basis, and the prices are quite affordable. For example, you might expect to pay around ¥300 to ¥500 per hour or ¥1,000 to ¥1,500 for a full day. This makes renting a bike a cost-effective way to explore the city, especially if you plan to visit multiple locations that aren't far from each other.

One popular bike rental service is the Docomo Bike Share system, which operates in various locations throughout Tokyo. This service allows you to rent a bicycle from one of their docking stations and return it at any other station in the city. This flexibility makes it incredibly convenient, especially if you want to ride around a neighborhood like Shibuya or Asakusa and then drop the bike off near a different station when you're done. The Docomo bikes are also electric-assisted, which can be very helpful if you're cycling in areas with hills or if you want to cover longer distances without getting too tired. The rental process is simple, and you can register online or use the service through a mobile app, where you can also find the nearest available bikes and docking stations. Prices for Docomo Bike Share are usually around ¥150 for 30 minutes, and you can pay with a credit card.

Another rental option is Tokyo Bike Rentals Yanaka, located in the historic Yanaka district. This rental shop specializes in providing bicycles to tourists who want to explore the quieter, more traditional parts of the city. Yanaka is one of Tokyo's best-preserved old neighborhoods, known for its temples, narrow streets, and a slower pace of life compared to the bustling city center. Renting a bike from this shop allows you to ride through Ueno Park, visit the famous Yanaka Cemetery, and stop by small, locally-owned shops and restaurants. The staff at Tokyo Bike Rentals Yanaka can provide recommendations on routes and sightseeing spots, making it a great choice for first-time visitors. Rates here are typically around ¥1,500 for a day's rental, and helmets are available if you prefer to use one.

If you're staying in areas like Odaiba or near the Sumida River, you'll find that these areas are ideal for cycling because of their flat terrain and wide open spaces. In Odaiba, for instance, you can enjoy a relaxed ride along the waterfront, taking in views of the Rainbow Bridge and Tokyo Bay. There are bike rental services available near Odaiba's parks and attractions, and many of these rentals offer comfortable bikes that are easy to handle, even if you're not an experienced cyclist. Renting a bike here is a good way to spend a leisurely afternoon exploring the futuristic architecture and enjoying the fresh air by the bay.

Before renting a bicycle in Tokyo, it's important to understand some basic rules and etiquette for cycling in the city. Although Tokyo is a safe and orderly place to ride a bike, it's essential to follow traffic rules to ensure that your ride is smooth and hassle-free. In most parts of the city, you'll be riding on the sidewalk rather than the road, as bikes are generally allowed on sidewalks unless there are specific signs prohibiting it. However, it's crucial to be mindful of pedestrians, especially in busy areas. Cyclists are expected to ride slowly and carefully when sharing sidewalks with pedestrians, and you should always ring your bell or announce your presence when approaching someone from behind to avoid collisions.

If you're riding on the road, keep in mind that bicycles are treated like vehicles under Japanese traffic law, meaning you are expected to follow the same rules as cars. Always ride on the left side of the road, obey traffic signals, and avoid riding against the flow of traffic. At intersections, be cautious and follow the signals for pedestrians or cyclists if they are available. Also, note that cycling while using a mobile phone, riding under the influence of alcohol, and carrying an umbrella while riding are all illegal in Japan. Following these rules will not only help you avoid accidents but also ensure that your cycling experience in Tokyo is enjoyable and stress-free.

When it comes to parking your bicycle, Tokyo has specific rules and designated areas for bike parking. Many popular areas and stations have bicycle parking lots or racks where you can safely leave your bike while you explore. These parking spots may charge a small fee, typically around ¥100 to ¥200 for a few hours. It's important not to park your bicycle in unauthorized areas, such as on sidewalks or outside shops, as illegally parked bikes can be impounded. If your bike is impounded, you'll need to pay a fine and go to a designated location to retrieve it, so it's best to park only in designated areas.

If you prefer a more guided experience, there are also cycling tours available in Tokyo. These tours are a great way to see the city with the help of a knowledgeable guide who can take you to some of the best sightseeing spots while sharing information about the history and culture of Tokyo. Many of these tours are designed for small groups, and they offer different routes that cater to a variety of interests. For example, you can join a tour that focuses on Tokyo's historic sites, or you can choose one that takes you through the city's parks and gardens. Cycling tours often provide the bikes, helmets, and even snacks, so you don't need to worry about renting equipment separately.

Walking Tips: Navigating Tokyo's Streets

Walking is one of the best ways to explore Tokyo, especially since the city is designed with pedestrians in mind. Despite being a massive metropolis, Tokyo is full of interesting neighborhoods, hidden alleys, quiet parks, and unique sights that are often best experienced on foot.

Tokyo's streets are an intricate mix of wide avenues, narrow alleyways, and quiet residential lanes. Unlike many Western cities that follow a grid-like pattern, Tokyo's street layout can seem disorganized and maze-like. It's important to know that Tokyo doesn't use a traditional street address system. Instead of streets having names, addresses are typically organized by neighborhood (called chome) and block numbers. For example, you might see an address like "Shibuya 2-14-8," which refers to the specific area (Shibuya), the neighborhood subdivision (2), the block (14), and the building number (8). This system can be confusing at first, especially if you're relying on street signs, but it's something you get used to with a bit of practice. In addition, buildings are often numbered in the order they were built, not in a linear or logical sequence, so even with a precise address, it might take some time to locate your destination.

Using a reliable map or navigation app is essential when walking around Tokyo. Google Maps is widely used in Japan and provides accurate walking directions, which are invaluable when trying to navigate the city's complex streets. Many Japanese map apps, such as Navitime, are also helpful, though they may not be available in English. GPS will be your best friend while navigating Tokyo's streets, but don't be surprised if you need to adjust your route a few times as you get closer to your destination. It's common to follow a general route on a map and then have to ask for directions or look for specific landmarks when you arrive in the vicinity of your destination.

When walking around Tokyo, it's important to be aware of pedestrian etiquette. Tokyo is an incredibly orderly city, and its residents follow specific unwritten rules about walking that help keep things moving smoothly, especially in crowded areas. In most places, people walk on the left side of the sidewalk, although in some neighborhoods or stations, walking on the right may be the norm. Pay attention to the flow of foot traffic around you and try to follow along. Tokyo's train stations and popular areas like Shibuya and Shinjuku can get extremely busy, so it's important to keep pace with the crowd and avoid stopping in the middle of sidewalks or walkways. If you need to stop to check your map or take a photo, it's best to move to the side to avoid blocking others.

Crosswalks are an essential part of navigating Tokyo's streets, and it's important to use them properly. Tokyo has very strict pedestrian rules, and jaywalking (crossing the street outside of designated crosswalks) is strongly discouraged. Crosswalks in busy areas often have traffic lights specifically for pedestrians, and it's important to wait for the green light before crossing. In quieter areas, you may find crosswalks without signals, in which case it's important to wait for cars to stop before crossing. Drivers in Tokyo are generally very respectful of pedestrians, but it's always a good idea to make eye contact with drivers before stepping into the road to ensure they've seen you.

One of the most enjoyable aspects of walking around Tokyo is discovering the city's mix of traditional and modern architecture. You can easily stumble upon centuries-old temples, shrines, and traditional houses hidden among towering skyscrapers and futuristic shopping complexes. Neighborhoods like Asakusa and Yanaka are known for their preserved historic streets, where you can explore narrow alleys lined with traditional machiya houses, small shops, and local eateries. On the other hand, areas like Shinjuku and Shibuya are filled with towering buildings, neon lights, and modern architecture that give you a glimpse into the fast-paced, high-tech side of the city.

Walking is also a great way to experience Tokyo's vibrant street life and local culture. Neighborhoods like Harajuku, Shimokitazawa, and Akihabara are known for their lively atmosphere, where you can see people dressed in colorful fashion, street performers, and bustling markets. These areas are filled with small shops, cafes, and galleries that you can easily miss if you're not walking through them. Exploring these parts of the city on foot allows you to stop and explore as you please, whether it's browsing through a vintage clothing store or grabbing a quick snack from a local street vendor.

Tokyo's parks and gardens are also ideal for exploring on foot. Walking through Ueno Park, Yoyogi Park, or the Shinjuku Gyoen National Garden provides a peaceful escape from the busy city streets. These parks are large and beautifully maintained, making them perfect for leisurely walks. If you're visiting during the spring, you'll be treated to the sight of cherry blossoms in full bloom, especially in places like Ueno Park and Chidorigafuchi. These parks often have well-marked paths, and you can spend hours walking through the grounds, visiting small shrines, or enjoying a picnic under the trees.

It's important to be mindful of where you walk in residential areas. While exploring quieter neighborhoods can give you a unique insight into daily life in Tokyo, it's crucial to be respectful of residents. Keep your voice low, especially in the early morning or late at night, and avoid taking photos of private homes or people without permission. Tokyo is a densely populated city, and while it's generally safe to walk around any time of day, being considerate of the local culture and customs is important.

One thing to keep in mind when walking in Tokyo is that many of the streets and sidewalks are narrow, particularly in older parts of the city. Sidewalks are not always present, and you may find yourself walking directly on the road in some areas. In these cases, stay as close to the edge as possible and be aware of vehicles, bicycles, and delivery scooters that may be passing by. In busy shopping areas or near train stations, some streets are designated as pedestrian-only during certain hours of the day, allowing you to walk freely without worrying about traffic. These pedestrian zones are usually marked with signs, and you'll notice that many of the busiest streets in places like Shibuya or Ginza become car-free during weekends or holidays.

Tokyo is a city that values cleanliness and order, and you'll notice that the streets are remarkably clean despite the lack of public trash cans. When walking around, it's important to carry a small bag for your trash and dispose of it properly when you find a bin, often located near vending machines or convenience stores. Smoking on the street is also prohibited in most areas of Tokyo, and designated smoking areas are available instead. You'll find these areas marked with signs, and they are usually located near train stations or inside large shopping complexes.

Another important consideration when walking in Tokyo is footwear. Since you'll likely be spending a lot of time on your feet, it's essential to wear comfortable shoes that can handle long distances and uneven surfaces. Tokyo's streets are well-maintained, but you may find yourself walking on cobblestone paths, gravel roads, or up and down stairs, especially in areas like temples or shrines. Having comfortable shoes will make your walking experience much more enjoyable and prevent foot fatigue as you explore the city.

Public restrooms are readily available throughout Tokyo, making it easy to find facilities while you're out walking. Most large train stations, parks, and shopping malls have clean and free public restrooms that are well-maintained. Convenience stores also often have restrooms available for customers. If you're walking through more residential areas or smaller neighborhoods, it's a good idea to take advantage of restrooms when you see them, as they may be less frequent in these parts of the city.

CHAPTER 6

MUST-VISIT TOKYO ATTRACTIONS

Historic Landmarks: Shrines, Temples, and Palaces

Tokyo is not only a bustling metropolis of modern skyscrapers and cutting-edge technology, but it is also a city rich with history and tradition. The city is home to many historic landmarks, including ancient shrines, temples, and palaces that offer a glimpse into Japan's past. These sites are not just important cultural and historical treasures, but they also provide visitors with a tranquil escape from the fast-paced energy of Tokyo. Visiting these landmarks is a must for anyone interested in learning about Japan's heritage, and the experiences you can have at these places will leave lasting memories of your trip.

One of the most iconic historic sites in Tokyo is the Meiji Shrine, or Meiji Jingu, which is located in the Shibuya district. This Shinto shrine is dedicated to Emperor Meiji and Empress Shoken, who played a pivotal role in Japan's modernization during the late 19th and early 20th centuries. The shrine was completed in 1920 and has since become a symbol of Japan's spiritual and historical legacy. Meiji Shrine is set in a large forested area, making it a peaceful oasis in the heart of the city. When you visit, you'll enter through massive wooden torii gates and walk along wide gravel paths lined with towering trees, which give the entire area a sense of calm and reverence.

To get to Meiji Shrine, you can take the JR Yamanote Line or the Tokyo Metro to Harajuku Station, which is just a short walk from the shrine's entrance. The shrine is free to enter, and visitors are welcome to participate in traditional Shinto rituals, such as offering a prayer at the main hall, purchasing omamori (protective charms), or writing wishes on wooden plaques called ema. One of the best times to visit Meiji Shrine is during the New Year, when millions of people gather here to pray for good fortune in the coming year, but it is a serene and meaningful experience at any time of the year. A visit to Meiji Shrine is also a great opportunity to explore nearby Yoyogi Park, where you can relax or have a picnic under the shade of the trees.

Another must-visit historical landmark in Tokyo is the Senso-ji Temple, located in the Asakusa district. Senso-ji is Tokyo's oldest and most famous Buddhist temple, dating back to the year 628 AD. The temple is dedicated to Kannon, the Buddhist goddess of mercy, and it attracts millions of visitors each year. As you approach Senso-ji, you'll first pass through the Kaminarimon, or Thunder Gate, which is the temple's grand entrance and features a giant red lantern that has become a symbol of the area. From there, you'll walk along Nakamise Shopping Street, a lively street lined with shops selling traditional snacks, souvenirs, and local crafts.

Senso-ji is not just a place of worship, but also a vibrant cultural center. Once you reach the main temple building, you can offer prayers, light incense, and admire the beautiful architecture. Don't miss the Five-Story Pagoda, which stands next to the temple and is an iconic feature of the complex. Another important part of the Senso-ji experience is drawing a fortune from one of the temple's omikuji boxes. For a small donation, you can shake a container until a numbered stick falls out, and you'll be given a fortune based on that number. If you receive a good fortune, you can keep it with you, but if the fortune is bad, you can tie it to a designated rack in the temple grounds to leave the bad luck behind.

Senso-ji is easily accessible by public transportation. You can take the Tokyo Metro Ginza Line or Toei Asakusa Line to Asakusa Station, which is just a short walk from the temple grounds. The temple and its surrounding area are especially beautiful at night when the buildings are illuminated, creating a magical atmosphere.

For those interested in Japan's imperial history, the Tokyo Imperial Palace is another significant landmark to visit. Located in the Chiyoda district, the Imperial Palace is the primary residence of Japan's Imperial Family. The palace stands on the site of the former Edo Castle, which was the seat of power for the Tokugawa shogunate during the Edo period. While much of the palace grounds are not open to the public, the surrounding East Gardens and outer grounds are free to explore and offer a fascinating look at the remains of the original Edo Castle, including its moats, stone walls, and gates.

The East Gardens of the Imperial Palace are particularly beautiful during the spring cherry blossom season and in the autumn when the leaves change color. Visitors can walk along well-maintained paths that take them through lush gardens, around ancient ruins, and past the foundations of the old castle keep. The gardens also house the Museum of Imperial Collections, where you can see art and artifacts from the Imperial Family's private collection. One of the most popular times to visit the Imperial Palace is on January 2nd and December 23rd, when the inner grounds are opened to the public, and the Emperor makes a special appearance to greet well-wishers.

To get to the Imperial Palace, you can take the Tokyo Metro Tozai Line or the JR Chuo Line to Otemachi Station. From there, it's just a short walk to the palace grounds. Visiting the Imperial Palace offers a unique glimpse into Japan's imperial past and the opportunity to explore a peaceful, historical area in the heart of modern Tokyo.

For a different type of historical experience, you can visit the Nezu Shrine, one of Tokyo's oldest Shinto shrines, located in the Bunkyo district. Nezu Shrine dates back over 1,900 years and is known for its beautiful architecture and tranquil gardens. One of the highlights of the shrine is its tunnel of red torii gates, similar to the famous gates at Fushimi Inari Shrine in Kyoto. These gates lead up to the main shrine building, where visitors can offer prayers and enjoy the peaceful surroundings. Nezu Shrine is especially popular in the spring when it hosts the annual Azalea Festival, and the grounds are covered in vibrant flowers.

To reach Nezu Shrine, you can take the Tokyo Metro Chiyoda Line to Nezu Station, and the shrine is just a few minutes' walk from there. The shrine is relatively small and less crowded than some of the other major tourist spots, making it a perfect place to relax and reflect while taking in traditional Japanese architecture.

Finally, the Hie Shrine in Akasaka is another beautiful Shinto shrine worth visiting. Perched on a hill, the shrine is dedicated to the guardian deity of Tokyo and is surrounded by trees, offering a quiet retreat from the city's busy streets. Hie Shrine is particularly famous for its annual Sanno Matsuri, one of Tokyo's three great festivals, which includes elaborate processions through the city. The shrine is also known for its red torii gates, which form a path up the hillside and make for a picturesque walk.

Hie Shrine is located near Akasaka Station on the Tokyo Metro Chiyoda Line and Tameike-Sanno Station on the Ginza Line. It's an easy stop if you're exploring the Akasaka or Roppongi areas and offers a blend of traditional culture and natural beauty.

Tokyo Skytree and Tokyo Tower

Tokyo is home to two iconic towers that stand tall in the city's skyline: Tokyo Skytree and Tokyo Tower. These landmarks are must-visit tourist attractions that offer stunning views of the sprawling metropolis and provide visitors with a unique way to experience Tokyo from above. While both towers serve as observation points and symbols of the city, each has its own distinct history, design, and set of features that make the experience of visiting them memorable.

Tokyo Skytree, the tallest structure in Japan and the second tallest in the world, is located in the Sumida district of Tokyo. Completed in 2012, it stands at a staggering 634 meters (2,080 feet) and has quickly become one of Tokyo's most recognizable landmarks. The tower was originally built as a television broadcasting tower, replacing the older Tokyo Tower, but it also serves as a popular tourist destination with two observation decks that offer breathtaking views of the city.

The first observation deck, known as the Tembo Deck, is located 350 meters above the ground. This deck features floor-to-ceiling glass windows, allowing visitors to take in a 360-degree view of the city. On a clear day, you can see landmarks such as the Tokyo Bay, Mount Fuji in the distance, and the surrounding Kanto region. One of the highlights of the Tembo Deck is its glass floor section, where visitors can look directly down to the ground far below, giving you a thrilling perspective of the height. The experience here is one of awe and amazement as you get a bird's-eye view of Tokyo's vast urban landscape.

The second observation deck, called the Tembo Galleria, is located at 450 meters above the ground and offers an even more impressive view. The Galleria is a spiraling ramp that gradually ascends around the tower, giving you the sensation of walking in the sky. This part of the tower is designed to offer a more intimate viewing experience, where you can see the city in greater detail. The higher vantage point and unique design of the Galleria make it a favorite for visitors who want to capture incredible photos of the Tokyo skyline, especially at sunset or in the evening when the city lights up.

In addition to the observation decks, Tokyo Skytree is home to a shopping complex called Tokyo Solamachi, located at the base of the tower. Solamachi has over 300 shops and restaurants, making it a great place to explore before or after your visit to the observation decks. Whether you're looking for unique souvenirs, traditional Japanese sweets, or international brands, Solamachi has something for everyone. You can also find a variety of restaurants offering local and international cuisine, some of which have views of the tower or the city. For those interested in science, the Sumida Aquarium, located within the Solamachi complex, is a fantastic place to learn about marine life, with exhibits featuring creatures from Tokyo Bay and other parts of Japan.

Getting to Tokyo Skytree is easy. You can take the Tokyo Metro Hanzomon Line or the Tobu Skytree Line to Oshiage Station, which is directly connected to the Skytree complex. Alternatively, the Toei Asakusa Line also stops at Oshiage Station. Once you arrive, you can spend hours exploring the tower, the observation decks, and the surrounding shopping and entertainment areas.

Tokyo Tower, on the other hand, is a symbol of Tokyo's post-war rebirth and modernization. Completed in 1958, it was modeled after the Eiffel Tower in Paris and stands 333 meters (1,093 feet) tall. Located in the Minato district, near the Zojoji Temple, Tokyo Tower was once the tallest structure in Japan and served as the city's primary television broadcasting tower until it was replaced by Tokyo Skytree. Despite its age, Tokyo Tower remains one of the city's most beloved landmarks and continues to draw millions of visitors each year.

The main attraction of Tokyo Tower is its two observation decks, which offer panoramic views of the city. The Main Deck is located 150 meters above the ground and provides a fantastic view of central Tokyo, including landmarks like the Imperial Palace, Roppongi Hills, and Rainbow Bridge. The Main Deck is particularly popular at night when the city is illuminated by thousands of lights, creating a stunning view of the urban landscape. Like Tokyo Skytree, Tokyo Tower also has sections of glass flooring, where you can stand and look down at the streets far below, adding a touch of excitement to the experience.

For an even higher view, you can visit the Top Deck, located 250 meters above the ground. The Top Deck offers a more exclusive viewing experience and features a futuristic, mirrored interior that enhances the feeling of floating above the city. The Top Deck Tour is a guided experience that includes access to special elevators, multimedia displays about the tower's history, and a more personalized look at the city's skyline.

One of the unique features of Tokyo Tower is its lighting. The tower is illuminated with different colors throughout the year, depending on the season or special events. For example, during the winter months, Tokyo Tower is often lit up with warm, orange lights, while in the summer, cooler white lights are used to create a refreshing atmosphere. The tower also celebrates holidays and events with special light shows, making it a beautiful sight to see from both near and far.

At the base of Tokyo Tower, you'll find the FootTown building, which houses a variety of attractions, including souvenir shops, cafes, and a small amusement area. One of the highlights is the Tokyo Tower Wax Museum, which features wax figures of famous personalities from Japan and around the world. There is also a One Piece-themed amusement park called Tokyo One Piece Tower, which is based on the popular manga and anime series. This attraction is particularly popular with fans of the series and offers interactive exhibits, games, and live shows.

To reach Tokyo Tower, you can take the Toei Oedo Line to Akabanebashi Station, the Tokyo Metro Hibiya Line to Kamiyacho Station, or the JR Yamanote Line to Hamamatsucho Station. Each station is a short walk from the tower, and as you approach, you'll be able to spot Tokyo Tower rising above the city's buildings, creating an impressive sight against the skyline.

Visiting both Tokyo Skytree and Tokyo Tower offers a unique opportunity to see Tokyo from different heights and perspectives. While Tokyo Skytree provides a more modern and futuristic experience, Tokyo Tower is steeped in history and nostalgia. Both towers offer unforgettable views of Tokyo, and each has its own charm and features that make them must-visit destinations for tourists.

Exploring Asakusa and Senso-ji Temple

Asakusa is one of Tokyo's most historic and culturally rich neighborhoods, offering visitors a unique chance to experience traditional Japan amidst the backdrop of the modern city. At the heart of Asakusa lies Senso-ji Temple, Tokyo's oldest and most iconic Buddhist temple. This area is a must-visit for anyone looking to immerse themselves in Japan's spiritual heritage, explore ancient architecture, and enjoy a lively and vibrant atmosphere filled with shops, street food, and traditional festivals. A visit to Asakusa and Senso-ji Temple is more than just sightseeing; it's an experience that connects you to the roots of Japanese culture and history.

Senso-ji Temple, also known as Asakusa Kannon Temple, was founded in 628 AD and is dedicated to Kannon, the Buddhist goddess of mercy. Legend has it that two fishermen discovered a statue of Kannon in the Sumida River, and despite returning it to the water, the statue kept reappearing. This led to the construction of the temple, which has since become a major pilgrimage site and one of Tokyo's most popular attractions. Over the centuries, Senso-ji has grown into a sprawling temple complex with multiple halls, gates, and pagodas, each with its own historical and religious significance.

As you approach Senso-ji, the first thing you'll notice is the Kaminarimon, or Thunder Gate. This is the outer gate of the temple and serves as the grand entrance to the complex. The Kaminarimon is an imposing structure, featuring a giant red paper lantern that hangs in the center, with the characters for "thunder gate" written on it. Flanking the lantern are statues of the Shinto gods of wind and thunder, who are believed to protect the temple. The gate is one of the most photographed spots in Tokyo, and it sets the tone for the rest of your visit.

After passing through the Kaminarimon, you'll find yourself on Nakamise-dori, a bustling shopping street that leads directly to the temple's main hall. Nakamise-dori is lined with shops selling traditional Japanese snacks, souvenirs, and crafts. Here, you can try treats like freshly made taiyaki (fish-shaped cakes filled with sweet red bean paste), rice crackers, and melonpan (a sweet bread with a crisp outer layer). You'll also find shops selling yukata (casual summer kimonos), folding fans, and other traditional goods, making it a great place to pick up unique souvenirs. Walking down Nakamise-dori is a sensory experience—between the aroma of food being prepared, the vibrant colors of the stalls, and the sound of tourists and locals chatting, it feels like stepping into an older, more traditional Tokyo.

At the end of Nakamise-dori, you'll reach Hozomon, the inner gate of the temple, which leads to the main hall. The Hozomon is an impressive two-story gate, flanked by massive lanterns and statues of guardians who protect the temple. As you pass through the gate, you'll come into the temple courtyard, which is dominated by the main hall (Hondo) and a five-story pagoda.

The main hall of Senso-ji is where worshippers come to offer prayers to Kannon. The hall is grand and beautifully decorated, with intricate carvings and gold accents. Visitors are welcome to participate in the traditional practice of offering a prayer at the altar by tossing a coin into the offering box, bowing, and clapping twice before making a wish or prayer. The atmosphere inside the hall is one of reverence, with the smell of incense filling the air and the soft sound of chanting occasionally heard in the background.

Before entering the main hall, many visitors stop at the large incense burner located in the courtyard in front of the temple. This is called the jokoro, and it is believed that wafting the smoke over your body can bring health and good fortune. You'll see people waving the smoke toward themselves, especially over areas where they might have aches or pains. This is another deeply spiritual aspect of visiting Senso-ji, as it connects visitors to the traditions and beliefs that have been practiced at this temple for over a thousand years.

Another popular activity at Senso-ji is drawing omikuji fortunes. For a small donation, you can shake a metal box until a numbered stick falls out. The number corresponds to a fortune that you can pull from a drawer. If you receive a good fortune, you keep it as a token of good luck. If you draw a bad fortune, it is customary to tie it to a special rack at the temple to leave the bad luck behind. This ritual is a fun and interactive way to engage with Japanese temple culture, and it's a favorite activity for both locals and tourists.

To the side of the main hall is the Five-Story Pagoda, one of the most striking features of the Senso-ji complex. The pagoda is a symbol of Buddhist enlightenment and serves as a spiritual beacon for the temple. While you can't enter the pagoda itself, it is a beautiful structure to admire, especially when framed against the sky or illuminated at night. The surrounding garden area is also worth exploring, offering a peaceful escape from the busy temple grounds.

Senso-ji Temple is also famous for its festivals, the most important of which is the Sanja Matsuri, held every May. This is one of Tokyo's largest and most energetic festivals, where portable shrines (mikoshi) are paraded through the streets of Asakusa in honor of the three founders of Senso-ji. The festival draws huge crowds, and the streets come alive with music, dancing, and lively celebrations. If you happen to be in Tokyo during Sanja Matsuri, it's an unforgettable experience to witness.

Beyond the temple itself, the surrounding Asakusa neighborhood is filled with things to see and do. One of the highlights is the Sumida River, which runs just a short distance from the temple. You can take a relaxing walk along the riverbank or enjoy a boat cruise that offers views of Tokyo's skyline, including the Tokyo Skytree in the distance. There are also several parks nearby, such as Sumida Park, which is a popular spot for cherry blossom viewing in the spring.

Asakusa is also known for its traditional rickshaw rides, where you can sit in a hand-pulled cart while a guide takes you on a tour of the area. The rickshaw drivers, known as shafu, are knowledgeable about the history of Asakusa and can share interesting facts and stories as they take you through the neighborhood's narrow streets and alleys. It's a fun and nostalgic way to explore the area, and it adds to the overall experience of stepping back in time while visiting Asakusa.

To get to Senso-ji and Asakusa, the easiest way is by taking the Tokyo Metro Ginza Line or Toei Asakusa Line to Asakusa Station. From the station, it's just a short walk to the temple grounds. Alternatively, you can take the Tobu Skytree Line, which also stops at Asakusa Station. The area is well-connected by public transportation, making it an easy destination to reach from other parts of Tokyo.

The Imperial Palace: A Glimpse into Japan's History

The Imperial Palace in Tokyo is one of the most historically significant and culturally important landmarks in Japan. Located in the heart of the city, the Imperial Palace is the residence of Japan's Emperor and the site of the former Edo Castle, which was the center of political power during the Edo period. While much of the palace grounds are closed to the public, the surrounding gardens and historic structures offer visitors a unique glimpse into Japan's imperial history and the opportunity to explore a beautiful and tranquil space amid the hustle and bustle of central Tokyo. A visit to the Imperial

Palace is a journey through Japan's history, architecture, and tradition, and it is one of the most memorable experiences for any tourist in Tokyo.

The Imperial Palace stands on the site of Edo Castle, which was originally built in the 15th century and later became the seat of power for the Tokugawa shogunate, Japan's ruling military government, during the Edo period (1603-1868). After the Meiji Restoration, when power was restored to the emperor, the Imperial Family moved from Kyoto to Tokyo, and the former Edo Castle became the Imperial Palace. While the original castle structures were largely destroyed over time, the palace grounds retain many of the original moats, stone walls, and gates, offering a fascinating glimpse into Japan's feudal past.

One of the main attractions of the Imperial Palace is the East Gardens, which are open to the public year-round and free to enter. The East Gardens cover a large area of the palace grounds and include the ruins of Edo Castle, beautiful landscaped gardens, and several historic buildings. As you walk through the East Gardens, you'll come across the massive stone foundations of the former castle keep, which was once the tallest structure in Edo (modern-day Tokyo). Though the keep itself no longer exists, the stone base remains and serves as a reminder of the grandeur of the castle that once stood here.

The East Gardens are also home to Ninomaru Garden, a traditional Japanese landscape garden that features a pond, stone lanterns, and meticulously manicured trees and plants. The garden is especially beautiful during the spring cherry blossom season and the autumn when the leaves change color. Visitors can take a leisurely walk along the garden's paths, enjoy the tranquility of the surroundings, and take in the carefully designed natural beauty that characterizes traditional Japanese gardens.

Another important historical site within the East Gardens is the Museum of the Imperial Collections, which houses art and artifacts from the Imperial Family's private collection. The museum offers visitors a rare chance to see works of art, ceramics, calligraphy, and other cultural treasures that are not typically on display to the public. The collection reflects the deep cultural heritage of the Imperial Family and provides insight into Japan's artistic traditions over the centuries.

While the East Gardens are open to the public, the inner grounds of the Imperial Palace are only accessible on two special occasions each year: January 2nd for New Year's greetings and December 23rd for the Emperor's birthday. On these days, the Imperial Family makes a public appearance, and visitors can enter the inner grounds to offer their greetings. Thousands of people gather for these events, making it a once-in-a-lifetime experience to witness a unique part of Japan's imperial tradition.

One of the most iconic features of the Imperial Palace is the Nijubashi Bridge, a beautiful double-arched stone bridge that leads to the palace's inner grounds. While visitors cannot cross the bridge, it offers one of the best photo opportunities in the area, with the bridge reflecting in the surrounding moat and the palace buildings visible in the background. The bridge, combined with the lush greenery and the calm waters of the moat, creates a picturesque scene that is especially stunning in the early morning or late afternoon when the light is soft.

The palace grounds are also surrounded by the remnants of Edo Castle's massive moats, which still encircle much of the area. These moats, filled with water and lined with trees, add to the peaceful atmosphere of the area and serve as a reminder of the castle's original defensive design. Walking along the paths that follow the moat offers a sense of serenity, and it's a great way to explore the perimeter of the palace grounds while enjoying the natural beauty of the area.

For those interested in learning more about the history of the Imperial Palace and its role in Japanese history, guided tours are available. The Imperial Household Agency offers free tours of the palace grounds in both Japanese and English, although advance reservations are required. These tours provide detailed explanations of the various structures, gates, and historical sites within the palace grounds, and they give visitors a deeper understanding of the importance of the Imperial Palace in Japan's political and cultural history.

One of the most accessible areas of the palace grounds is Kokyo Gaien, a large open plaza located in front of the Imperial Palace. This expansive space is a popular spot for both locals and tourists to relax, jog, or simply take in the view of the palace. Kokyo Gaien offers unobstructed views of the palace's outer buildings and moats, and it is a great place to start your exploration of the area. The plaza is also home to several important statues, including a statue of the famous samurai Kusunoki Masashige, who is revered for his loyalty to the emperor during the 14th century.

To reach the Imperial Palace, there are several convenient transportation options. The palace is located in the Chiyoda district, right in the center of Tokyo. The closest subway station is Otemachi Station, which is served by multiple lines, including the Tokyo Metro Chiyoda, Hanzomon, and Marunouchi lines. From Otemachi Station, it's just a short walk to the palace grounds. Alternatively, you can take the JR Yamanote Line to Tokyo Station, which is also within walking distance of the palace. If you're coming from other parts of the city, the palace is easily accessible by train or subway, making it a convenient destination for a day of exploration.

In addition to its historical significance, the Imperial Palace is also a place of natural beauty, and visiting the palace grounds offers a peaceful retreat from the busy streets of Tokyo. The area surrounding the palace is full of wide, tree-lined avenues and open spaces, making it an ideal place for a leisurely walk or a bike ride. You'll often see locals jogging around the perimeter of the palace, taking advantage of the quiet and scenic environment. The contrast between the modern skyscrapers of central Tokyo and the traditional architecture and gardens of the Imperial Palace creates a unique atmosphere that captures the essence of Tokyo's blend of old and new.

For those who enjoy photography, the Imperial Palace offers plenty of opportunities to capture stunning images. Whether you're photographing the reflection of Nijubashi Bridge in the moat, the cherry blossoms in the East Gardens, or the towering walls of Edo Castle's remnants, the palace grounds provide a wealth of picturesque scenes. In the spring, the palace area is one of Tokyo's best spots for viewing cherry blossoms, particularly along the moats and in the East Gardens, where the delicate pink flowers create a striking contrast against the ancient stone walls.

Odaiba and Its Futuristic Sights

Odaiba is one of Tokyo's most unique and futuristic areas, offering a variety of attractions that blend cutting-edge technology, modern architecture, and entertainment with beautiful waterfront views. This artificial island, located in Tokyo Bay, was originally developed in the 19th century as part of the city's coastal defense system, but today it has transformed into a popular leisure and shopping destination that draws millions of visitors each year. Odaiba's modern skyline, iconic structures, and numerous attractions make it a must-visit destination for anyone looking to experience a different side of Tokyo.

Odaiba is situated in the Tokyo Bay area and is accessible by several different modes of transportation. One of the most popular and scenic ways to get to Odaiba is by taking the

Yurikamome Line, an automated elevated train that departs from Shimbashi Station and travels across the iconic Rainbow Bridge, offering stunning views of the Tokyo skyline and the bay. The Yurikamome Line makes several stops throughout Odaiba, making it convenient to access various attractions. Another option is the Rinkai Line, which connects Odaiba to central Tokyo and the rest of the city's extensive rail network. If you prefer a more scenic route, you can take a water bus from locations such as Asakusa or Hinode Pier, which gives you the opportunity to enjoy a leisurely boat ride across Tokyo Bay before arriving at Odaiba's shores.

One of the first sights that will catch your eye when you arrive in Odaiba is the futuristic architecture of the Fuji TV Building. This iconic building is one of the most recognizable landmarks in Odaiba, featuring a large silver sphere that appears to float above the structure. The sphere houses an observation deck, which offers panoramic views of Odaiba, Tokyo Bay, and the city skyline. Visitors can also explore exhibitions related to Fuji TV's programming, making it an interesting stop for fans of Japanese television. The observation deck is especially popular at sunset and in the evening, when the lights of the city and Rainbow Bridge create a beautiful backdrop.

Another must-see attraction in Odaiba is the teamLab Borderless digital art museum. Located in the Mori Building Digital Art Museum, teamLab Borderless is an immersive and interactive experience that uses cutting-edge technology to create stunning digital art installations. The exhibits are designed to blur the boundaries between the physical and digital worlds, with rooms filled with projections of flowing waterfalls, colorful flowers, and glowing lights that respond to the movement of visitors. The experience is unlike any traditional museum, as the artwork changes and evolves as you move through the space, making each visit unique. TeamLab Borderless is one of the most popular attractions in Odaiba, and it's recommended to purchase tickets in advance due to its popularity.

For those interested in science and technology, the National Museum of Emerging Science and Innovation, known as Miraikan, is another highlight of Odaiba. This museum offers interactive exhibits on a wide range of topics, from robotics and artificial intelligence to space exploration and environmental sustainability. One of the main attractions at Miraikan is ASIMO, Honda's advanced humanoid robot, which performs demonstrations for visitors. The museum also features a large spherical display called the Geo-Cosmos, which projects real-time images of the Earth and provides information about global environmental changes. Miraikan is a great place to learn about Japan's contributions to science and technology, and its hands-on exhibits make it a fun and educational experience for visitors of all ages.

Odaiba is also home to some of Tokyo's most unique shopping experiences. One of the largest and most popular shopping centers is DiverCity Tokyo Plaza, which is best known for the life-sized Unicorn Gundam statue that stands outside the mall. This giant robot statue is a must-see for fans of the Gundam anime series, and it periodically transforms, with different parts of the statue lighting up and moving. Inside DiverCity, you'll find a wide range of shops, from high-end fashion brands to popular Japanese and international retailers. The mall also has a food court with a variety of dining options, including local favorites like ramen and sushi.

Another shopping and entertainment complex in Odaiba is Aqua City Odaiba. This mall offers a more relaxed shopping experience, with a variety of stores, cafes, and restaurants that overlook Tokyo Bay. One of the best features of Aqua City is its outdoor terrace, which provides a stunning view of the Rainbow Bridge and the Statue of Liberty replica, which is located just outside the mall. This replica of the famous American monument was originally erected as a temporary display but became so popular that it was made a permanent feature. Aqua City is also home to a cinema complex that shows the latest movies, including Japanese films and international blockbusters.

Speaking of the Rainbow Bridge, this impressive suspension bridge is one of Odaiba's most famous landmarks. Spanning Tokyo Bay, the bridge connects Odaiba to the mainland and is illuminated at night with colorful lights, making it a stunning sight to see from various viewpoints around the area. You can walk across the Rainbow Bridge via a pedestrian walkway, which offers fantastic views of both Tokyo's cityscape and the bay. The walk takes about 30 minutes, and it's especially enjoyable during the evening when the city lights begin to twinkle.

For those looking to relax by the water, Odaiba Seaside Park offers a pleasant escape with its sandy beach and waterfront promenade. While swimming is not allowed, the park is a great place to take a walk, enjoy a picnic, or watch the sunset over Tokyo Bay. The park's beach area is popular with families, and you'll often see people flying kites, playing beach volleyball, or simply sitting on the sand enjoying the view. The park also offers great photo opportunities, with the Rainbow Bridge and Tokyo Tower visible in the distance. The beach's calm atmosphere and scenic views make it a perfect spot to unwind after a day of exploring Odaiba's many attractions.

For those who enjoy thrilling rides and amusement parks, Odaiba is home to the Odaiba Oedo-Onsen Monogatari, a hot spring theme park that offers a traditional Japanese onsen (hot spring) experience in a fun and family-friendly environment. The complex is designed to resemble a historic Edo-period town, and visitors can walk around in yukata (casual summer kimonos) while enjoying the various indoor and outdoor baths. The baths are filled with natural hot spring water, and there are also foot baths, relaxation areas, and traditional Japanese games to enjoy. Oedo-Onsen Monogatari is a great place to relax and experience Japanese onsen culture without having to leave Tokyo.

In addition to its many attractions, Odaiba is known for hosting various events and festivals throughout the year. The area often serves as a venue for concerts, exhibitions, and seasonal festivals that draw both locals and tourists. One of the most popular annual events is the Odaiba Rainbow Fireworks, held on Saturday evenings during the winter months. These fireworks displays light up the night sky over Tokyo Bay, with the Rainbow Bridge serving as a stunning backdrop. Attending one of these fireworks shows is a magical experience and a highlight for anyone visiting Odaiba during the winter season.

Cultural Gems: Museums and Galleries

Tokyo is a city that is not only known for its futuristic skyline, bustling streets, and modern technology, but also for its deep-rooted cultural heritage. This heritage is preserved and celebrated through a wide variety of museums and galleries spread across the city. These cultural gems offer visitors a chance to explore Japanese art, history, and culture in a meaningful and engaging way.

One of the most significant cultural institutions in Tokyo is the Tokyo National Museum, located in Ueno Park. Established in 1872, the Tokyo National Museum is Japan's oldest and largest museum, housing a vast collection of over 110,000 pieces of art and artifacts, including national treasures and important cultural properties. The museum is a must-visit for anyone interested in Japan's history and art, as it offers a comprehensive overview of the country's cultural development from ancient times to the present day. The collection spans a wide range of mediums, including ceramics, swords, samurai armor, textiles, sculptures, and more.

One of the highlights of the Tokyo National Museum is the Honkan, or Japanese Gallery, which features exhibits on the history of Japanese art. Here, you can explore a rich array of ancient Buddhist sculptures, calligraphy, and traditional paintings, as well as exquisite examples of Japanese pottery and lacquerware. The gallery provides an immersive journey through Japan's artistic evolution, from the early Jomon period to the Edo period. Another must-see section is the Heiseikan, which focuses on Japan's archeological history and includes a fascinating collection of artifacts from Japan's ancient past.

The Tokyo National Museum is located in Ueno Park, one of the city's most popular public parks, which is also home to several other cultural attractions. To get to the museum, you can take the JR Yamanote Line or Tokyo Metro Ginza Line to Ueno Station, from where it's just a short walk to the museum entrance. Spending a day in Ueno Park, exploring the museum and its surroundings, is a wonderful way to immerse yourself in Tokyo's cultural heritage.

Another cultural landmark in Tokyo is the Edo-Tokyo Museum, located in the Ryogoku district. This museum offers visitors an in-depth look at the history of Tokyo (formerly known as Edo) and how it has transformed from a small fishing village to the modern metropolis it is today. The museum's exhibits cover the Edo period (1603-1868) as well as the rapid modernization that occurred during the Meiji Restoration and beyond. Through life-size reconstructions, models, and interactive displays, visitors can get a sense of what life was like in old Edo, from the daily lives of samurai and merchants to the development of traditional arts and theater.

One of the most impressive features of the Edo-Tokyo Museum is its full-scale replica of Nihonbashi Bridge, which was a central hub of commerce and trade during the Edo period. Walking across the bridge and exploring the recreated Edo-period townscape is like stepping back in time. The museum also showcases artifacts such as scrolls, clothing, and tools that were used during the Edo period, giving you a deeper understanding of Tokyo's roots. To get to the Edo-Tokyo Museum, you can take the JR Sobu Line to Ryogoku Station, which is just a short walk from the museum.

For those with an interest in modern and contemporary art, the Mori Art Museum, located in the Roppongi Hills complex, is one of Tokyo's premier destinations for contemporary art. The museum is known for its rotating exhibitions of both Japanese and international artists, and it regularly hosts groundbreaking and thought-provoking exhibitions on a variety of themes, from contemporary sculpture and installations to video art and photography. The Mori Art Museum is located on the 53rd floor of the Mori Tower, and in addition to the art on display, visitors can enjoy breathtaking views of the Tokyo skyline from the museum's observation deck, known as Tokyo City View.

What makes the Mori Art Museum stand out is its commitment to showcasing global contemporary art alongside Japanese art. The museum often hosts exhibitions that explore societal issues such as technology, environmental concerns, and the relationship between tradition and modernity. These exhibitions are designed to engage visitors on a deeper level and encourage reflection on the world around them. After visiting the museum, you can explore the surrounding Roppongi Hills area, which is home to numerous restaurants, shops, and cultural attractions. To get to the Mori Art Museum, take the Tokyo Metro Hibiya Line to Roppongi Station.

For lovers of traditional Japanese art, the Nezu Museum in the Aoyama district is another must-visit cultural gem. The museum houses the private collection of Nezu Kaichiro, a businessman and art collector who was passionate about preserving traditional Japanese art. The Nezu Museum is renowned for its extensive collection of Japanese and East Asian art, including calligraphy, paintings, ceramics, and textiles. The museum also has a beautiful traditional garden that visitors can stroll through, offering a serene escape from the city.

One of the highlights of the Nezu Museum is its collection of byobu (folding screens), which depict scenes from nature, mythology, and everyday life in ancient Japan. The museum's collection of Buddhist art is also impressive, featuring sculptures, ritual objects, and paintings that date back centuries. The Nezu Museum's garden is designed in the traditional stroll garden style, with winding paths, ponds, and carefully placed stones and plants that create a harmonious atmosphere. After exploring the museum's exhibits, a walk through the garden provides a peaceful conclusion to your visit. To get to the Nezu Museum, take the Tokyo Metro Ginza Line to Omotesando Station, and it's a short walk from there.

For a more modern art experience, the National Art Center, Tokyo, located in the Roppongi area, is one of the city's largest and most unique museums. Unlike most museums, the National Art Center does not have a permanent collection. Instead, it hosts temporary exhibitions, showcasing a wide range of art from both Japanese and international artists. The museum's distinctive architecture, designed by Kisho Kurokawa, is a work of art in itself, with its undulating glass façade and open, airy interior.

The National Art Center is known for hosting large-scale exhibitions that cover everything from contemporary art to fashion, design, and photography. Visitors can check the museum's schedule to see what exhibitions are on during their visit, and with the museum's constantly changing lineup, there's always something new to discover. The museum also has a stylish café where you can relax and enjoy a cup of coffee after exploring the exhibitions. To reach the National Art Center, you can take the Tokyo Metro Hibiya Line or Toei Oedo Line to Roppongi Station.

In addition to these major cultural institutions, Tokyo is home to many smaller galleries and museums that offer intimate and specialized experiences. For example, the Sumida Hokusai Museum, located in the Sumida district, is dedicated to the life and work of Katsushika Hokusai, one of Japan's most famous ukiyo-e (woodblock print) artists. The museum showcases Hokusai's iconic works, including his famous series Thirty-Six Views of Mount Fuji, and offers insights into the techniques and themes that defined his art.

Visiting museums and galleries in Tokyo not only provides an opportunity to explore Japan's rich artistic and cultural history but also offers a deeper understanding of the country's modern art scene and its contributions to global culture. Whether you're admiring ancient artifacts at the Tokyo National Museum, walking through the recreated streets of Edo at the Edo-Tokyo Museum, or contemplating contemporary installations at the Mori Art Museum, each experience adds a new layer to your understanding of Japan.

CHAPTER 7

NEIGHBORHOODS AND DISTRICTS TO EXPLORE

Shibuya: The Heart of Modern Tokyo

Shibuya is often regarded as the beating heart of modern Tokyo. It is one of the city's most vibrant and dynamic districts, known for its bustling streets, iconic landmarks, and an electric atmosphere that captures the energy of urban life in Japan's capital. Shibuya is not only a center for fashion, shopping, and nightlife, but it also serves as a cultural hub where the latest trends and innovations are born.

Located in the southwestern part of central Tokyo, Shibuya is easily accessible from nearly all parts of the city. The primary gateway to the area is Shibuya Station, one of Tokyo's busiest and most important transportation hubs. Shibuya Station is served by several major train and subway lines, including the JR Yamanote Line, the Tokyo Metro Ginza Line, the Tokyo Metro Hanzomon Line, and the Keio Inokashira Line. This makes Shibuya incredibly convenient to reach from districts like Shinjuku, Tokyo Station, or even from further away in suburban areas. From Shibuya Station, you'll find yourself right in the middle of the action, with all of the area's attractions within walking distance.

One of Shibuya's most famous landmarks is the Shibuya Scramble Crossing, often considered the busiest pedestrian crossing in the world. Every few minutes, as the traffic lights change, hundreds or even thousands of people converge from all directions to cross the street at the same time. This chaotic yet orderly flow of people has become a symbol of Tokyo's fast-paced life, and watching it from one of the nearby buildings or standing right in the midst of it is an unforgettable experience. Many visitors make their way to the second-floor windows of the Starbucks located in the QFRONT building, which offers a prime view of the crossing. The best time to see the crossing is at night, when the surrounding neon signs and advertisements light up the entire area, giving it an even more vibrant atmosphere.

Just a short walk from the crossing is the Hachiko Statue, one of Shibuya's most beloved meeting spots. The statue commemorates the famous story of Hachiko, a loyal dog who waited at Shibuya Station every day for his owner, even after the owner's death. Hachiko's loyalty touched the hearts of many, and today, the statue serves as a popular spot where friends and families meet before heading into the district. The area around Hachiko is always bustling with people, but taking a moment to visit this iconic landmark is a meaningful way to connect with Shibuya's history and the story that has become part of Tokyo's cultural fabric.

Shibuya is also a fashion mecca, especially for young people. The district is known for its cutting-edge fashion, and this is evident in the numerous shopping centers that line the streets.

One of the most famous is Shibuya 109, a towering department store that has been at the forefront of Japanese youth fashion for decades. The store houses multiple floors of boutiques that sell trendy clothing, accessories, and cosmetics aimed primarily at young women. Shibuya 109 has played a major role in shaping fashion trends in Japan, and it remains a must-visit for anyone interested in the latest styles. Even if you're not planning on buying anything, simply walking through the store is a fun way to experience the lively and colorful world of Japanese fashion.

For those looking for a more high-end shopping experience, Shibuya has plenty to offer as well. Shibuya Hikarie is a sleek and modern shopping complex that caters to a more sophisticated crowd. Inside Hikarie, you'll find a wide range of shops, from designer boutiques to home goods stores, as well as a variety of restaurants and cafes. Hikarie is also home to an art gallery and a theater, making it a cultural destination in its own right. The building's observation floor offers fantastic views of the surrounding area, providing visitors with a quiet retreat from the bustling streets below.

Another key attraction in Shibuya is the vibrant nightlife. The district comes alive after dark, with countless bars, clubs, and restaurants catering to all kinds of tastes. One area that is particularly well-known for its nightlife is Nonbei Yokocho, a narrow alley lined with tiny bars and eateries. Nonbei Yokocho, which translates to "Drunkard's Alley," is a nostalgic throwback to post-war Tokyo, where you can experience a more intimate side of the city's nightlife. The bars here are small, often seating just a handful of customers, but this creates a cozy and friendly atmosphere where you can enjoy drinks and conversation with locals and fellow travelers. Nonbei Yokocho offers a refreshing contrast to Shibuya's more modern and high-energy clubs, making it a perfect spot for those looking for a quieter, more authentic experience.

Shibuya is also a hub for Japanese pop culture, particularly in terms of music and entertainment. Tower Records Shibuya is a must-visit for music lovers, as it is one of the largest music stores in the world. The multi-floor store has an impressive selection of Japanese and international music, as well as books, merchandise, and DVDs. Tower Records often hosts live performances, album release events, and artist signings, making it a key location for experiencing Tokyo's vibrant music scene.

If you're interested in discovering Shibuya's subcultures, visiting Cat Street is highly recommended. Cat Street, which runs between Shibuya and the neighboring Harajuku district, is a trendy and alternative shopping street known for its independent boutiques, vintage stores, and quirky cafes. The atmosphere here is more laid-back compared to the main streets of Shibuya, and it's a great place to find unique fashion pieces or enjoy a leisurely stroll. The street is particularly popular with Tokyo's creative and artistic crowd, and it offers a different side of Shibuya that contrasts with the busier shopping centers.

Beyond its shopping and nightlife, Shibuya also offers several opportunities to relax and enjoy green spaces. Yoyogi Park, located just a short distance from Shibuya Station, is one of Tokyo's largest and most popular parks. The park is a favorite spot for picnics, jogging, and people-watching, and it's especially beautiful during the cherry blossom season in spring. On weekends, you'll often find street performers, musicians, and various cultural events taking place in the park, adding to its lively atmosphere. Yoyogi Park is also adjacent to the famous Meiji Shrine, one of Tokyo's most important Shinto shrines, providing a perfect combination of nature, history, and culture all in one visit.

Another cultural highlight in Shibuya is the Bunkamura cultural complex, which houses a theater, concert hall, cinema, and museum. Bunkamura hosts a variety of performances, from classical concerts and opera to contemporary art exhibitions and film screenings. For those looking to enjoy the arts while in Shibuya, Bunkamura offers a diverse range of cultural experiences, making it a key destination for theater and music lovers.

Food is another major attraction in Shibuya, with an endless variety of dining options ranging from casual street food to high-end restaurants. One of the best ways to experience Shibuya's food scene is by exploring the many small eateries and izakayas (Japanese pubs) scattered throughout the district. You can find everything from yakitori (grilled chicken skewers) and okonomiyaki (savory pancakes) to ramen and sushi. Many of these restaurants are tucked away in narrow streets or basement levels, offering hidden gems that cater to both locals and visitors.

Shinjuku: Entertainment, Skyscrapers, and Nightlife

Shinjuku is one of Tokyo's most exciting and diverse neighborhoods, offering a blend of entertainment, towering skyscrapers, and a vibrant nightlife that make it a must-visit destination for anyone exploring the city. As one of the busiest and most dynamic districts in Tokyo, Shinjuku has something for everyone, whether you're a fan of modern architecture, interested in high-end shopping, or looking to experience the city's famous after-dark entertainment scene. The area is famous for its neon-lit streets, towering buildings, massive department stores, and unique cultural spots that make it a key attraction for both locals and tourists alike.

Shinjuku is located in the western part of central Tokyo and is centered around Shinjuku Station, which is one of the busiest train stations in the world. Shinjuku Station serves as a major transportation hub and is easily accessible from nearly every part of Tokyo. The station is served by numerous train lines, including the JR Yamanote Line, the Chuo Line, the Tokyo Metro Marunouchi Line, and the Toei Oedo Line. With such a vast array of train and subway options, getting to Shinjuku is incredibly convenient, whether you're coming from neighboring districts like Shibuya or further out in the suburbs. From the station, it's easy to explore the district's various attractions, as most are within walking distance or a short train ride away.

One of Shinjuku's defining features is its impressive skyline, dominated by skyscrapers that house offices, hotels, and commercial spaces. The most iconic of these buildings is the Tokyo Metropolitan Government Building, a towering structure that offers panoramic views of the city from its observation decks, which are free to enter. The observation decks, located on the 45th floor of each tower, provide a stunning 360-degree view of Tokyo, with clear days offering a glimpse of Mount Fuji in the distance. Visiting the Tokyo Metropolitan Government Building is an excellent way to start your exploration of Shinjuku, as it gives you a bird's-eye view of the sprawling district below and the rest of Tokyo stretching out to the horizon.

Just a short walk from the government building is the Shinjuku Skyscraper District, where you'll find an array of impressive high-rise buildings, many of which house upscale hotels, restaurants, and offices. This area is particularly beautiful at night, when the buildings are illuminated, creating a striking contrast against the dark sky. For visitors looking to experience Shinjuku's high-end dining and luxury accommodations, many of these skyscrapers house some of the city's finest hotels, including the Park Hyatt Tokyo, which was famously featured in the movie Lost in Translation. The Park Hyatt's New York Bar, located on the 52nd floor, offers not only world-class cocktails but also one of the best night views of the city.

Shinjuku is also renowned for its shopping, with countless department stores, boutiques, and electronics shops lining its streets. Some of the most popular shopping destinations include Isetan, a luxury department store known for its high-end fashion brands and gourmet food hall, and Takashimaya Times Square, a massive shopping complex that offers everything from clothing and accessories to home goods and electronics. For those interested in Japanese pop culture and electronics, Yodobashi Camera in Shinjuku is a multi-floor megastore that offers an extensive selection of gadgets, cameras, and gaming equipment. You can easily spend hours wandering through the store's various departments, exploring the latest in Japanese technology.

Beyond shopping and skyscrapers, Shinjuku is also home to some of Tokyo's most famous entertainment districts. One of the most iconic is Kabukicho, known as Tokyo's premier nightlife area. Kabukicho is often referred to as the city's red-light district, but it's much more than that—it's a vibrant entertainment hub filled with restaurants, bars, nightclubs, and themed entertainment venues. The streets of Kabukicho come alive after dark, with neon signs lighting up the area and people flocking to its many attractions. From karaoke bars to host and hostess clubs, Kabukicho offers a wide range of nightlife experiences for visitors looking to enjoy Tokyo's legendary after-hours scene.

A unique and quirky attraction in Kabukicho is the Robot Restaurant, a one-of-a-kind dinner show that features robots, lasers, dancers, and over-the-top performances. The show is a sensory overload, with colorful lights, loud music, and larger-than-life robots taking the stage in an epic spectacle. While the Robot Restaurant has become one of the more touristy attractions in the area, it remains a fun and unforgettable experience that captures the eccentric side of Tokyo's entertainment culture.

For those looking for a quieter but equally captivating nightlife experience, Golden Gai is a hidden gem within Shinjuku. This small area, located just a short walk from Kabukicho, is made up of narrow alleys lined with tiny, atmospheric bars. Each bar in Golden Gai has its own unique theme and character, often only seating a handful of customers at a time. Golden Gai is known for its intimate and nostalgic feel, and many of the bars attract a loyal crowd of locals, artists, and musicians. Some of the bars are open to tourists, while others cater more to regulars, but the area as a whole offers a charming glimpse into Shinjuku's post-war drinking culture.

Shinjuku is not only about nightlife and entertainment; it also offers plenty of green spaces where visitors can relax and take a break from the busy streets. One of the most beautiful parks in Tokyo, Shinjuku Gyoen National Garden, is located just a short walk from Shinjuku Station. This expansive park covers over 58 hectares and features a mix of traditional Japanese, French, and English-style gardens. Shinjuku Gyoen is particularly famous for its cherry blossoms in the spring, drawing large crowds of visitors who come to enjoy hanami (flower viewing) under the park's numerous cherry trees. The park's serene ponds, manicured lawns, and tea houses provide a peaceful retreat in the middle of one of Tokyo's busiest districts.

Another important cultural landmark in Shinjuku is the Samurai Museum, which offers a fascinating look at Japan's samurai heritage. The museum displays an impressive collection of samurai armor, swords, and weapons, providing visitors with insight into the history and culture of these legendary warriors. The museum also offers live demonstrations of swordsmanship and opportunities to try on samurai armor, making it a hands-on experience for anyone interested in Japan's feudal past.

For fans of anime and manga, Shinjuku is also home to several themed cafes and stores that cater to the city's vibrant otaku (pop culture fan) scene. Animate Shinjuku, for example, is a multi-floor store filled with anime merchandise, manga, and collectibles. The store is a must-visit for anyone interested in Japanese pop culture, and it regularly hosts events and signings with popular anime voice actors and creators. Nearby, you'll also find cafes and restaurants themed after popular anime and gaming franchises, offering unique dining experiences for fans.

Food is a major part of the Shinjuku experience, and the district is home to countless restaurants that cater to all tastes and budgets. Whether you're looking for high-end dining or casual street food, Shinjuku has it all. Omoide Yokocho, also known as Memory Lane, is a narrow alley filled with tiny restaurants serving yakitori (grilled chicken skewers), ramen, and other Japanese comfort foods. This area is particularly popular with locals, and it offers a glimpse into Tokyo's traditional food culture. Dining at one of the small, smoky yakitori stands in Omoide Yokocho is a great way to experience authentic Japanese food in a lively and atmospheric setting.

For those looking to try something unique, the Shinjuku area also offers themed restaurants that provide an entertaining dining experience. One such restaurant is the Ninja Akasaka, where guests are served by ninja-clad waiters in a setting designed to resemble a feudal Japanese village. The food is often presented with theatrical flair, and the restaurant's themed decor adds to the overall experience.

Harajuku: Youth Culture and Fashion

Harajuku is one of Tokyo's most vibrant and eclectic neighborhoods, known worldwide for its cutting-edge fashion, youthful energy, and unique blend of modern pop culture with traditional elements. It has become a symbol of Tokyo's creativity and is the epicenter of youth culture in Japan. Located in the Shibuya ward, Harajuku is a must-visit destination for anyone interested in fashion, street culture, art, or simply exploring a district that captures the essence of Tokyo's ever-evolving urban scene. The district's colorful streets are filled with independent boutiques, trendy shops, and cafes, making it a lively and visually captivating area that appeals to both locals and tourists alike.

Harajuku is conveniently located near several major train and subway lines, making it easily accessible from anywhere in Tokyo. The main hub is Harajuku Station, which is served by the JR Yamanote Line, one of Tokyo's key transportation routes. From Harajuku Station, visitors are immediately within walking distance of many of the area's main attractions. Another nearby station is Meiji-jingumae Station, which is served by the Tokyo Metro Chiyoda Line and Fukutoshin Line, providing additional access points to the neighborhood. Once you arrive, Harajuku is a district best explored on foot, as the narrow streets and vibrant atmosphere invite you to wander and discover everything the area has to offer.

One of the most iconic and famous streets in Harajuku is Takeshita Street, or Takeshita-dori, which has become synonymous with youth culture and street fashion. This pedestrian-only street is a bustling hub of activity, packed with trendy clothing stores, accessory shops, and a wide variety of cafes and food stalls. Takeshita Street is the place to go if you're looking to experience the latest in Japanese street fashion, from bold and colorful outfits to avant-garde styles. Many of the shops here cater to teenagers and young adults, offering affordable yet fashionable clothing that embodies the playful and experimental spirit of Harajuku fashion. The stores range from well-known chain stores to small independent boutiques, each offering unique and often quirky items that you won't find anywhere else.

Takeshita Street is also known for its abundance of themed cafes and street food stalls, which add to the lively atmosphere.

One of the must-try treats is the famous Harajuku crepe, which comes in an endless variety of flavors and fillings, from sweet options like strawberries and whipped cream to savory options like ham and cheese. You'll find several crepe stands along Takeshita Street, each offering their own signature creations. Another popular street food in Harajuku is taiyaki, a fish-shaped pastry filled with sweet red bean paste or custard, which is a favorite among locals and tourists alike.

Aside from its fashion and food, Harajuku is also home to a wide range of unique and quirky attractions that reflect its status as a cultural hotspot. One of these is the Kawaii Monster Café, an eye-poppingly colorful themed café that embraces the "kawaii" (cute) culture that Harajuku is famous for. The café is filled with vibrant, surreal decorations, from rainbow-colored furniture to giant candy-shaped sculptures. It's a visual feast, and the menu is just as playful, with dishes and drinks designed to look like colorful works of art. The Kawaii Monster Café is a popular destination for those looking to experience the whimsical and imaginative side of Harajuku's pop culture scene.

For those interested in high fashion and more upscale shopping, Harajuku also has plenty to offer. Omotesando, often referred to as Tokyo's Champs-Élysées, is a tree-lined avenue that runs parallel to Takeshita Street. While Takeshita-dori is known for its youthful and affordable fashion, Omotesando is where you'll find luxury brands and high-end designer boutiques. This area is home to flagship stores of international brands like Louis Vuitton, Dior, and Prada, as well as Japanese fashion designers who have made their mark on the global fashion scene. The contrast between the youthful chaos of Takeshita Street and the sophisticated elegance of Omotesando highlights the diversity of Harajuku's fashion landscape.

In addition to fashion, Harajuku is also known for its vibrant art scene, with numerous galleries and spaces showcasing both established and emerging artists. One notable venue is the Watari Museum of Contemporary Art, also known as the Watari-um, located just a short walk from Harajuku Station. This small but influential museum focuses on contemporary art from both Japan and abroad, offering thought-provoking exhibitions that challenge the boundaries of art and culture. The museum often hosts installations, multimedia exhibits, and experimental projects that attract art lovers from all over the city. Visiting the Watari-um provides a glimpse into the cutting-edge art world that thrives in Harajuku, reflecting the district's creative and boundary-pushing ethos.

While Harajuku is best known for its modern pop culture, it is also home to one of Tokyo's most significant historical landmarks: the Meiji Shrine. Located in a large forested park just steps away from Harajuku Station, Meiji Shrine offers a peaceful and spiritual retreat from the bustling streets of Harajuku. The shrine is dedicated to Emperor Meiji and Empress Shoken, who played a key role in modernizing Japan during the late 19th and early 20th centuries. The shrine complex is surrounded by over 170 acres of lush greenery, making it an ideal place for a quiet walk or reflection.

Visitors to Meiji Shrine can participate in traditional Shinto practices, such as offering prayers at the main hall, writing wishes on wooden plaques called ema, or purchasing protective charms known as omamori. One of the highlights of visiting Meiji Shrine is walking through its massive torii gates, which mark the entrance to the sacred grounds. The serene atmosphere of the shrine, combined with its historical significance, offers a stark contrast to the lively streets of Harajuku, providing a deeper connection to Japan's cultural and spiritual heritage.

For those who love to explore green spaces, Harajuku is also home to Yoyogi Park, one of Tokyo's largest and most popular public parks. Yoyogi Park is a great place to relax and enjoy nature, especially during the spring cherry blossom season or in the fall when the leaves change color. The park is a popular spot for picnics, jogging, and people-watching, and on weekends, it often comes alive with street performers, musicians, and various cultural events. Yoyogi Park is also a favorite gathering place for Tokyo's cosplayers, who dress up as their favorite anime, manga, or video game characters and come to the park to take photos and socialize. Visiting Yoyogi Park is a fun way to experience the unique blend of nature, culture, and performance that characterizes Harajuku.

In addition to its contemporary attractions, Harajuku is also steeped in historical and architectural interest. One such example is Togo Shrine, a Shinto shrine located near Omotesando. Togo Shrine is dedicated to Admiral Togo Heihachiro, one of Japan's most celebrated naval heroes who led Japan to victory in the Russo-Japanese War. The shrine is less crowded than the nearby Meiji Shrine, making it a peaceful spot to explore for those interested in learning more about Japan's modern history and the role of Shinto in everyday life.

Exploring Harajuku is not only about fashion and pop culture but also about uncovering the many layers of history, creativity, and tradition that coexist in this eclectic district. Whether you're shopping for the latest trends on Takeshita Street, admiring the high fashion of Omotesando, or seeking out the artistic flair of the area's galleries and cafes, Harajuku offers a diverse range of experiences that will leave a lasting impression. The district's ability to blend the old with the new, the traditional with the avant-garde, makes it one of Tokyo's most fascinating and essential places to visit.

Ginza: Luxury Shopping and Fine Dining

Ginza is one of Tokyo's most prestigious neighborhoods, renowned for its luxury shopping, fine dining, and sophisticated atmosphere. It is often considered the epitome of high-end Tokyo, where some of the world's most famous brands have set up flagship stores, and Michelin-starred restaurants are as common as casual eateries in other parts of the city. If you're looking to experience the lavish side of Tokyo, Ginza is the place to be. The area's wide, tree-lined streets are a blend of historical charm and modern elegance, and the district has long been a center of commerce and culture. A visit to Ginza offers an opportunity to indulge in luxury while also appreciating the district's deep historical roots and cultural significance.

Located in the heart of Tokyo, Ginza is easily accessible from various parts of the city. The area is served by several subway lines, including the Tokyo Metro Ginza Line, the Hibiya Line, and the Marunouchi Line. Ginza Station is the main hub for the district, and from there, you can explore the neighborhood's many attractions on foot. Alternatively, you can take the JR Yamanote Line or the Keihin-Tohoku Line to Yurakucho Station, which is just a short walk from Ginza. The district is well connected to other major areas in Tokyo, such as Shibuya, Shinjuku, and Tokyo Station, making it a convenient stop for both tourists and locals.

One of the main draws of Ginza is its reputation as one of the world's most famous shopping districts. The neighborhood is lined with luxury boutiques, flagship stores, and high-end department stores, making it a paradise for those who love fashion and luxury goods. International brands like Chanel, Louis Vuitton, and Gucci have large stores in Ginza, and many of these flagship locations offer exclusive items that can't be found anywhere else. The main street of Ginza, known as Chuo-dori, is where most of these luxury brands are located, and walking down this street feels like walking through a catalog of the world's most renowned fashion houses.

One of Ginza's most iconic shopping destinations is Ginza Six, a massive shopping complex that opened in 2017. Ginza Six is home to over 240 shops, including high-end fashion brands, beauty stores, and lifestyle boutiques. The building itself is a marvel of modern architecture, with sleek, futuristic design elements that make it stand out even in a neighborhood known for its elegance. Inside, you'll find not only luxury shops but also an art gallery, a rooftop garden, and a variety of gourmet restaurants. The shopping experience at Ginza Six is truly comprehensive, combining fashion, culture, and fine dining all in one place.

Another famous department store in Ginza is Mitsukoshi, one of Japan's oldest and most prestigious department stores. Mitsukoshi Ginza has been a landmark in the area for over a century and continues to attract shoppers with its wide selection of luxury goods, from high-end fashion and accessories to traditional Japanese crafts. The store's basement food hall is a must-visit for food lovers, offering a range of gourmet products, including beautifully packaged sweets, premium sushi, and delicacies from across Japan. Mitsukoshi is also known for its exceptional customer service, making shopping here a truly enjoyable experience.

For those looking to explore more local and unique stores, Ginza is also home to a number of boutique shops that specialize in Japanese craftsmanship. One such place is Wako, another long-established department store with a focus on luxury items, including fine jewelry, watches, and home goods. Wako's iconic clock tower is one of Ginza's most recognizable landmarks, and its refined selection of goods makes it a favorite among both locals and visitors. The store's emphasis on quality and traditional craftsmanship provides a more intimate and culturally rich shopping experience.

Beyond its reputation as a shopping haven, Ginza is also known for its world-class dining scene. The district is home to numerous Michelin-starred restaurants, offering everything from traditional Japanese cuisine to international fare. Whether you're in the mood for sushi, tempura, kaiseki (a traditional multi-course Japanese meal), or French haute cuisine, Ginza's dining options are some of the best in Tokyo. One of the most famous sushi restaurants in the area is Sushi Jiro, run by the legendary sushi master Jiro Ono. With three Michelin stars, Sushi Jiro has earned a reputation as one of the finest sushi restaurants in the world, although getting a reservation can be extremely difficult due to its popularity.

For those looking for a more accessible dining experience, Ginza offers a wide range of options that cater to all tastes and budgets. The area is filled with izakayas (Japanese pubs), ramen shops, and small cafes that serve up delicious meals at a fraction of the price of the more exclusive establishments. One popular spot for casual dining is Ginza Kagari, a small ramen shop that has gained a following for its rich and flavorful chicken broth ramen. Despite its modest setting, Ginza Kagari is often packed with both locals and tourists, and it's worth the wait to try one of the best bowls of ramen in the city.

In addition to its shopping and dining, Ginza also offers a number of cultural attractions that reflect the district's historical significance and artistic heritage. One of the key cultural sites in Ginza is the Kabukiza Theatre, the main theater for kabuki, a traditional Japanese performing art that dates back to the Edo period. Kabuki performances are known for their elaborate costumes, exaggerated movements, and dramatic storytelling, and attending a show at Kabukiza is a great way to experience one of Japan's most iconic art forms. The theater itself is an architectural gem, blending traditional Japanese design with modern elements. Even if you don't have time to watch a full kabuki performance, you can visit the Kabukiza Gallery, which offers an introduction to the history and artistry of kabuki, or explore the theater's gift shop for unique souvenirs.

Another cultural gem in Ginza is the Pola Museum Annex, a contemporary art gallery that regularly hosts exhibitions featuring both Japanese and international artists. The gallery is located within the Pola Ginza Building, and its exhibitions are known for their innovative and thought-provoking works. Visiting the Pola Museum Annex is a great way to explore the modern art scene in Ginza while taking a break from shopping and dining. The gallery's intimate space and rotating exhibitions make it a must-visit for art lovers looking for something off the beaten path.

For those interested in architecture, Ginza is also home to several buildings that showcase the district's unique blend of traditional and modern design. The Mikimoto Ginza 2 Building, for example, is a stunning example of contemporary architecture, with its distinctive façade that features irregularly shaped windows resembling a cluster of pearls. Designed by architect Toyo Ito, the building houses Mikimoto, Japan's premier pearl jeweler, and is a popular spot for architecture enthusiasts. Ginza's skyline is a mix of sleek modern skyscrapers and historic buildings, making it a visually captivating area to explore.

In addition to its daytime attractions, Ginza also comes alive at night, when the district's elegant buildings are illuminated, and the streets take on a more glamorous ambiance. The area's high-end restaurants, cocktail bars, and lounges make it a popular destination for nightlife, particularly among those looking for a more refined and sophisticated experience. Many of Ginza's bars offer stunning views of the city, making it an ideal place to unwind with a drink while taking in the sights of Tokyo's glittering skyline.

One of the unique features of Ginza is that on weekends, the main street, Chuo-dori, is closed to vehicle traffic, turning it into a pedestrian paradise known as "Hokosha Tengoku" (Pedestrian Heaven). This allows visitors to leisurely stroll down the street, enjoying the shopping and dining options without the usual hustle and bustle of city traffic. The pedestrian-only hours create a relaxed and enjoyable atmosphere, making it an ideal time to explore Ginza's many attractions.

Akihabara: The World of Electronics and Anime

Akihabara, often referred to as "Akiba," is a neighborhood in Tokyo that has earned worldwide recognition as the epicenter of electronics, anime, and gaming culture. Known for its vibrant streets filled with multi-story electronics stores, anime shops, and gaming arcades, Akihabara is a must-visit district for technology enthusiasts and fans of Japanese pop culture. This neighborhood is where cutting-edge technology meets the colorful world of anime and manga, making it a unique and fascinating area to explore.

Akihabara is located in the Chiyoda ward, just a short distance northeast of central Tokyo. It is conveniently accessible by train, with Akihabara Station being served by several major lines, including the JR Yamanote Line, JR Keihin-Tohoku Line, and the Tokyo Metro Hibiya Line. The area surrounding Akihabara Station is packed with electronics stores, anime shops, and themed cafes, making it easy to explore the district on foot. The neighborhood's proximity to other popular areas, such as Ueno and Asakusa, also makes it a convenient stop on any Tokyo itinerary.

Akihabara's reputation as a center for electronics dates back to the post-World War II era, when the area became a hub for selling radios and electronic parts. Over time, it evolved into a mecca for all things technology-related, and today it is home to countless stores selling everything from the latest gadgets to retro tech. One of the largest and most famous electronics retailers in Akihabara is Yodobashi Camera, a massive multi-floor megastore that offers an extensive selection of electronics, including computers, cameras, smartphones, home appliances, and gaming consoles. Yodobashi Camera is a one-stop shop for tech enthusiasts, and its sheer size and variety of products make it a must-visit destination for anyone looking to explore Akihabara's electronics scene.

In addition to large retailers like Yodobashi Camera, Akihabara is also known for its smaller specialty stores that cater to hobbyists and collectors. These shops sell a wide range of electronic components, tools, and rare parts that are often hard to find elsewhere. For those interested in building their own computers, robots, or other DIY electronics projects, Akihabara is the perfect place to find the necessary components and expertise. Many of these smaller stores are tucked away in side streets and narrow alleys, giving the area a maze-like quality that invites exploration.

While Akihabara's history is rooted in electronics, the district has also become a global hub for anime, manga, and gaming culture. The area is filled with shops that specialize in anime merchandise, from figurines and posters to DVDs and cosplay costumes. One of the most famous anime stores in the area is Animate, a multi-story shop dedicated to anime, manga, and gaming merchandise. Animate Akihabara is a paradise for anime fans, offering an extensive selection of character goods, limited-edition items, and exclusive collaborations that can't be found anywhere else. The store also frequently hosts events, such as signings and exhibitions, making it a lively and engaging place to visit.

Another must-visit location for anime enthusiasts is Mandarake, one of the largest second-hand stores in Akihabara. Mandarake specializes in rare and vintage anime and manga collectibles, making it a treasure trove for collectors. The store spans multiple floors, each dedicated to different types of merchandise, including action figures, manga volumes, art books, and cosplay items. Whether you're a seasoned collector or just getting started, Mandarake is a fascinating place to browse and discover hidden gems from Japan's rich pop culture history.

For fans of video games, Akihabara is home to numerous gaming arcades and stores that offer a wide range of both modern and retro gaming experiences. One of the most iconic arcades in the area is Club SEGA, a towering building filled with rows of arcade machines offering everything from classic fighting games to rhythm games. The arcade's multiple floors cater to different gaming tastes, making it a great place to spend a few hours playing and experiencing the unique atmosphere of a Japanese arcade. Retro game enthusiasts will also find a haven in Akihabara, as the district is known for its shops selling vintage consoles, games, and accessories from the 1980s and 1990s. Stores like Super Potato are famous for their selection of retro gaming gear, including rare cartridges, old-school consoles like the Famicom (Nintendo Entertainment System), and collectible memorabilia.

Beyond shopping and gaming, Akihabara is also famous for its themed cafes, particularly the iconic maid cafes. These cafes offer a whimsical experience in which customers are served by staff dressed in elaborate maid costumes who refer to them as "master" or "mistress" and perform various playful rituals to enhance the experience. Maidreamin is one of the most well-known maid cafes in Akihabara, offering a fun and interactive atmosphere where guests can enjoy drinks, food, and performances by the maids. While maid cafes are often seen as quirky or unusual to first-time visitors, they are a quintessential part of Akihabara's unique culture and offer a glimpse into the playful, fantasy-driven side of Japanese entertainment.

In addition to maid cafes, Akihabara is home to several other themed cafes, including cafes based on popular anime and gaming franchises. For example, the Gundam Cafe, dedicated to the famous mecha anime series Mobile Suit Gundam, offers themed food, drinks, and exclusive merchandise related to the series. The cafe's decor is inspired by the futuristic world of Gundam, making it a must-visit for fans of the anime. The district also has numerous other themed cafes, ranging from animal cafes, where you can interact with cats, owls, or rabbits, to cafes that feature virtual reality experiences.

For those interested in the artistic side of Japanese pop culture, Akihabara also offers opportunities to explore anime and gaming from a more creative perspective. The Akihabara UDX building houses the Akiba Square event space, which regularly hosts exhibitions, art shows, and conventions related to anime, manga, and gaming. These events often feature industry professionals, artists, and voice actors, providing visitors with a deeper understanding of the creative processes behind their favorite series and games.

While Akihabara is primarily known for its electronics and pop culture, the district also has historical and cultural significance. One notable location is Kanda Myojin Shrine, a Shinto shrine located just a short walk from the main Akihabara shopping area. Kanda Myojin Shrine has a history dating back over 1,200 years and is dedicated to three deities, including the god of good fortune and prosperity. The shrine is a popular place for both locals and tourists to visit, particularly those seeking blessings for success in business or protection for their electronic devices, which has become a modern twist on the traditional purposes of the shrine. The contrast between the ancient shrine and the modern streets of Akihabara offers a fascinating juxtaposition of old and new, reflecting Tokyo's ability to blend tradition with innovation.

Akihabara is also home to several unique museums and galleries that showcase the history and culture of electronics and gaming in Japan. The Tokyo Anime Center, located in Akihabara UDX, is a cultural facility dedicated to promoting Japanese animation both domestically and internationally. The center features exhibitions on popular anime series, sells exclusive merchandise, and hosts events and screenings that highlight the latest trends in the anime industry. Visiting the Tokyo Anime Center is a great way to gain insight into the behind-the-scenes world of anime production and learn more about the cultural impact of Japanese animation.

To fully experience Akihabara's vibrant atmosphere, it's best to visit on the weekend, when Chuo-dori, the main street running through the district, is closed to vehicle traffic, turning it into a pedestrian-only area. This allows visitors to freely walk through the bustling streets and explore the numerous shops, cafes, and arcades without the usual traffic congestion. The lively energy of Akihabara is even more palpable during these pedestrian-only hours, making it the ideal time to experience the district's unique charm.

Ueno: Parks, Museums, and History

Ueno is one of Tokyo's most culturally rich and historically significant neighborhoods, offering visitors a perfect blend of nature, art, and history. Situated in the northeastern part of central Tokyo, Ueno is home to Ueno Park, one of the largest and most famous public parks in the city, as well as a host of important museums, historical landmarks, and vibrant markets. This district has long been a hub of cultural and educational institutions, making it a must-visit destination for those looking to explore the deeper layers of Tokyo's history and artistic heritage.

Ueno is easily accessible from various parts of Tokyo, with Ueno Station serving as the main gateway to the area. Ueno Station is a major transportation hub, served by several train and subway lines, including the JR Yamanote Line, the JR Keihin-Tohoku Line, the Tokyo Metro Ginza Line, and the Hibiya Line. From Ueno Station, it's just a short walk to Ueno Park and many of the neighborhood's main attractions, making it a convenient stop for tourists and locals alike. The station itself is located near Ameya-Yokocho, a lively market street that offers a stark contrast to the more serene and contemplative atmosphere of the park and museums.

Ueno Park, also known as Ueno Onshi Koen, is the heart of the district and one of Tokyo's most popular green spaces. The park was established in 1873 on the former grounds of Kan'ei-ji Temple, a large Buddhist temple that was destroyed during the Boshin War of the late 19th century. Today, Ueno Park serves as a cultural and recreational center, attracting millions of visitors each year with its expansive lawns, tree-lined pathways, and numerous cultural institutions. The park is especially famous for its cherry blossoms in the spring, drawing large crowds during the hanami (cherry blossom viewing) season. In fact, Ueno Park is one of Tokyo's top spots for cherry blossom viewing, with over 1,000 cherry trees creating a stunning display of pink blossoms every spring.

As you explore Ueno Park, you'll find several ponds, shrines, and statues that add to the park's serene and historical atmosphere. One of the most notable landmarks is Shinobazu Pond, a large body of water divided into three sections: one for boating, one for lotus flowers, and one for wildlife. Visitors can rent rowboats or pedal boats and enjoy a leisurely ride on the pond, which offers a peaceful escape from the busy city streets. In the center of the pond is Benten-do, a small temple dedicated to Benzaiten, the goddess of fortune, music, and knowledge. The temple is located on an island and is connected to the shore by a small bridge, making it a picturesque spot to visit.

Another historical landmark within Ueno Park is the statue of Saigo Takamori, one of the most famous figures of the Meiji Restoration. Saigo Takamori was a samurai who played a key role in the fall of the Tokugawa shogunate and the modernization of Japan. The statue, which depicts Saigo walking his dog, is a beloved symbol of Ueno Park and serves as a reminder of the area's historical significance during Japan's transition from a feudal society to a modern nation.

Ueno Park is also home to several of Tokyo's most important museums, making it a cultural hub for art, history, and science. The Tokyo National Museum, located in the northeastern corner of the park, is the oldest and largest museum in Japan. Established in 1872, the Tokyo National Museum houses an extensive collection of art and artifacts that span Japan's history, from ancient times to the modern era. The museum's collection includes everything from traditional Japanese ceramics, swords, and armor to Buddhist sculptures, calligraphy, and paintings. One of the museum's highlights is its collection of national treasures and important cultural properties, which offer a fascinating insight into Japan's artistic and cultural heritage.

The Tokyo National Museum consists of several buildings, each dedicated to different aspects of Japanese and Asian art. The Honkan, or Japanese Gallery, focuses on the history of Japanese art, while the Toyokan houses collections from other parts of Asia, including China, Korea, and India. The Heiseikan building features exhibits on Japan's archaeological history, with displays of artifacts from prehistoric times through the early feudal period. A visit to the Tokyo National Museum is an enriching experience that allows visitors to explore Japan's artistic traditions and historical evolution in great depth.

Another major museum in Ueno Park is the National Museum of Nature and Science, which offers a comprehensive look at Japan's natural history and scientific achievements. The museum features exhibits on a wide range of topics, from geology and biology to space exploration and robotics. One of the highlights is the dinosaur exhibit, which includes life-size models of dinosaurs as well as actual fossils. The museum also has a planetarium and interactive displays that make it a great destination for families and those interested in science and technology.

For art lovers, the Tokyo Metropolitan Art Museum is another must-visit destination within Ueno Park. This museum hosts rotating exhibitions of modern and contemporary art, showcasing works by both Japanese and international artists. The museum's temporary exhibitions cover a wide range of artistic genres, from painting and sculpture to photography and digital art. The Tokyo Metropolitan Art Museum is known for its diverse and engaging exhibitions, making it a dynamic and inspiring space for art enthusiasts.

One of the more specialized museums in Ueno is the Ueno Royal Museum, which focuses on traditional Japanese art and culture. The museum often hosts exhibitions on Nihonga, a style of Japanese painting that emphasizes traditional techniques and materials. The Ueno Royal Museum is a smaller, more intimate museum compared to the larger institutions in the park, but it offers a deep dive into Japan's artistic heritage and is well worth a visit.

In addition to its museums, Ueno Park is home to Ueno Zoo, Japan's oldest zoo, which first opened in 1882. Ueno Zoo is a popular attraction for families and animal lovers, offering a chance to see a wide variety of animals, including giant pandas, tigers, elephants, and gorillas. The zoo's most famous residents are its giant pandas, which have been a major draw for visitors since they were first introduced to the zoo in the 1970s. Ueno Zoo is divided into different sections, each focusing on animals from different regions of the world, and it also has a petting zoo where children can interact with small animals. A visit to Ueno Zoo is a fun and educational experience that complements the more cultural and historical attractions in the park.

After spending time in Ueno Park and its many museums, visitors can explore the surrounding areas, which offer even more to see and do. One of the most famous nearby attractions is Ameya-Yokocho, also known as Ameyoko, a bustling market street located just south of Ueno Station. Ameyoko was originally a black market after World War II, but today it's a lively shopping street filled with vendors selling everything from fresh seafood and snacks to clothing and electronics. The atmosphere in Ameyoko is energetic and chaotic, making it a fun place to shop, eat, and soak in the local culture. The market's narrow streets are lined with small shops and food stalls, offering an authentic Tokyo street market experience.

Ueno is also home to several historical temples and shrines that offer a glimpse into the area's religious and cultural past. One of the most significant is Kan'ei-ji Temple, which was once one of the largest and most powerful temples in Tokyo during the Edo period. Although much of the temple was destroyed during the Boshin War, a few structures remain, including the five-story pagoda, which now stands within the grounds of Ueno Zoo. Kan'ei-ji Temple played an important role in the religious and political life of Edo (the former name of Tokyo), and its remnants offer a fascinating look into the city's historical landscape.

Another nearby temple is Kiyomizu Kannon-do, a Buddhist temple located on a hill within Ueno Park. The temple is modeled after the famous Kiyomizu-dera in Kyoto and offers a beautiful view of Shinobazu Pond and the surrounding park. Kiyomizu Kannon-do is known for its statue of Kannon, the goddess of mercy, and is a peaceful spot to reflect and enjoy the natural beauty of the park.

Roppongi: Art, Nightlife, and International Vibe

Roppongi is one of Tokyo's most dynamic and cosmopolitan districts, known for its vibrant blend of art, nightlife, and international flair. Located in the heart of Minato ward, Roppongi is a neighborhood that offers something for everyone—from world-class art galleries and museums to lively bars, clubs, and a range of international dining options. The area has long been associated with Tokyo's expatriate community and remains a popular destination for foreign residents and visitors. Its reputation as a hub of art and nightlife has evolved over the years, with Roppongi transitioning from a party district to a more sophisticated area that combines culture, entertainment, and a cosmopolitan atmosphere. A visit to Roppongi provides a comprehensive experience that captures the essence of modern Tokyo's multicultural spirit.

Getting to Roppongi is easy, as the area is well-connected by public transportation. Roppongi Station is the main access point and is served by both the Tokyo Metro Hibiya Line and the Toei Oedo Line. The district is also easily reachable from other key parts of Tokyo, including Shibuya, Shinjuku, and Tokyo Station. The surrounding neighborhoods of Azabu, Akasaka, and Aoyama are just a short distance away, making Roppongi a convenient location for those looking to explore multiple parts of the city in one day.

One of Roppongi's main attractions is its thriving art scene, which is anchored by two of Tokyo's most important cultural complexes: Roppongi Hills and Tokyo Midtown. Both of these developments are home to major art museums and galleries that have established Roppongi as a cultural destination.

Roppongi Hills, a large urban development that opened in 2003, is a city within a city, combining residential, office, shopping, and cultural spaces. At the heart of Roppongi Hills is the Mori Art Museum, one of Japan's most prominent contemporary art institutions. Located on the 53rd floor of the Mori Tower, the museum offers stunning panoramic views of Tokyo in addition to its ever-changing exhibitions of modern and contemporary art. The Mori Art Museum showcases the work of both Japanese and international artists, with a focus on thought-provoking exhibitions that explore global and societal themes. The museum is known for its bold and innovative displays, which often include large-scale installations, multimedia works, and interactive pieces. Visiting the Mori Art Museum is an immersive experience that provides a deep dive into the world of contemporary art while also offering breathtaking views of the city from its observation deck, Tokyo City View.

In addition to the Mori Art Museum, Roppongi Hills also features the Mori Garden, a beautifully landscaped traditional Japanese garden that offers a peaceful retreat from the surrounding urban environment. The garden is particularly beautiful in the spring when the cherry blossoms are in bloom, and in the autumn, when the leaves turn vibrant shades of red and orange. Strolling through the Mori Garden provides a serene contrast to the modern architecture of Roppongi Hills, making it a perfect spot to relax after exploring the museum or shopping in the nearby luxury boutiques.

Another key art destination in Roppongi is Tokyo Midtown, a large multi-use complex that opened in 2007. Like Roppongi Hills, Tokyo Midtown combines shopping, dining, office spaces, and cultural institutions. The main cultural attraction at Tokyo Midtown is the Suntory Museum of Art, which focuses on traditional Japanese art and crafts. The museum's collection includes ceramics, lacquerware, glass, textiles, and paintings, with an emphasis on the beauty of everyday objects.

The museum's exhibitions change regularly, offering visitors the chance to explore different aspects of Japan's artistic heritage. The Suntory Museum of Art is a quieter and more contemplative experience compared to the Mori Art Museum, making it a great place to appreciate the craftsmanship and aesthetics of traditional Japanese art.

Tokyo Midtown is also home to 21_21 Design Sight, a museum dedicated to design and architecture. Founded by renowned Japanese designers Issey Miyake and Taku Satoh, along with architect Tadao Ando, 21_21 Design Sight hosts exhibitions that explore the relationship between design and everyday life. The museum's minimalist architecture, designed by Ando, is a work of art in itself, and the exhibitions often feature interactive elements that engage visitors in the design process. 21_21 Design Sight is a must-visit for anyone interested in contemporary design, architecture, and the intersection of art and function.

While Roppongi's art scene is a major draw, the district is perhaps even more famous for its nightlife. Roppongi has long been known as one of Tokyo's top destinations for after-dark entertainment, with a wide variety of bars, nightclubs, and lounges that cater to both locals and the international crowd. The area's nightlife scene is diverse, ranging from upscale cocktail bars and live music venues to lively nightclubs where you can dance until the early hours of the morning.
One of the most popular nightlife spots in Roppongi is the iconic Roppongi Kaguwa, a fusion of nightclub and traditional Japanese cabaret. At Kaguwa, visitors can enjoy a dinner show

that blends modern performance with traditional Japanese theater, complete with elaborate costumes, acrobatic stunts, and energetic dance routines. The club's unique fusion of old and new makes it a memorable experience for anyone looking to enjoy Tokyo's nightlife in a more theatrical setting.

For those looking for a more relaxed evening, Roppongi offers a number of sophisticated bars and lounges where you can enjoy a quiet drink while taking in the city views. One of the most popular spots is the rooftop bar at the Ritz-Carlton Tokyo, located in Tokyo Midtown. The bar offers sweeping views of Tokyo's skyline, including Tokyo Tower and Mount Fuji on clear days, making it a perfect place to enjoy a cocktail while watching the sun set over the city. The Ritz-Carlton's bar is known for its elegant ambiance, expertly crafted drinks, and attentive service, making it a popular destination for those seeking a more refined nightlife experience.

In addition to its upscale bars and nightclubs, Roppongi also has a vibrant expat scene, with a number of international pubs and sports bars that attract both locals and foreigners. These establishments offer a more casual and laid-back atmosphere, making them great places to meet people and enjoy a drink in a friendly, international environment. The Hub, for example, is a British-style pub that has become a staple of Roppongi's expat community, offering a wide selection of beers, cocktails, and pub food. The friendly atmosphere and reasonable prices make it a popular spot for both after-work drinks and late-night gatherings.

Roppongi's international vibe extends beyond its nightlife, as the district is home to a number of embassies, international schools, and foreign companies, which has contributed to its cosmopolitan atmosphere. This diversity is reflected in the wide range of dining options available in the area, with restaurants serving everything from traditional Japanese cuisine to international dishes from around the world. Whether you're in the mood for sushi, Italian pasta, French pastries, or Indian curry, Roppongi offers a culinary tour of the globe.

One of the most popular spots for fine dining in Roppongi is Sukiyabashi Jiro, a Michelin-starred sushi restaurant that has become famous worldwide thanks to the documentary Jiro Dreams of Sushi. While the restaurant's main location is in Ginza, the Roppongi branch offers an equally exceptional sushi experience, with each piece carefully prepared by master chefs. Reservations are difficult to secure, but for sushi lovers, dining at Sukiyabashi Jiro is a once-in-a-lifetime experience.

For those looking for something a bit more casual, Roppongi is also home to a wide variety of izakayas, Japanese-style pubs that offer a more relaxed dining experience. At an izakaya, you can enjoy small plates of food, such as grilled meats, sashimi, and tempura, along with beer, sake, or shochu. One popular izakaya in Roppongi is Gonpachi, which is known for its lively atmosphere and delicious skewers. Gonpachi has become famous as the inspiration for the fight scene in Quentin Tarantino's Kill Bill, and the restaurant's interior resembles a traditional Japanese teahouse. The combination of good food, lively conversation, and a fun atmosphere makes Gonpachi a great place to enjoy a casual meal with friends or family.

In addition to its art, dining, and nightlife, Roppongi also offers a number of unique attractions that make it a fun and diverse neighborhood to explore. One such attraction is Tokyo Tower, located just a short walk from Roppongi Hills. Tokyo Tower is one of the city's most iconic landmarks and offers visitors the chance to enjoy panoramic views of the city from its observation decks. At night, the tower is illuminated in vibrant colors, creating a stunning backdrop to the city's skyline. Climbing to the top of Tokyo Tower provides a fantastic view of Roppongi and the surrounding areas, making it a great way to round out your visit to the neighborhood.

Yokohama and Day Trips Beyond Tokyo

Yokohama is a bustling port city located just south of Tokyo and offers a fascinating mix of modern attractions, historical sites, and stunning waterfront views. As Japan's second-largest city, Yokohama is often considered an ideal destination for a day trip from Tokyo. It provides a break from the fast-paced energy of the capital while still offering plenty of cultural, shopping, and dining experiences. The city's proximity to Tokyo makes it an easy and convenient escape, with a host of sights and activities that can cater to all types of travelers.

Yokohama is easily accessible from Tokyo, with multiple train options that make traveling between the two cities quick and hassle-free. The JR Tokaido Line, the JR Yokosuka Line, and the Tokyu Toyoko Line all connect central Tokyo to Yokohama, with a journey that typically takes between 25 and 45 minutes depending on the departure station and the train line used. The JR Keihin-Tohoku Line is also a popular choice for visitors traveling from areas such as Ueno or Shinagawa. Yokohama Station is one of the main entry points into the city, and from there, it's easy to access many of the city's key attractions either on foot or by using local public transportation.

One of the main draws of Yokohama is its scenic waterfront, particularly the Minato Mirai 21 district. Minato Mirai, which translates to "Port of the Future," is a sprawling, modern urban development that combines shopping, entertainment, dining, and cultural attractions. The area's iconic skyline, featuring the futuristic Yokohama Landmark Tower and other high-rise buildings, makes it one of the most recognizable parts of the city. The Landmark Tower, standing at 296 meters, is Japan's second-tallest building and offers an observation deck on the 69th floor. From here, visitors can enjoy panoramic views of Yokohama, Tokyo, and on a clear day, even Mount Fuji in the distance. The observation deck, known as the Sky Garden, provides a stunning vantage point, particularly at sunset when the city lights begin to sparkle and the bay takes on a serene glow.

At the base of the Landmark Tower, you'll find the Yokohama Landmark Plaza, a large shopping complex that offers a wide range of stores, from high-end fashion brands to unique Japanese boutiques. Connected to the plaza is the Queen's

Square Yokohama, another expansive shopping and dining complex that provides visitors with even more options for leisure. These two shopping centers are at the heart of the Minato Mirai area and are a great place to enjoy some retail therapy or sample local and international cuisine in one of the many restaurants.

One of the most unique attractions in the Minato Mirai district is the Yokohama Cosmo World amusement park, which is home to the iconic Cosmo Clock 21 Ferris wheel. Once the world's largest Ferris wheel, Cosmo Clock 21 remains a major symbol of Yokohama and is a must-visit for those looking to experience the city's lively waterfront from above. The Ferris wheel offers breathtaking views of the harbor and cityscape, especially when it lights up in the evening. Yokohama Cosmo World also features various other rides and games, making it a fun stop for families and thrill-seekers alike.

For those interested in exploring the maritime history of Yokohama, the Nippon Maru, a museum ship anchored in the harbor, offers visitors a glimpse into Japan's nautical past. The Nippon Maru was a training ship used by the Japanese merchant marine, and today it serves as a floating museum where you can tour the decks, learn about life at sea, and see exhibits related to Japan's maritime industry. Nearby, the Yokohama Port Museum offers further insights into the history of Yokohama as a port city, tracing its development from the opening of Japan to international trade in the 19th century to its current status as one of Japan's busiest and most important ports.

Another cultural highlight in Yokohama is the Red Brick Warehouse, a historic building that has been repurposed into a shopping, dining, and event space. Originally used as a customs building in the early 20th century, the Red Brick Warehouse has been beautifully preserved and now hosts a variety of shops selling unique crafts, souvenirs, and local products. It is also home to several cafes and restaurants where you can relax and enjoy the views of Yokohama Bay. The Red Brick Warehouse often hosts seasonal events, concerts, and festivals, adding to its lively and welcoming atmosphere. Its blend of history and modern usage makes it a popular destination for both locals and tourists.

Yokohama is also known for its rich cultural diversity, particularly its large Chinatown, which is one of the biggest in Japan. Yokohama Chinatown, located just a short distance from the Minato Mirai area, is a bustling district filled with colorful streets, Chinese temples, and a wide variety of restaurants and food stalls. The vibrant gates at the entrance to Chinatown mark the beginning of a lively area where you can sample delicious Chinese cuisine, including dumplings, steamed buns, and noodle dishes. The streets are lined with souvenir shops and vendors selling everything from traditional Chinese goods to Yokohama-themed trinkets. Yokohama Chinatown is not only a great place to enjoy authentic Chinese food but also a fascinating area to explore the multicultural influences that have shaped Yokohama's history as an international port city.

For art lovers, Yokohama offers a number of excellent museums and galleries. One of the most prominent is the Yokohama Museum of Art, located near Minato Mirai. The museum's collection includes works from both Japanese and international artists, with a focus on modern and contemporary art. The Yokohama Museum of Art also hosts temporary exhibitions that cover a wide range of artistic styles and periods, making it an engaging stop for those looking to experience the city's cultural side. The museum's striking architecture, designed by famed Japanese architect Kenzo Tange, is a notable attraction in itself, and the spacious galleries provide a serene setting for art appreciation.

Beyond Yokohama's central attractions, the city also offers several beautiful parks and green spaces where you can relax and enjoy nature. Yamashita Park, located along the waterfront, is one of Yokohama's most famous parks and offers stunning views of the harbor, including the iconic Hikawa Maru, a historic ocean liner turned museum. The park is a favorite spot for locals to take leisurely walks, enjoy picnics, and watch the ships pass by in the bay. In the spring, the park is a great place to view cherry blossoms, and its well-maintained gardens make it a peaceful retreat from the more urban parts of the city.

Another popular park in Yokohama is Sankeien Garden, a traditional Japanese garden located a bit further from the city center. Sankeien is known for its meticulously designed landscapes, featuring ponds, streams, and historic buildings that were relocated from other parts of Japan. The garden offers a tranquil setting for strolling, and its tea houses, pagodas, and seasonal flowers provide a beautiful backdrop for photography and relaxation. Sankeien Garden is particularly stunning in the autumn when the leaves turn vibrant shades of red and orange, making it a popular destination for nature lovers and photographers.

For those looking to explore beyond Yokohama and experience more of the greater Tokyo region, there are several fantastic day trips that can easily be combined with a visit to the city. One of the most popular destinations is Kamakura, a coastal town known for its historic temples, shrines, and the famous Great Buddha (Daibutsu). Located just under an hour from Yokohama by train, Kamakura is a peaceful retreat from the urban environment and offers visitors a chance to explore Japan's rich religious and cultural heritage. Some of the highlights of Kamakura include the Tsurugaoka Hachimangu Shrine, the Hasedera Temple, and the scenic hiking trails that wind through the hills surrounding the town. Kamakura's proximity to the ocean also makes it a great place to enjoy the beach, particularly in the summer months.

Another nearby destination is the hot spring resort town of Hakone, located to the southwest of Yokohama. Hakone is famous for its natural hot springs, stunning views of Mount Fuji, and the scenic Lake Ashi. A day trip to Hakone offers visitors the chance to relax in a traditional Japanese onsen (hot spring) while also enjoying the beautiful mountain scenery. The Hakone Open-Air Museum, which features outdoor sculptures set against the backdrop of the surrounding mountains, is another popular attraction in the area. Hakone is easily accessible from Yokohama via train, making it a perfect destination for those looking to experience Japan's natural beauty and hot spring culture.

For travelers interested in exploring the more rural side of Japan, the Miura Peninsula offers a scenic escape just a short train ride from Yokohama. The peninsula is home to small fishing villages, quiet beaches, and rugged coastal landscapes. Miura's Kannonzaki Park is a great spot for hiking, offering panoramic views of Tokyo Bay and the surrounding countryside. The peninsula is also known for its fresh seafood, particularly tuna, and the local markets and restaurants are great places to sample delicious, freshly caught fish.

CHAPTER 8

FOOD AND DINING IN TOKYO

Traditional Japanese Dishes to Try

When visiting Tokyo, one of the most exciting and culturally enriching experiences is exploring the traditional Japanese dishes that form the backbone of the country's culinary heritage. Japan is globally renowned for its cuisine, and Tokyo, as its capital, offers an incredible range of food that reflects both time-honored techniques and regional flavors.

Sushi is perhaps the most well-known Japanese dish internationally, and there is no better place to experience authentic sushi than in Tokyo. Sushi refers to vinegared rice paired with seafood, usually raw, and it can range from simple bites at a casual stand to meticulously crafted pieces at Michelin-starred restaurants. Tokyo's Tsukiji Fish Market, now moved to Toyosu Market, is one of the most famous locations to try fresh sushi. The Toyosu Market is the largest wholesale fish and seafood market in the world, and many of Tokyo's top sushi restaurants source their fish from here. For visitors, sushi breakfast at the market is a highly recommended experience. Some of the most notable sushi restaurants, such as Sushi Dai and Daiwa Sushi, serve up fresh cuts of tuna, salmon, and sea urchin in an intimate setting. The journey to Toyosu Market is easily accessible via the Yurikamome Line, and a meal here offers a sensory dive into one of Tokyo's culinary institutions.

Another iconic Japanese dish to try in Tokyo is ramen, a noodle soup that has become a comfort food for people all over Japan. Ramen typically consists of wheat noodles served in a rich broth, which can be flavored with soy sauce, miso, or pork-based tonkotsu. Toppings such as slices of pork, seaweed, bamboo shoots, and a boiled egg complete the dish. Tokyo is home to numerous ramen shops, ranging from small local stalls to famous chains. One of the best places to experience ramen is at Ramen Street in Tokyo Station. This underground street features several renowned ramen shops, each offering a different regional take on this beloved dish. Getting to Tokyo Station is straightforward, as it is a major transportation hub accessible by the JR Yamanote Line, among others. For those seeking a more immersive experience, consider visiting the Shin-Yokohama Ramen Museum, a short train ride from Tokyo, where you can explore the history of ramen and sample different varieties from across Japan.

Tempura is another traditional dish that has its roots in Tokyo, where it was first developed as a street food during the Edo period. Tempura consists of seafood and vegetables that are lightly battered and deep-fried to a delicate crisp. The key to great tempura lies in the batter, which should be light and airy, allowing the freshness of the ingredients to shine through. In Tokyo, one of the best places to enjoy high-quality tempura is at Tempura Kondo, a Michelin-starred restaurant located in the upscale district of Ginza. Kondo is known for its meticulous preparation and its use of seasonal ingredients like shrimp, sweet potato, and even rare vegetables. Ginza itself is a luxury shopping and dining district, easily accessible via the Tokyo Metro Ginza Line, and exploring this neighborhood is a worthwhile experience in itself.

For a taste of traditional Japanese cuisine that emphasizes the beauty of simplicity and natural flavors, kaiseki is a must-try dining experience. Kaiseki is a multi-course meal that is often considered the pinnacle of Japanese fine dining. Each course is crafted to highlight seasonal ingredients and is presented with an emphasis on aesthetics and balance. Kaiseki meals typically start with a light appetizer, followed by sashimi, grilled fish, a simmered dish, and rice, often concluding with a delicate dessert. One of the most highly regarded places to experience kaiseki in Tokyo is at the restaurant Ryugin, located in the Roppongi district. Ryugin is famous for its innovative approach to kaiseki, blending traditional Japanese techniques with modern culinary methods. Roppongi is known for its international flair and is easily reached via the Tokyo Metro Hibiya Line or Oedo Line. Dining at a kaiseki restaurant provides not just a meal but a cultural experience, with each dish reflecting the seasons and the chef's philosophy.

For a more casual but equally important Japanese dish, yakitori is something you should not miss. Yakitori refers to skewered and grilled chicken, often served at izakayas (Japanese pubs) or specialized yakitori restaurants. These skewers can include various cuts of chicken, such as thighs, wings, and even more adventurous parts like liver or gizzards, all seasoned with salt or a soy-based sauce called tare. Yakitori is a popular dish for pairing with beer or sake, making it a staple of Tokyo's vibrant nightlife. One of the best places to experience yakitori is in the neighborhood of Omoide Yokocho in Shinjuku, where narrow alleys are filled with small yakitori shops serving freshly grilled skewers. Omoide Yokocho is a short walk from Shinjuku Station, one of Tokyo's busiest transportation hubs, making it easy to reach and perfect for an evening of dining and exploring.

Another must-try dish in Tokyo is tonkatsu, a breaded and deep-fried pork cutlet that is both crispy on the outside and juicy on the inside. Tonkatsu is often served with shredded cabbage, rice, and miso soup, and it is a comforting and hearty meal. While tonkatsu can be found in many places around Tokyo, one of the most famous spots is Maisen, located in the Aoyama district. Maisen has been serving tonkatsu since 1965 and is known for its perfectly cooked, tender pork cutlets. Aoyama is a chic neighborhood known for its fashion boutiques and art galleries, making it a great place to visit before or after enjoying a meal at Maisen. You can reach Aoyama by taking the Tokyo Metro Ginza Line or Hanzomon Line to Omotesando Station.

If you are looking for something distinctly regional to Tokyo, monjayaki is a dish that originated in the city's Tsukishima neighborhood. Monjayaki is a type of savory pancake made with a variety of ingredients, including cabbage, seafood, and vegetables, mixed with a batter that is thinner than traditional okonomiyaki. The batter is cooked on a hot griddle at the table, resulting in a gooey, crispy pancake that is both flavorful and interactive to eat. Tsukishima's Monja Street is lined with restaurants specializing in this dish, and visiting this area offers a unique opportunity to taste a true Tokyo specialty. Tsukishima is accessible via the Tokyo Metro Yurakucho Line or Toei Oedo Line, and the neighborhood itself has a quaint, old-fashioned charm that contrasts with the bustling city center.

For dessert, one cannot leave Tokyo without trying wagashi, traditional Japanese sweets that are often served with tea. Wagashi are typically made from natural ingredients such as rice flour, red bean paste, and seasonal fruits, and they are known for their delicate appearance and subtle sweetness. One of the best places to experience wagashi is at Toraya, a renowned confectioner that has been making traditional Japanese sweets for centuries. Toraya's flagship store in Tokyo is located in the prestigious Akasaka district, which is easily reachable via the Tokyo Metro Ginza Line. Here, you can enjoy beautifully crafted sweets alongside a cup of matcha tea, making for a relaxing and authentic Japanese experience.

Another essential part of Japanese dining culture is the drink. While sake (Japanese rice wine) is well known, Tokyo also offers opportunities to try shochu, a distilled spirit that can be made from barley, sweet potatoes, or rice. Shochu is often enjoyed neat, on the rocks, or mixed with water, and it is a popular choice in izakayas. Many izakayas in Tokyo will offer a variety of shochu brands, allowing you to sample different regional varieties. Some izakayas, like those in Ebisu or Nakameguro, offer tasting flights of shochu, making it easy to explore the diverse flavors of this traditional Japanese spirit. Ebisu and Nakameguro are both trendy neighborhoods, accessible via the JR Yamanote Line, and are known for their excellent dining and nightlife options.

Sushi, Ramen, and Tempura: Must-Try Delicacies

When visiting Tokyo, it is impossible to miss out on three of the most iconic Japanese dishes: sushi, ramen, and tempura. These foods have become synonymous with Japan's culinary identity and offer some of the most delicious, authentic experiences you can have in the city. Tokyo is home to some of the finest examples of these dishes, ranging from simple and affordable street food to Michelin-starred restaurants that have taken these dishes to new heights. Each dish reflects Japan's deep respect for ingredients, craftsmanship, and presentation.

Let's start with sushi, arguably Japan's most famous culinary export. Sushi, in its most traditional form, consists of vinegared rice topped with slices of fresh, high-quality seafood, such as tuna, salmon, or sea urchin. The balance between the rice and the fish, the texture, and the temperature of the ingredients are all crucial elements that make sushi an art form in Japan. Tokyo, especially with its proximity to the sea, offers some of the freshest and most exquisite sushi you can find. The city has a wide range of sushi options, from conveyor belt sushi joints to exclusive, reservation-only restaurants.

One of the best places to experience sushi in Tokyo is at the Toyosu Market, the world's largest wholesale fish and seafood market. Toyosu Market replaced the historic Tsukiji Fish Market and is now the center for seafood distribution in Tokyo. Visiting Toyosu offers not only the chance to taste some of the freshest sushi imaginable but also the opportunity to observe the famous tuna auctions, where massive fish are auctioned off to top sushi chefs and restaurants. Some of the best sushi restaurants around Toyosu Market include Sushi Dai and Daiwa Sushi, both of which are renowned for their superb offerings and the skill of their chefs. Although the lines can be long, especially in the early morning, the quality of the sushi makes it well worth the wait.

Getting to Toyosu Market is easy via the Yurikamome Line, which connects the market to central Tokyo. Once there, you can take your pick of sushi restaurants located in and around the market, many of which have built a reputation for serving sushi that is both fresh and flavorful, directly sourced from the market's seafood suppliers.

For a more upscale sushi experience, Ginza is home to some of the finest sushi restaurants in Tokyo, many of which have been awarded Michelin stars. Sukiyabashi Jiro is perhaps the most famous sushi restaurant in the world, made legendary by the documentary Jiro Dreams of Sushi. While getting a reservation here is notoriously difficult, those who manage to dine at Jiro's restaurant are treated to an unforgettable omakase (chef's choice) experience, where each piece of sushi is carefully crafted and served one by one. Ginza is easily accessible by the Tokyo Metro Ginza Line, and exploring this district also provides an opportunity to enjoy luxury shopping and dining in one of Tokyo's most sophisticated areas.

If you're looking for sushi that is more affordable yet still high quality, conveyor belt sushi, or kaiten-zushi, is a great option. In these restaurants, plates of sushi travel around the counter on a conveyor belt, allowing you to pick and choose what you'd like to try. Places like Sushiro and Uobei in Shibuya offer a fun and casual way to enjoy sushi without breaking the bank. Shibuya Station, on the JR Yamanote Line, is a major hub, making it easy to reach these popular restaurants and enjoy the famous Shibuya Crossing while you're in the area.

Next on the list is ramen, another dish that has gained immense popularity worldwide. Ramen is a noodle soup dish that comes in various styles, with the most common types being shoyu (soy sauce-based), miso (fermented soybean paste-based), and tonkotsu (pork bone-based). The beauty of ramen lies in the complexity of its broth, the texture of its noodles, and the array of toppings, which can include slices of pork, soft-boiled eggs, green onions, bamboo shoots, and nori (seaweed).

Tokyo is considered one of the best places to enjoy ramen because the city offers a huge variety of ramen styles, each with its own regional twist. One of the best places to start your ramen journey is Tokyo Ramen Street, located in the underground mall of Tokyo Station. Here, you'll find several famous ramen shops, each specializing in a different type of ramen. One of the most popular spots is Rokurinsha, known for its rich, thick tsukemen (dipping noodles), where the noodles are served separately from the broth, allowing you to dip them as you eat. The savory, umami-packed broth and chewy noodles make this a standout dish that many consider a must-try.

Tokyo Station is a major transportation hub and easily accessible by multiple train lines, including the JR Yamanote Line. After enjoying a hearty bowl of ramen, you can explore the nearby Marunouchi and Ginza districts, which are home to high-end shopping, historic buildings, and iconic sites such as the Imperial Palace.

For those who prefer a more authentic local experience, many ramen shops are scattered across the city, each offering their own take on this beloved dish. In the Shinjuku area, Ichiran Ramen is a chain that allows diners to customize their ramen to their liking. At Ichiran, you can adjust the richness of the broth, the firmness of the noodles, and the spiciness of the soup. What makes Ichiran unique is its single-seat booths, which provide a private, focused dining experience where you can concentrate solely on enjoying your ramen. Shinjuku is easily accessible via the JR Yamanote Line, and the vibrant atmosphere of this area, combined with the delicious ramen, makes for a great day or night out.

Another popular ramen shop is Nakiryu, located in the Otsuka neighborhood. Nakiryu earned a Michelin star for its tantanmen, a spicy ramen variation influenced by Chinese cuisine. The creamy broth, spiced with sesame and chili oil, is perfectly balanced and has become a favorite among ramen enthusiasts. The shop is small, and there is often a wait, but the quality of the ramen makes it worth the effort. Otsuka Station, on the JR Yamanote Line, is the best way to reach Nakiryu.

Tempura, the third must-try dish, is a traditional Japanese technique of deep-frying seafood and vegetables in a light, airy batter. Despite its simple ingredients, tempura is an art form that requires skill and precision. The best tempura is crispy, not greasy, with a delicate batter that enhances the flavor of the ingredients rather than overpowering them. Tempura is typically served with a dipping sauce made from soy sauce, mirin, and dashi, along with grated daikon radish on the side.

One of the most famous places to try tempura in Tokyo is Tempura Kondo, a Michelin-starred restaurant located in the upscale district of Ginza. Tempura Kondo is known for its perfectly fried seasonal vegetables, such as sweet potatoes, lotus roots, and mushrooms, as well as its fresh seafood, including shrimp, eel, and scallops. The attention to detail and the use of the freshest ingredients make dining at Tempura Kondo a memorable experience. After enjoying your meal, you can explore the elegant streets of Ginza, which are lined with luxury shops, cafes, and galleries. Getting to Ginza is easy, with Ginza Station being a major stop on the Tokyo Metro Ginza Line, Hibiya Line, and Marunouchi Line.

For a more traditional experience, Tenmatsu in Nihonbashi is another excellent choice. Founded in 1885, Tenmatsu has been serving high-quality tempura for generations. The restaurant maintains a classic ambiance, and its set menus feature a variety of tempura dishes, including seasonal vegetables and delicate fish. After your meal, you can take a stroll through the Nihonbashi area, which is rich in history and known for its traditional shops and centuries-old establishments. Nihonbashi is accessible via the Tokyo Metro Ginza Line, Tozai Line, or Asakusa Line.

Another option for enjoying tempura in a casual setting is Tempura Tendon Tenya, a popular chain known for serving tempura bowls, or tendon, at affordable prices. A tendon consists of tempura served over a bowl of rice, topped with a sweet and savory sauce. Tenya offers a variety of tempura, from shrimp and fish to vegetables like eggplant and pumpkin. With locations all over Tokyo, including in major shopping districts like Shibuya and Ueno, Tenya is an easy, budget-friendly way to experience tempura. Shibuya Station, on the JR Yamanote Line and Tokyo Metro Ginza Line, is a convenient way to reach one of Tenya's central locations.

As you explore Tokyo's culinary landscape, trying sushi, ramen, and tempura will give you a deeper appreciation for the diversity and skill behind Japanese cooking. Whether you're enjoying sushi at Toyosu Market, slurping ramen in Shinjuku, or savoring tempura in Ginza, these dishes offer a window into Japan's rich culinary traditions. Each dish is more than just food; it represents a centuries-old craft that has been refined and perfected over generations. Tokyo, with its endless dining options, provides the perfect setting to experience these iconic dishes in their most authentic form.

Street Food and Market Experiences

Exploring the street food and markets in Tokyo is one of the best ways to experience the city's rich culinary traditions and local culture. Tokyo is known for its variety of food offerings, and while high-end restaurants and sushi bars may come to mind first, the vibrant street food scene and bustling markets are equally captivating.

One of the best-known markets in Tokyo is the Toyosu Fish Market, which replaced the historic Tsukiji Fish Market as the largest wholesale seafood market in the city. While Toyosu is known for its tuna auctions and wholesale seafood, it also offers visitors a chance to explore food stalls and small eateries where you can sample fresh seafood dishes. Sushi lovers often visit Toyosu early in the morning to witness the tuna auctions, but the real highlight for food enthusiasts is the opportunity to enjoy a sushi breakfast at one of the market's many restaurants. These eateries source their fish directly from the auction floor, ensuring that what you eat is some of the freshest sushi available in Tokyo.

The market is accessible via the Yurikamome Line, and after arriving at the Toyosu Market Station, you can explore the market's various food offerings at your leisure. While sushi is the star of the show, you'll also find other street food favorites such as tamago-yaki, a Japanese rolled omelet often served on a stick. This dish is slightly sweet and fluffy, making it a delicious snack to try as you explore the market. Many stalls offer samples, so you can try different variations of this simple yet flavorful dish as you make your way through the food area.

Although Toyosu has taken over much of the wholesale seafood business from the original Tsukiji Market, the outer market of Tsukiji is still very much alive and remains one of the top destinations for street food in Tokyo. The outer market consists of narrow streets filled with small shops, stalls, and restaurants offering a wide range of food, from fresh seafood to prepared street food. Tsukiji's outer market is a food lover's paradise, where you can try grilled scallops, uni (sea urchin), grilled eel, and other seafood specialties right on the street. One of the most popular items is the kaisen-don, or seafood rice bowl, which features fresh sashimi piled high on a bowl of rice. You can customize your bowl with your choice of seafood, from salmon to tuna to shrimp, creating a satisfying meal that's full of flavor and freshness.

Getting to Tsukiji Market is easy, with Tsukiji Station on the Tokyo Metro Hibiya Line or Tsukijishijo Station on the Toei Oedo Line being the nearest stops. The market is a lively and colorful place to explore, and it's best to visit in the morning when the stalls are freshly stocked and the energy is at its peak.

Another must-visit area for street food in Tokyo is Ameya-Yokocho, often referred to simply as "Ameyoko." This bustling market street is located near Ueno Station and is known for its vibrant atmosphere and diverse food options.

Originally a black market after World War II, Ameyoko has evolved into a popular shopping street where you can find everything from clothing and cosmetics to fresh produce and seafood. For food lovers, the real draw is the street food, with stalls offering a wide range of snacks and dishes that reflect both Japanese and international influences.

At Ameyoko, you can try takoyaki, a popular street food that consists of small, round balls of batter filled with pieces of octopus. These savory snacks are typically topped with a drizzle of mayonnaise, takoyaki sauce (similar to Worcestershire sauce), and bonito flakes. The crispy exterior and soft, flavorful center make takoyaki a favorite among locals and visitors alike. You'll also find grilled skewers of meat, such as yakitori (grilled chicken), and kushiyaki (skewered grilled items), which are perfect for snacking as you stroll through the market.

Ameyoko's proximity to Ueno Station, on the JR Yamanote Line and Tokyo Metro Ginza Line, makes it a convenient stop on your Tokyo itinerary. After exploring the market, you can also visit nearby Ueno Park, home to several museums and the Ueno Zoo, or take a leisurely walk through the park's cherry blossom trees if you're visiting in the spring.

Another street food hotspot is the Nakamise Shopping Street in Asakusa, which leads to the famous Senso-ji Temple. Nakamise is one of the oldest shopping streets in Tokyo, and its long row of stalls offers a mix of traditional crafts, souvenirs, and of course, delicious street food. As you make your way toward the temple, you'll find an array of snacks that reflect both the traditional flavors of Japan and the local specialties of the area. One of the most famous street foods here is ningyo-yaki, small, doll-shaped cakes filled with sweet red bean paste. These soft, bite-sized treats are made fresh on the spot, and you can watch as the vendors expertly pour batter into molds, fill them with red bean paste, and cook them to golden perfection.

Another local favorite in Asakusa is senbei, traditional Japanese rice crackers that are often grilled over charcoal and brushed with soy sauce. These crunchy, savory snacks come in a variety of flavors, from sweet and salty to spicy, and they make a great souvenir to take home. Nakamise is also a great place to try taiyaki, a fish-shaped cake filled with either sweet red bean paste or custard. The soft, warm cake and the sweet filling create a satisfying combination that is perfect for enjoying as you explore the temple grounds.

Asakusa is easily accessible via Asakusa Station on the Tokyo Metro Ginza Line or Toei Asakusa Line, and the Nakamise Shopping Street is located just a short walk from the station. After sampling the street food, take the time to visit Senso-ji Temple, one of Tokyo's most famous landmarks, where you can experience the spiritual atmosphere of this historic site and explore the nearby Asakusa Shrine.

For a more modern street food experience, head to the trendy Harajuku district, particularly Takeshita Street, which is famous for its youth culture and fashion. Takeshita Street is lined with small shops, cafes, and street food vendors, and it's a great place to try creative and colorful snacks that reflect Harajuku's playful and vibrant spirit. One of the most iconic street foods in Harajuku is the crepe. Harajuku crepes are thin, crispy pancakes that are filled with a variety of sweet or savory ingredients, such as whipped cream, strawberries, chocolate, or even ice cream. The crepes are rolled into a cone shape, making them easy to eat on the go, and their endless variety of fillings makes them a favorite among both tourists and locals.

In addition to crepes, Harajuku is also known for its cotton candy, which comes in bright, rainbow colors and is often served in huge, fluffy portions. This whimsical treat is a must-try for those with a sweet tooth and adds to the fun and quirky atmosphere of Takeshita Street. Harajuku is located just a short walk from Harajuku Station on the JR Yamanote Line or Meiji-jingumae Station on the Tokyo Metro Chiyoda Line, making it an easy and enjoyable destination for a day of shopping, eating, and people-watching.

For those seeking a more traditional market experience, the Omoide Yokocho (Memory Lane) in Shinjuku offers a glimpse into post-war Tokyo and is a fantastic spot to try some of Japan's most beloved street food dishes. Located just steps from Shinjuku Station, Omoide Yokocho is a narrow alleyway filled with small eateries and izakayas (Japanese pubs) that serve up classic dishes such as yakitori (grilled chicken skewers), oden (a type of hotpot with various ingredients simmered in broth), and nikomi (stewed beef or pork). The atmosphere here is cozy and nostalgic, with smoky grills, dim lighting, and close-quartered seating giving the area a distinctly old-fashioned charm.

While yakitori is one of the most popular items on the menu in Omoide Yokocho, don't miss the chance to try oden if it's in season. Oden is a winter comfort food in Japan, and it consists of various ingredients, such as tofu, daikon radish, boiled eggs, and fish cakes, all simmered in a light soy-flavored broth. Each restaurant has its own variation, and you can often customize your bowl by choosing the ingredients you like best.

Omoide Yokocho is best visited in the evening when the alley comes alive with locals and tourists alike looking for a bite to eat after work. The izakayas are small, so be prepared to share a table or sit elbow-to-elbow with fellow diners. The lively, down-to-earth atmosphere makes it a memorable dining experience and a great way to experience a different side of Tokyo's food culture.

Finally, the Yanaka Ginza shopping street offers a more relaxed and local street food experience. Located in the traditional neighborhood of Yanaka, this retro shopping street is lined with small shops selling everything from groceries and snacks to clothing and household goods. The food stalls here offer an array of classic street foods, such as korokke (Japanese croquettes), menchi-katsu (fried ground meat cutlet), and yakitori. Yanaka Ginza's atmosphere feels like stepping back in time, and it's a great place to explore if you want to experience a more laid-back side of Tokyo.

Yanaka Ginza is easily accessible from Nippori Station on the JR Yamanote Line or Tokyo Metro Chiyoda Line, and it's an excellent spot to explore if you're looking for an authentic, neighborhood feel. As you walk through the street, you'll see locals shopping for their daily groceries, and the slower pace of life here is a refreshing contrast to the hustle and bustle of central Tokyo.

Michelin-Starred Restaurants and Fine Dining

Tokyo is renowned as one of the world's premier dining destinations, and the city holds the highest number of Michelin-starred restaurants anywhere on the globe. The combination of Japanese precision, attention to detail, and reverence for ingredients has created a dining scene that is unmatched in variety and quality. The fine dining culture in Tokyo spans both traditional Japanese cuisine and international influences, offering something unique for any food lover who wants to experience some of the most memorable meals of their life.

One of the most famous Michelin-starred restaurants in Tokyo is Sukiyabashi Jiro, run by Jiro Ono, one of the world's most celebrated sushi chefs. Sukiyabashi Jiro has earned three Michelin stars and gained international recognition through the documentary Jiro Dreams of Sushi, which tells the story of Jiro's pursuit of perfection in his craft. Dining at Sukiyabashi Jiro is an intimate and highly curated experience, with only a small number of seats available at the counter, and Jiro himself personally preparing the sushi for each guest. The meal is an omakase (chef's choice), meaning the chef selects each piece of sushi to be served based on the freshest ingredients of the day. The meal typically lasts around 30 minutes, but every second is a sensory journey into the purity of Japanese sushi-making.

The restaurant is located in the Ginza district, one of Tokyo's most luxurious areas, known for its high-end shopping and refined dining establishments. Ginza is easily accessible by the Tokyo Metro Ginza Line, and Sukiyabashi Jiro itself is located in the basement of an unassuming office building. While getting a reservation here is notoriously difficult—often requiring bookings months in advance—it remains one of the ultimate dining experiences in Tokyo for those lucky enough to secure a seat.

For those who may not manage to get into Sukiyabashi Jiro but still want an exceptional sushi experience, Sushi Saito is another three-Michelin-starred restaurant that is widely regarded as one of the best sushi places in the city. Saito's sushi is known for its delicate balance of flavors and textures, with each piece of fish and rice perfectly seasoned and served at the ideal temperature. Sushi Saito is also a small, intimate restaurant, where the chef serves each guest directly, creating a personal and attentive dining experience. Like Sukiyabashi Jiro, Sushi Saito is located in the Minato ward and can be reached via Roppongi Station on the Tokyo Metro Hibiya Line or Toei Oedo Line.

If you're interested in exploring the broader range of traditional Japanese cuisine, kaiseki dining is an experience not to be missed. Kaiseki is a multi-course meal that celebrates seasonal ingredients and meticulous presentation. Each course in a kaiseki meal is carefully designed to showcase the natural flavors and textures of the ingredients, with an emphasis on balance and harmony. One of the most renowned kaiseki restaurants in Tokyo is Kanda, which has been awarded three Michelin stars. Chef Hiroyuki Kanda's approach to kaiseki is rooted in simplicity and respect for tradition, but he also incorporates subtle modern touches that make each dish feel fresh and innovative. The meal at Kanda is an immersive experience in Japanese fine dining, where the beauty of each dish matches the extraordinary flavors.

Kanda is located in the Aoyama district, which is known for its art galleries, fashion boutiques, and refined atmosphere. To reach Kanda, you can take the Tokyo Metro Ginza Line to Omotesando Station, from where it's a short walk to the restaurant. The elegance of both the food and the setting makes dining at Kanda a serene and memorable occasion.

For those looking to experience fine dining with a more contemporary or international twist, Tokyo has no shortage of Michelin-starred French restaurants that have successfully integrated Japanese sensibilities into their cuisine. Quintessence, a three-Michelin-starred restaurant in the Shinagawa ward, is one of the most famous examples of this fusion. Chef Shuzo Kishida trained in France and brought back his deep understanding of French techniques, which he now pairs with Japanese ingredients to create exquisite, innovative dishes. Quintessence is known for its ever-changing menu, which reflects the chef's commitment to using only the finest seasonal ingredients. The focus on purity of flavor and the precision in cooking techniques make each meal at Quintessence a masterclass in fine dining.

Getting to Quintessence is convenient, as the restaurant is located in the Shinagawa area, close to Gotanda Station on the JR Yamanote Line or Toei Asakusa Line. The restaurant's minimalist décor and focus on food allow the dishes to take center stage, making the experience both sophisticated and deeply satisfying.

Another top destination for French cuisine in Tokyo is L'Atelier de Joël Robuchon, located in the Roppongi Hills development. The restaurant has earned two Michelin stars and is part of the global network of restaurants created by the late French chef Joël Robuchon. L'Atelier de Joël Robuchon offers a more relaxed yet still luxurious dining atmosphere, with an open kitchen that allows diners to watch the chefs at work. The menu features French dishes that have been crafted with exceptional attention to detail, using both French and Japanese ingredients. From perfectly seared foie gras to delicate desserts, every course is a work of art. Roppongi Hills is a lively area filled with shops, galleries, and nightlife, so you can easily plan to spend an entire day or evening in the area after enjoying your meal at L'Atelier de Joël Robuchon. To get there, you can take the Tokyo Metro Hibiya Line to Roppongi Station.

For those looking to experience more casual but equally refined Michelin-starred dining, Tempura Kondo is an excellent option. Located in the Ginza district, Tempura Kondo is a two-Michelin-starred restaurant that specializes in tempura, the Japanese art of deep-frying seafood and vegetables in a light, crispy batter. Tempura may seem like a simple dish, but at Kondo, it is elevated to a fine art. The chef uses only the freshest seasonal ingredients, such as shrimp, eel, and sweet potato, and carefully fries each piece to perfection. The tempura is served with a side of rice, miso soup, and dipping sauce, creating a meal that is both elegant and comforting. Tempura Kondo's minimalist interior allows you to focus entirely on the food, and the chef's skill and precision make this a must-visit for tempura lovers.

Ginza is home to many of Tokyo's finest restaurants, and Tempura Kondo is just one of the many Michelin-starred options in the area. After your meal, you can explore the upscale shopping streets of Ginza or visit one of the nearby art galleries, making it an ideal location for a day of luxury dining and cultural exploration.

For those interested in exploring both traditional Japanese cuisine and modern innovations, Nihonryori RyuGin is an exceptional choice. Located in the upscale Roppongi district, RyuGin is a three-Michelin-starred restaurant that combines traditional Japanese flavors with contemporary techniques. Chef Seiji Yamamoto is known for his creative and boundary-pushing approach to kaiseki, blending seasonal ingredients with elements of molecular gastronomy to create a dining experience that is both surprising and deeply rooted in Japanese culinary traditions. The restaurant's kaiseki menu changes with the seasons, and each course is a reflection of Japan's natural beauty and its cultural heritage. From perfectly cooked fish to inventive desserts, every dish at RyuGin is designed to engage all the senses, making it a memorable and immersive dining experience.

Roppongi is easily accessible via the Tokyo Metro Hibiya Line or Toei Oedo Line, and the vibrant atmosphere of the district makes it a perfect place to explore before or after your meal. Whether you're visiting the Mori Art Museum, strolling through the nearby shopping streets, or enjoying the nightlife, Roppongi offers a variety of activities that complement the world-class dining experience at RyuGin.

In addition to Japanese and French cuisine, Tokyo is also home to some of the finest Italian restaurants in Asia. Heinz Beck Tokyo, located in the Marunouchi area, has earned two Michelin stars and is known for its refined Italian dishes that incorporate Japanese ingredients. Chef Heinz Beck is celebrated for his modern approach to Italian cuisine, using techniques that highlight the freshness and purity of the ingredients. Dishes such as handmade pasta, delicate seafood, and beautifully presented desserts make dining at Heinz Beck Tokyo an elegant and unforgettable experience.

The Marunouchi area, located near Tokyo Station, is a hub of business, shopping, and dining, making it an ideal location for fine dining. After your meal at Heinz Beck Tokyo, you can explore the nearby Imperial Palace grounds or visit one of the many luxury shops in the area. Tokyo Station is a major transportation hub, making it easy to reach this part of the city from almost anywhere in Tokyo.

Izakayas: Experience Local Nightlife

Izakayas are one of the best ways to immerse yourself in Tokyo's local nightlife and experience a side of Japan that is both casual and deeply rooted in tradition. An izakaya is often compared to a pub or a small bar, but it is distinctly Japanese in its atmosphere, food, and drinking culture. It is a place where people gather after work to enjoy drinks, share small plates of food, and unwind with friends, colleagues, or even strangers. Izakayas vary in style, from tiny, hole-in-the-wall establishments tucked into narrow alleys to larger, more modern venues.

Tokyo is home to countless izakayas, with each neighborhood offering its own variation of the izakaya experience. One of the most famous areas for izakayas is Shinjuku's Omoide Yokocho, also known as "Memory Lane." This narrow alleyway is lined with small, traditional izakayas, each seating only a handful of people at a time. The area is rich in post-war nostalgia, with smoky grills, paper lanterns, and the smell of grilled meat wafting through the air. Omoide Yokocho offers a snapshot of old Tokyo, where patrons sit elbow to elbow on stools, chatting while enjoying skewers of yakitori (grilled chicken) and sipping on cold beer or sake.

Located just a short walk from Shinjuku Station, Omoide Yokocho is easy to reach, making it a popular destination for both locals and tourists. Shinjuku Station is one of Tokyo's busiest hubs and is accessible via the JR Yamanote Line, the Tokyo Metro Marunouchi Line, and several other lines. After stepping off the train, it's just a few minutes to the lively streets of Omoide Yokocho. Visiting this area in the evening, when the alley comes to life with chatter, clinking glasses, and the scent of grilled food, is a truly atmospheric experience.

One of the highlights of an izakaya experience is the wide variety of dishes on offer. Izakayas are known for serving small plates, which are meant to be shared among the group. These dishes range from traditional Japanese fare to more creative, fusion-style offerings. Common items include yakitori, which are skewers of grilled chicken seasoned with either salt or a sweet-savory tare sauce, and karaage, which are deep-fried pieces of marinated chicken that are crispy on the outside and juicy on the inside. You'll also find edamame (steamed soybeans), tamago-yaki (a sweet rolled omelet), and various types of sashimi. For heartier options, you can try oden, a simmered dish consisting of items like boiled eggs, fish cakes, and daikon radish in a flavorful broth.

Drinking is, of course, central to the izakaya experience. Most izakayas offer a wide selection of beverages, including beer, sake, shochu (a distilled spirit often made from barley or sweet potatoes), and chu-hi (a highball made with shochu and flavored soda water). The drinks are typically served in large mugs or bottles, making it easy to share and enjoy the social aspect of drinking. Many izakayas also offer all-you-can-drink options, known as nomihoudai, where for a set price, you can drink as much as you like for a certain amount of time. This is a popular choice for groups looking to celebrate or unwind after a long day.

While Omoide Yokocho offers a more traditional and nostalgic izakaya experience, Shibuya is another fantastic neighborhood to explore if you want a more modern take on Tokyo nightlife. Shibuya is famous for its vibrant energy, and this extends to its izakaya scene, which tends to attract a younger crowd. Nonbei Yokocho, which translates to "Drunkard's Alley," is located just a few minutes from the iconic Shibuya Crossing. Much like Omoide Yokocho, Nonbei Yokocho is a collection of narrow streets filled with tiny izakayas and bars, each offering its own unique atmosphere. The bars here are cozy and often only accommodate a few patrons at a time, giving you an intimate and personal experience.

Shibuya Station is a major stop on the JR Yamanote Line, Tokyo Metro Ginza Line, and other lines, making it an easily accessible destination. Once you've taken in the electric atmosphere of Shibuya Crossing, a visit to Nonbei Yokocho allows you to wind down in a more laid-back setting, where you can share drinks and small plates of food with locals. The contrast between the hustle and bustle of Shibuya and the quiet, tucked-away izakayas in Nonbei Yokocho is part of what makes the experience so enjoyable.

For a more upscale izakaya experience, Ebisu is another neighborhood worth exploring. Ebisu is known for its chic, sophisticated dining and drinking establishments, and its izakayas are no exception. Here, you'll find modern izakayas that combine traditional Japanese flavors with contemporary presentation and high-quality ingredients. One such place is Ebisu Yokocho, a lively, indoor alleyway packed with izakayas, where the atmosphere is vibrant and the food is top-notch. The area is popular among Tokyo's young professionals and offers a wide variety of food and drink options, from grilled skewers to fresh seafood and innovative fusion dishes.

Ebisu is easily accessible via the JR Yamanote Line, with Ebisu Station just a short walk from the heart of the neighborhood. The area is known for its sophisticated nightlife, with stylish bars, restaurants, and cafes lining the streets, making it a great spot to explore both before and after your izakaya visit.

Another neighborhood that offers a rich izakaya experience is Nakameguro, known for its trendy, bohemian vibe and beautiful cherry blossom-lined canal. Nakameguro has a number of stylish izakayas that reflect the neighborhood's relaxed, creative atmosphere. Here, you'll find izakayas that emphasize fresh, seasonal ingredients, often with a focus on organic or locally sourced produce. The dining experience in Nakameguro is a bit more refined compared to the casual, rowdy atmosphere of other areas, making it a great spot for those looking to enjoy a more leisurely and thoughtful izakaya meal.

Nakameguro Station is located on the Tokyo Metro Hibiya Line, and the neighborhood is just a short train ride from central Tokyo. In the spring, the area becomes a popular spot for cherry blossom viewing, and dining at an izakaya along the canal while the cherry blossoms are in full bloom is a magical experience.

For visitors who want to experience the local nightlife without venturing into the bustling neighborhoods of central Tokyo, the area of Koenji offers a more laid-back and retro izakaya scene. Koenji, located in the Suginami ward, is known for its bohemian atmosphere and its thriving music and art culture. The izakayas in Koenji are often smaller, independent establishments that reflect the neighborhood's quirky and creative spirit. One of the highlights of dining in Koenji is the opportunity to explore places that cater to locals, offering an authentic experience that feels worlds away from the more tourist-heavy areas of the city.

Koenji is accessible via the JR Chuo Line, and the area is just a short ride from Shinjuku Station. After visiting an izakaya, you can explore Koenji's many vintage shops, music venues, and second-hand stores, making it a fun and offbeat destination for an evening out.

No discussion of izakayas would be complete without mentioning Golden Gai, a unique and historic nightlife district located in Shinjuku. Golden Gai is a collection of tiny, interconnected alleyways packed with over 200 bars and izakayas, each with its own distinct personality. The establishments in Golden Gai are famously small—many can only seat a handful of people at a time—and the atmosphere is friendly and intimate. Golden Gai is known for its quirky, eclectic vibe, with bars and izakayas catering to a wide range of tastes and interests. Some establishments are themed, while others focus on specific drinks or food, making Golden Gai a fascinating place to explore.

Golden Gai is located in Kabukicho, Shinjuku's famous red-light district, and is just a short walk from Shinjuku Station. The area has a slightly gritty but charming feel, and the narrow alleys lined with lanterns and neon lights create a distinctly old Tokyo ambiance. Visiting Golden Gai is a memorable way to experience a more unusual side of Tokyo's nightlife, and it's an especially popular spot for those who want to get to know the locals over drinks and food in a relaxed, casual setting.

Vegetarian and Vegan Options in Tokyo

Tokyo is a city known for its incredible diversity when it comes to food, and in recent years, the demand for vegetarian and vegan options has grown significantly. While traditional Japanese cuisine is often centered around fish and meat, Tokyo has embraced the global rise of plant-based diets and now offers a wide range of vegetarian and vegan-friendly restaurants. From casual eateries to more refined dining establishments, there are plenty of places where you can enjoy delicious meals that cater to both vegetarians and vegans without sacrificing the flavors that make Japanese food so unique. Exploring Tokyo's vegetarian and vegan options allows you to experience the city's culinary creativity while sticking to your dietary preferences.

One of the best neighborhoods for vegetarian and vegan food in Tokyo is the bustling district of Shibuya. Shibuya is not only famous for its lively nightlife and fashion scene, but it also has some excellent plant-based dining options. One standout restaurant is Nagi Shokudo, a cozy and welcoming spot that offers a fully vegan menu. Located about a 10-minute walk from Shibuya Station, Nagi Shokudo is known for its creative Japanese-inspired vegan dishes, which often incorporate seasonal ingredients. The menu features a variety of set meals, such as vegan curry, fried soy meat, and miso-based soups. Each dish is thoughtfully prepared, and the portions are generous, making it a great place to enjoy a hearty vegan meal in a relaxed, laid-back atmosphere. Nagi Shokudo's proximity to Shibuya Crossing makes it an ideal stop for lunch or dinner after exploring the area's famous landmarks.

For a more upscale vegan experience in Shibuya, you can visit the restaurant called 8ablish. 8ablish is a chic and modern eatery located near Omotesando, offering a menu that combines Japanese and Western flavors with a focus on plant-based ingredients. The dishes here are beautifully presented and include options such as vegan pasta, salads, and creative desserts made without animal products. 8ablish is known for its attention to detail and use of high-quality ingredients, making it a popular choice among both locals and visitors. The restaurant's elegant yet casual vibe makes it perfect for a relaxing meal, and the Omotesando area itself is great for shopping and strolling through trendy streets. To get to 8ablish, you can take the Tokyo Metro Ginza Line or Chiyoda Line to Omotesando Station, and from there it's just a short walk to the restaurant.

If you're looking for a vegetarian or vegan option with a more traditional Japanese feel, T's Tantan is a must-visit. Located within Tokyo Station, T's Tantan specializes in vegan ramen, offering a variety of flavors, from rich and creamy sesame-based broths to lighter, spicier versions. The ramen is entirely plant-based, using soy meat as a substitute for pork, and the noodles are perfectly cooked to complement the flavorful broth. T's Tantan has gained a loyal following due to its delicious vegan ramen that doesn't compromise on taste or texture. This restaurant is especially convenient for travelers, as it's located in the bustling Tokyo Station, making it an excellent option if you're passing through the area or waiting for a train. Tokyo Station is one of the city's major transportation hubs, accessible via the JR Yamanote Line, Shinkansen, and multiple Tokyo Metro lines.

In the trendy neighborhood of Harajuku, you'll find another vegan gem called Ain Soph. Journey. This restaurant is part of the Ain Soph group, which has several locations across Tokyo, all of which offer vegan menus that are both inventive and satisfying. Ain Soph. Journey in Harajuku is known for its hearty dishes such as vegan burgers, pancakes, and Japanese-style curry. One of the highlights of the menu is their vegan version of tonkatsu, a traditionally pork-based dish that they recreate using plant-based ingredients without losing any of the rich flavors. Ain Soph. Journey's location near Harajuku's famous Takeshita Street makes it a great place to stop after exploring the area's unique shops and attractions. Harajuku Station, located on the JR Yamanote Line, is just a short walk from the restaurant, making it easily accessible for both locals and tourists.

For those who want to experience more traditional Japanese vegetarian cuisine, Shojin Ryori, or Buddhist temple cuisine, offers a window into Japan's plant-based culinary heritage. Shojin Ryori is a style of vegetarian cooking that originated in Buddhist temples, where monks prepare meals using only plant-based ingredients as part of their spiritual practice. The food is simple, yet deeply flavorful, with an emphasis on balance and mindfulness. One of the best places to try Shojin Ryori in Tokyo is at a restaurant called Sougo, located in the upscale district of Roppongi. Sougo offers a refined dining experience with beautifully crafted dishes that showcase seasonal vegetables, tofu, and traditional Japanese ingredients like yuba (tofu skin) and miso. Each dish is prepared with care, reflecting the principles of Shojin Ryori, which focus on harmony between flavors, textures, and presentation.

Roppongi is a lively area known for its modern art museums, shopping, and nightlife, so a visit to Sougo can easily be combined with a day of cultural exploration. The restaurant is located near Roppongi Station, which is accessible via the Tokyo Metro Hibiya Line and Toei Oedo Line. Dining at Sougo is a peaceful and contemplative experience, offering a deeper understanding of the role that food plays in Japanese spirituality and culture.

For travelers exploring the Asakusa area, known for its historic temples and traditional atmosphere, there are also great vegetarian and vegan options to enjoy. One such place is Komaki Shokudo, a casual eatery located near Senso-ji Temple, which serves vegetarian Japanese home-cooked dishes. Komaki Shokudo specializes in teishoku, which are set meals that typically include rice, miso soup, and a variety of small dishes like tofu, pickles, and vegetables. The food is simple yet wholesome, making it an ideal stop after a day of sightseeing at Senso-ji Temple and exploring the nearby Nakamise Shopping Street. Asakusa Station, located on the Tokyo Metro Ginza Line and Toei Asakusa Line, is just a short walk away, making this restaurant a convenient and satisfying option for vegetarian travelers.

For those who love desserts, Tokyo has not forgotten its vegan sweet tooth. At Kousaiken Veganic To Go, located in the Nihonbashi area, you'll find a delightful range of vegan sweets and snacks, including wagashi (traditional Japanese sweets). This small takeaway spot offers vegan versions of classic treats, such as dorayaki (red bean-filled pancakes) and daifuku (mochi filled with sweet red bean paste). The treats here are made without animal products but still capture the authentic taste and texture of Japanese sweets. Nihonbashi is a district known for its historical significance and proximity to Tokyo Station, so you can easily stop by Kousaiken Veganic To Go for a quick snack while exploring the area's cultural landmarks.

Another dessert destination for vegans is Ain Soph. Ripple, located in the Ikebukuro neighborhood. This vegan restaurant specializes in burgers and casual fare, but they also offer an impressive selection of vegan desserts, including cakes, parfaits, and even vegan soft serve ice cream. Ikebukuro is a vibrant district filled with shopping centers, anime-themed stores, and entertainment options, so Ain Soph. Ripple is a great place to recharge with some vegan comfort food and desserts after a day of exploring the area's attractions. Ikebukuro Station is a major transit hub served by the JR Yamanote Line, the Tokyo Metro, and various other train lines, making it an easy and convenient stop.

Another option for those in search of plant-based sweets is Wired Bonbon, located in Shinjuku. This vegan-friendly cafe is known for its decadent desserts, including vegan parfaits layered with seasonal fruits, nuts, and plant-based cream. The cafe's creative approach to desserts makes it a popular spot for both vegans and non-vegans alike. Wired Bonbon is located in the LUMINE department store, which is directly connected to Shinjuku Station, making it a convenient stop for dessert lovers exploring the bustling Shinjuku area.

Exploring Tokyo as a vegetarian or vegan can be a rewarding experience, not only because of the growing number of plant-based dining options but also because of the city's focus on freshness and seasonal ingredients. Many restaurants in

Tokyo, even those not exclusively vegetarian or vegan, offer dishes that can be adapted to meet dietary preferences. The key to navigating Tokyo's plant-based dining scene is to explore the neighborhoods that interest you and take the time to try the variety of options available.

Budget-Friendly Eateries and Local Favorites

Tokyo is often seen as an expensive city, but when it comes to food, there are countless budget-friendly eateries that serve up delicious and authentic meals without breaking the bank. From hidden local favorites to popular chains, the city has a wide variety of affordable options that allow you to experience the rich flavors of Japanese cuisine. Exploring these eateries gives you an opportunity to eat like a local and discover the true essence of Tokyo's food culture, all while sticking to a budget.

One of the most beloved budget-friendly dishes in Tokyo is ramen. Ramen shops are everywhere in the city, offering steaming bowls of flavorful noodles in a variety of broths. One of the most famous ramen chains is Ichiran, known for its customizable ramen experience. At Ichiran, you can choose the richness of your broth, the firmness of your noodles, and the level of spice. This chain has several locations throughout Tokyo, including in Shibuya and Shinjuku, making it easy to find wherever you are in the city. The individual booth seating at Ichiran also allows you to fully focus on enjoying your bowl of ramen, which is made with a tonkotsu (pork bone) broth that is creamy, rich, and flavorful. A meal at Ichiran will typically cost you around 1,000 to 1,500 yen, making it an excellent choice for budget-conscious travelers.

If you're looking for something more traditional, soba is another affordable and popular option in Tokyo. Soba noodles are made from buckwheat flour and can be served either hot or cold, with dipping sauces or in a light broth. One of the best places to try soba on a budget is at Kanda Matsuya, a historic soba restaurant located in the Kanda district. Kanda Matsuya has been serving up soba for over a century, and its handmade noodles are famous for their chewy texture and subtle flavor. The restaurant's traditional decor, complete with wooden floors and sliding paper doors, adds to the experience of enjoying a meal that has been perfected over generations. A simple bowl of soba at Kanda Matsuya costs around 600 to 800 yen, making it a budget-friendly option for those looking to try authentic Japanese noodles.

To get to Kanda Matsuya, you can take the Tokyo Metro Ginza Line or JR Chuo Line to Kanda Station. The restaurant is just a short walk from the station, making it a convenient stop for lunch or dinner.

Another great option for budget dining in Tokyo is gyudon, or beef bowl, which consists of thinly sliced beef simmered with onions in a sweet and savory sauce, served over a bowl of rice. One of the most famous gyudon chains in Japan is Yoshinoya, which has locations all over Tokyo. Yoshinoya is known for its quick service and affordable prices, with a basic beef bowl costing as little as 400 to 500 yen. The menu also includes options like pork bowls and vegetable bowls for those looking for something different. Yoshinoya is popular among locals for its convenience and low prices, making it a great choice for a quick, satisfying meal when you're on the go. You'll find Yoshinoya branches in almost every major district of Tokyo, including Shibuya, Shinjuku, and Akihabara.

For a more unique Tokyo experience, Omoide Yokocho in Shinjuku is a must-visit destination. Omoide Yokocho, also known as "Memory Lane," is a narrow alleyway filled with tiny eateries that serve classic Japanese dishes like yakitori (grilled chicken skewers), oden (a type of hot pot), and nikomi (stewed beef or pork). The atmosphere here is lively and nostalgic, with smoky grills and the clinking of glasses filling the air as locals and tourists alike enjoy cheap, delicious food in a casual setting. The yakitori stalls are especially popular, with skewers starting at around 150 to 200 yen each. Omoide Yokocho is located just a short walk from Shinjuku Station, making it an easy stop after a day of sightseeing in one of Tokyo's busiest districts.

Another great area for budget-friendly food is Ameya-Yokocho, or "Ameyoko," located near Ueno Station. Ameyoko is a bustling market street where you'll find vendors selling everything from fresh produce to clothing, but it's also a fantastic spot for cheap eats. Here, you can sample a wide range of street food, such as takoyaki (octopus balls), taiyaki (fish-shaped cakes filled with sweet red bean paste), and gyoza (pan-fried dumplings). Many of the food stalls in Ameyoko offer snacks and small dishes for under 500 yen, making it a great place to try a variety of foods without spending too much. Ueno Station is easily accessible via the JR Yamanote

Line, Tokyo Metro Ginza Line, or Hibiya Line, and Ameyoko is just a few minutes' walk from the station.

For those interested in trying sushi without the high price tag, Tokyo has many conveyor belt sushi restaurants, known as kaiten-zushi, where plates of sushi travel around the counter on a conveyor belt, and you can pick whatever you'd like to try. One of the most popular kaiten-zushi chains in Tokyo is Sushiro, which offers a wide variety of sushi at extremely affordable prices, with most plates costing around 100 to 150 yen. Despite the low prices, the quality of the sushi is high, and Sushiro has become a favorite among both locals and tourists looking for an inexpensive sushi experience. There are several Sushiro locations throughout Tokyo, including in Akihabara and Shibuya, making it a convenient option for a budget-friendly meal.

Another budget sushi option is Genki Sushi, a modern kaiten-zushi chain with locations in Shibuya and Ueno. Genki Sushi takes the conveyor belt concept a step further, allowing diners to place their orders via a touchscreen, with the sushi delivered directly to their seat on a small automated train. The novelty of the ordering system, combined with the affordable prices and good quality sushi, makes Genki Sushi a fun and budget-friendly dining experience. Shibuya Station and Ueno Station are both major transportation hubs, making it easy to find Genki Sushi locations in these areas.

For those looking to try Japanese comfort food, okonomiyaki is a filling and budget-friendly option. Okonomiyaki is a savory pancake made with cabbage, flour, eggs, and a variety of other ingredients, such as pork, seafood, or vegetables. The dish is often cooked on a griddle at the table, allowing diners to customize their toppings and cook the pancake to their liking. One of the best places to try okonomiyaki in Tokyo is at Sometaro, a traditional okonomiyaki restaurant located in the Asakusa district. Sometaro has been serving okonomiyaki for decades, and the restaurant's rustic, old-fashioned atmosphere adds to the experience of enjoying this hearty dish. Prices at Sometaro are very reasonable, with most okonomiyaki costing around 800 to 1,200 yen.

Asakusa is known for its historic temples, including the famous Senso-ji Temple, and visiting Sometaro for a meal is a great way to end a day of sightseeing in the area. The restaurant is located about a 10-minute walk from Asakusa Station, which is served by the Tokyo Metro Ginza Line and Toei Asakusa Line.

Don't miss out on Tokyo's many convenience stores, or konbini, which offer surprisingly good food at very affordable prices. Chains like 7-Eleven, Lawson, and FamilyMart can be found all over the city, and they offer a wide variety of ready-to-eat meals, including rice balls (onigiri), sandwiches, bento boxes, and even hot food like fried chicken or noodles. Onigiri, which are rice balls filled with ingredients like salmon, pickled plum, or tuna, are a staple of convenience store food and typically cost around 100 to 150 yen each. Bento boxes, which contain a complete meal with rice, meat, and vegetables, usually cost between 400 and 600 yen, making them an excellent option for a quick, cheap lunch or dinner. Konbini food is not only affordable but also fresh and high quality, with many options available 24 hours a day.

Exploring Tokyo's budget-friendly eateries is a fantastic way to experience the city's diverse food culture without spending a lot of money. Each neighborhood in Tokyo has its own culinary specialties, and by visiting these budget eateries, you'll not only save money but also get a taste of the city's rich food traditions and local favorites.

CHAPTER 9

SHOPPING IN TOKYO

Department Stores, Malls, and Boutique Shops

Shopping in Tokyo is one of the most exciting and diverse experiences you can have in the city. Whether you're looking for high-end fashion, unique boutique finds, traditional Japanese goods, or cutting-edge technology, Tokyo has something for every shopper. The city is famous for its vast department stores, large shopping malls, and charming boutique shops, each offering a unique atmosphere and an extensive range of products. Tokyo's shopping scene is not just about buying things; it's about exploring the culture, style, and trends that define the city.

Let's begin with Ginza, Tokyo's premier luxury shopping district. Known for its upscale department stores, designer boutiques, and elegant atmosphere, Ginza is the go-to destination for high-end fashion and luxury goods. The wide, tree-lined streets of Ginza are home to some of the world's most famous luxury brands, such as Chanel, Louis Vuitton, and Gucci. One of the most iconic department stores in the area is Mitsukoshi, which has been a staple of Ginza shopping for over a century. Mitsukoshi Ginza offers an incredible selection of luxury fashion, accessories, and cosmetics spread across multiple floors. The department store also has an excellent food hall, where you can find gourmet sweets, pastries, and delicacies, as well as beautifully packaged souvenirs.

Another famous department store in Ginza is Wako, recognizable by its iconic clock tower. Wako specializes in luxury watches, jewelry, and leather goods, and its elegant, refined atmosphere makes it one of the most prestigious shopping destinations in Tokyo. Both Mitsukoshi and Wako are located along Chuo-dori, the main street that runs through Ginza, which is closed to cars on weekends, allowing visitors to leisurely stroll and enjoy the area.

To get to Ginza, you can take the Tokyo Metro Ginza Line to Ginza Station, or the JR Yamanote Line to Yurakucho Station, both of which are conveniently located near the shopping district. After shopping in Ginza, you can explore the nearby Kabuki-za Theater, one of Tokyo's most famous venues for traditional kabuki performances, or enjoy a meal at one of the many fine dining restaurants in the area.

If you're looking for a more modern and youthful shopping experience, Shibuya is the place to go. Shibuya is one of Tokyo's busiest and most vibrant neighborhoods, known for its fashion-forward atmosphere and lively streets. One of the most famous shopping destinations in Shibuya is Shibuya 109, a multi-level fashion mall that caters to young women. Shibuya 109 is packed with trendy clothing stores, accessories shops, and beauty products, making it a must-visit for anyone interested in Japanese street fashion. The mall's bold and colorful atmosphere reflects the youthful energy of the neighborhood, and it's a great place to discover the latest fashion trends in Tokyo.

Shibuya is also home to some of Tokyo's largest and most modern department stores, such as Seibu and Tokyu. Seibu Shibuya offers a wide range of fashion, home goods, and beauty products, while Tokyu Department Store, located near Shibuya Station, is known for its diverse selection of brands and its impressive food hall. Tokyu also operates the Shibuya Hikarie, a massive shopping and entertainment complex that includes high-end fashion, cosmetics, and dining options. Shibuya Hikarie is a sleek and modern space where you can browse both local and international brands while enjoying stunning views of the city from the upper floors.

Shibuya is easily accessible via Shibuya Station, which is served by multiple train lines, including the JR Yamanote Line, Tokyo Metro Ginza Line, and Hanzomon Line. The iconic Shibuya Crossing, one of the busiest pedestrian intersections in the world, is located right outside the station, making it a popular starting point for exploring the area.

For shoppers who prefer a more eclectic and unique experience, Harajuku is the perfect destination. Harajuku is famous for its quirky fashion, vibrant street culture, and its role as a hub for youth trends. Takeshita Street is the heart of Harajuku's shopping scene, and it's lined with boutique shops, trendy clothing stores, and fun accessories. Takeshita Street is also known for its affordable prices, making it a great spot for finding unique and playful fashion items without spending a fortune. In addition to clothing and accessories, Harajuku is famous for its colorful and creative street food, such as crepes and cotton candy, which you can enjoy while browsing the shops.

If you're looking for something more sophisticated, Omotesando, located just a short walk from Takeshita Street, offers a more upscale shopping experience. Omotesando is often referred to as Tokyo's Champs-Élysées, and its tree-lined boulevard is home to designer boutiques, luxury stores, and high-end department stores like Omotesando Hills. Omotesando Hills is a modern shopping complex that features both international luxury brands and local Japanese designers. The sleek, architectural design of the building, combined with its curated selection of stores, makes it a must-visit for anyone interested in fashion and design.

To reach Harajuku, you can take the JR Yamanote Line to Harajuku Station or the Tokyo Metro Chiyoda Line to Meiji-jingumae Station. After shopping, you can visit the nearby Meiji Shrine, one of Tokyo's most important Shinto shrines, or take a walk through the peaceful Yoyogi Park.

If you're interested in technology and electronics, Akihabara is the place to go. Akihabara, often referred to as "Electric Town," is Tokyo's premier destination for electronics, gadgets, and anime-related merchandise. Yodobashi Camera, one of the largest electronics stores in the world, is located in Akihabara and offers an incredible selection of cameras, computers, home appliances, and gaming consoles. Whether you're looking for the latest tech or just browsing the endless rows of gadgets, Yodobashi Camera is a must-visit for tech enthusiasts.

In addition to electronics, Akihabara is also known for its otaku (pop culture) scene, with many stores dedicated to anime, manga, and collectible figures. Shops like Mandarake and Animate offer a treasure trove of anime merchandise, from rare figurines to limited-edition art books. Akihabara is a paradise for fans of Japanese pop culture, and exploring its many shops and arcades can easily take up an entire day.

Akihabara is accessible via Akihabara Station on the JR Yamanote Line, Tokyo Metro Hibiya Line, and Tsukuba Express Line. The area is bustling with energy, and its neon signs and electronic billboards create a futuristic atmosphere that makes shopping in Akihabara a unique and exciting experience.

If you're looking for a more traditional shopping experience, Asakusa offers a glimpse into Tokyo's past. Asakusa is known for its historic temples and traditional craft shops, particularly around the famous Senso-ji Temple. Nakamise Shopping Street, which leads to the temple, is lined with small stalls and shops selling traditional Japanese goods, such as kimono, fans, and handmade crafts. The street is also a great place to find souvenirs, including local snacks, sweets, and traditional Japanese items like maneki-neko (beckoning cat statues) and daruma dolls.

Asakusa is also home to Kappabashi Street, a district known for its kitchenware shops. If you're interested in cooking or want to bring home some Japanese knives or ceramics, Kappabashi is the place to go. The shops here specialize in high-quality kitchen tools, including professional-grade knives, pots, and pans, as well as Japanese lacquerware and pottery.

Asakusa is easily accessible via Asakusa Station on the Tokyo Metro Ginza Line or Toei Asakusa Line. After shopping, you can take a relaxing stroll through Senso-ji Temple or enjoy a traditional boat ride along the Sumida River.

For those looking to explore more local and independent shops, Shimokitazawa is a neighborhood that offers a laid-back, bohemian shopping experience. Shimokitazawa is known for its vintage clothing stores, second-hand shops, and indie boutiques. The area has a relaxed and creative vibe, and it's a great place to find unique fashion items, records, and handmade accessories. In addition to shopping, Shimokitazawa has a thriving cafe culture, with many cozy coffee shops and small restaurants where you can take a break from shopping and enjoy the local atmosphere.

Shimokitazawa is located just a few stops from Shibuya on the Keio Inokashira Line or the Odakyu Line, and it's a popular destination for young people and artists looking for something off the beaten path. The neighborhood's narrow streets and vintage shops make it feel worlds away from the busy shopping districts of central Tokyo, offering a more intimate and personal shopping experience.

Lastly, for a truly comprehensive shopping experience, Roppongi Hills and Tokyo Midtown in the Roppongi district are modern shopping complexes that combine high-end fashion, art, and dining. Roppongi Hills is home to luxury boutiques, international brands, and the Mori Art Museum, while Tokyo Midtown offers a range of designer shops, art galleries, and upscale restaurants. Both complexes have a sleek, contemporary design and attract a sophisticated crowd. Roppongi Hills and Tokyo Midtown are easily accessible from Roppongi Station on the Tokyo Metro Hibiya Line and Toei Oedo Line.

Souvenirs and Unique Gifts from Tokyo

When it comes to shopping for souvenirs and unique gifts in Tokyo, the options are truly endless. From traditional Japanese crafts and local snacks to quirky pop culture items, the city offers an incredible variety of treasures that are perfect for bringing home a piece of Tokyo with you. Whether you're looking for something to commemorate your trip or searching for the perfect gift for friends and family, Tokyo has something for every taste and interest. The city's blend of modernity and tradition ensures that every shopping district has its own unique offerings, making the experience of finding the perfect souvenir a memorable part of your trip.

One of the most traditional and iconic souvenirs you can bring back from Tokyo is a maneki-neko, or "beckoning cat." This small statue of a cat with its paw raised is a symbol of good luck and prosperity in Japan, and you'll see them in shop windows, restaurants, and homes throughout the country. The most popular place to find maneki-neko is in the historic Asakusa district, particularly along Nakamise Shopping Street, which leads to the famous Senso-ji Temple. Nakamise Street is one of the oldest shopping streets in Tokyo and is filled with stalls selling traditional Japanese crafts, including maneki-neko of all sizes and colors. Some are simple, while others are intricately decorated with patterns and designs, making them a great souvenir that carries both cultural significance and charm.

Asakusa is easily accessible from Asakusa Station on the Tokyo Metro Ginza Line or Toei Asakusa Line. After browsing the shops on Nakamise Street, you can take the opportunity to explore Senso-ji Temple, one of Tokyo's most important historical landmarks. The bustling energy of the area, combined with the beautiful architecture of the temple, makes shopping for souvenirs here a truly enjoyable experience.

Another fantastic souvenir from Tokyo is traditional Japanese pottery and ceramics. Japan is known for its exquisite craftsmanship, and you'll find a wide variety of handcrafted ceramics, from delicate tea sets to intricately designed plates and bowls. A great place to find these treasures is in the Kappabashi Street area, also known as "Kitchen Town." Located near Asakusa, Kappabashi is famous for its stores specializing in kitchenware, but it's also a great place to find high-quality ceramics. Many of the shops here sell beautiful Japanese pottery, including hand-painted bowls, tea cups, and chopstick rests, which make for unique and practical gifts.

Kappabashi Street is located between Asakusa and Ueno, and you can easily walk there from either neighborhood. If you're coming by train, Tawaramachi Station on the Tokyo Metro Ginza Line is the closest stop. After exploring the shops, you can also check out Ueno's Ameya-Yokocho Market, which offers a more lively and eclectic shopping experience.

For those interested in bringing home a piece of Japanese fashion, Tokyo's vintage kimono shops offer a wonderful opportunity to purchase a piece of wearable art. A kimono is a traditional Japanese garment made from beautifully patterned silk, and while new kimonos can be quite expensive, there are many shops in Tokyo that sell vintage and second-hand kimonos at more affordable prices. One such store is Chicago, a well-known vintage clothing store located in Harajuku, which offers a range of vintage kimonos, yukatas (summer kimonos), and accessories like obi (kimono sashes). The colorful and intricate designs of these garments make them a truly special souvenir, whether you're buying one for yourself or as a gift.

Harajuku is also a great place to explore Tokyo's youth fashion scene, with its mix of quirky, bold, and eclectic styles. After shopping for a kimono, you can take a stroll down Takeshita Street to browse the many boutique shops offering everything from colorful accessories to playful streetwear.

Harajuku Station on the JR Yamanote Line is the best way to reach this area.

If you're looking for something more modern and tech-savvy, Akihabara is the perfect place to find unique gifts related to Japan's pop culture and electronics. Akihabara, also known as "Electric Town," is a shopping paradise for anime, manga, and gaming enthusiasts. You'll find countless stores selling figurines, plush toys, and collectibles from popular anime series, as well as retro video games and gaming consoles. Stores like Mandarake and Animate are particularly popular with fans of Japanese pop culture, offering a wide selection of rare and limited-edition items that are difficult to find outside Japan.

Akihabara is also the best place to find quirky electronic gadgets and high-tech souvenirs, from small robots to the latest headphones and cameras. Yodobashi Camera, one of the largest electronics stores in the world, is located here and offers everything from household appliances to the latest gadgets. Even if you're not a huge fan of anime or electronics, exploring the colorful and vibrant streets of Akihabara is an experience in itself, with its flashing neon signs and futuristic atmosphere. Akihabara Station on the JR Yamanote Line or the Tokyo Metro Hibiya Line will bring you right into the heart of this electric district.

For something truly special and handcrafted, Japanese lacquerware makes for an elegant and sophisticated souvenir. Lacquerware is a traditional Japanese craft that involves applying multiple layers of lacquer to wooden objects, creating a smooth and glossy finish. The most common items made from lacquerware include trays, bowls, and chopsticks, all of which are beautifully designed and often decorated with gold or intricate patterns. You can find high-quality lacquerware at department stores like Mitsukoshi in Ginza or in specialty craft shops across the city.

Ginza is known for its luxury shopping, but it's also home to many stores that specialize in traditional Japanese crafts. While you're in Ginza, you can also explore the area's famous food halls, which are located in the basement floors of department stores like Mitsukoshi and Takashimaya. These food halls, known as depachika, are filled with beautifully packaged sweets, snacks, and gourmet foods that make for excellent gifts. Japanese sweets like wagashi (traditional Japanese confections) or beautifully wrapped boxes of tea are popular choices. The presentation and attention to detail in depachika products make them perfect for gifting, and exploring these food halls is an experience not to be missed.

For those who want to bring home a taste of Japan, Tokyo is filled with specialty shops selling local snacks and sweets. One of the most popular souvenirs is Tokyo Banana, a banana-shaped sponge cake filled with creamy banana-flavored custard. Tokyo Banana has become an iconic souvenir, and you'll find it in every major train station and department store across the city. The cute packaging makes it an ideal gift for friends and family, and it's one of the most affordable and widely available souvenirs in Tokyo.

Another popular snack to bring home is senbei, or Japanese rice crackers. These crunchy snacks come in a variety of flavors, from soy sauce to seaweed, and are often sold in beautifully designed boxes or tins. You can find senbei at shops throughout Tokyo, especially in traditional areas like Asakusa and Ueno.

If you're looking for something truly one-of-a-kind, Tokyo's flea markets and antique shops are the best places to find unique vintage items and collectibles. The Oedo Antique Market, held twice a month near Tokyo International Forum in Yurakucho, is one of the largest and most famous flea markets in Tokyo. Here, you can browse stalls selling everything from antique pottery and lacquerware to old coins, jewelry, and vintage textiles. The market has a relaxed and friendly atmosphere, and it's a great place to find a special souvenir with a story behind it.

Yurakucho Station, located on the JR Yamanote Line and Tokyo Metro Yurakucho Line, is the closest station to the Oedo Antique Market. After browsing the market, you can explore the nearby Ginza district or enjoy a meal in one of the many izakayas (Japanese pubs) under the railway tracks near Yurakucho Station.

For visitors interested in beauty products, Japan is famous for its high-quality skincare and cosmetics, and Tokyo is home to countless stores where you can find the latest Japanese beauty trends. Shops like Matsumoto Kiyoshi and Don Quijote offer a wide range of affordable skincare and makeup products, including face masks, serums, and cleansing oils. Japanese beauty brands are known for their innovative formulations and attention to detail, making them popular souvenirs for those looking to bring home a piece of Japan's famous beauty culture.

Fashion Districts: From High-End to Vintage

Tokyo is one of the world's fashion capitals, offering a mix of high-end luxury, cutting-edge streetwear, and vintage treasures that attract fashion enthusiasts from all over the globe. Whether you're looking for the latest designer collections, seeking out unique vintage pieces, or simply wanting to explore the city's iconic fashion neighborhoods, Tokyo has something to offer every style and budget. Each district in the city has its own distinct fashion identity, and visiting these areas allows you to dive deep into Tokyo's vibrant and diverse fashion culture.

One of the most famous fashion districts in Tokyo is Ginza. Known for its luxury shopping and high-end boutiques, Ginza is where you'll find flagship stores for some of the world's top designers. The wide, elegant streets of Ginza are lined with global luxury brands like Chanel, Louis Vuitton, Dior, and Gucci, making it a paradise for those who are interested in designer fashion. The towering department stores in Ginza, such as Mitsukoshi and Matsuya, offer a curated selection of luxury goods, including high-end clothing, accessories, and cosmetics. Each floor is dedicated to different categories, with entire sections devoted to top international designers as well as Japanese brands.

Ginza is not just about shopping for luxury items, though. The experience itself is worth a visit, with its sleek and modern atmosphere that contrasts with the historical significance of the area. Many department stores feature beautifully designed interiors, with art exhibitions, cafes, and even rooftop gardens where you can take a break from shopping. The food halls, or depachika, located in the basements of these department stores, are also a highlight, offering an array of gourmet foods and sweets that are packaged beautifully—perfect for taking home as souvenirs.

To get to Ginza, you can take the Tokyo Metro Ginza Line, Hibiya Line, or Marunouchi Line to Ginza Station. Another option is to take the JR Yamanote Line to Yurakucho Station, which is just a short walk from the heart of the district. Once you've finished shopping, you can also visit the nearby Kabuki-za Theater to watch a traditional kabuki performance or explore the luxurious cafes and restaurants in the area.

For a more contemporary fashion scene, Shibuya is another must-visit district. Shibuya is known for its youthful and energetic atmosphere, and it's the place to go if you're interested in trendy street fashion. Shibuya 109, a famous multi-story fashion mall, is particularly popular among young women and offers a wide variety of shops selling the latest in Japanese street style. Each floor of Shibuya 109 is packed with boutiques that specialize in everything from casual everyday wear to bold and experimental fashion, making it a great place to discover Tokyo's ever-evolving youth trends. The mall is a symbol of Shibuya's vibrant fashion culture and has long been a destination for both locals and tourists looking for the latest fashion-forward clothing.

Shibuya's fashion scene is not limited to Shibuya 109, though. The area is also home to a number of large department stores, such as Seibu and Tokyu, which offer a broader selection of fashion, accessories, and beauty products. Shibuya Hikarie, a newer shopping complex, provides a more upscale shopping experience with a focus on sophisticated, modern fashion. Shibuya is also known for its sneaker shops, where you can find both mainstream and limited-edition shoes, making it a hotspot for sneaker enthusiasts.

The best way to reach Shibuya is by taking the JR Yamanote Line or Tokyo Metro Ginza Line to Shibuya Station. The iconic Shibuya Crossing, one of the busiest intersections in the world, is located just outside the station and serves as the perfect starting point for exploring the area's fashion offerings. After shopping, you can also check out the nearby Hachiko Statue, a popular meeting point, or visit the various cafes and restaurants that line the bustling streets of Shibuya.

For those interested in a more alternative and eclectic style, Harajuku is the place to be. Harajuku is synonymous with youth culture and street fashion, and it's where you'll find some of the most unique and playful clothing in the city. Takeshita Street, Harajuku's main shopping street, is lined with small boutiques and stores selling everything from colorful accessories to quirky, one-of-a-kind fashion pieces. The shops in Harajuku often cater to those who like to mix and match styles, combining elements of kawaii (cute) fashion with bold, edgy looks. It's a district where fashion knows no bounds, and you'll often see people dressed in elaborate outfits, taking inspiration from cosplay, punk, and gothic styles.

Aside from Takeshita Street, Omotesando, located just a short walk away, offers a more refined shopping experience. Omotesando is often referred to as Tokyo's Champs-Élysées, with its tree-lined boulevard and upscale boutiques. Omotesando Hills, a modern shopping complex, is home to high-end fashion brands and local Japanese designers. It's the perfect place to explore if you're looking for sophisticated, minimalist fashion or want to discover the latest collections from Tokyo's most talented designers.

Harajuku is easily accessible via the JR Yamanote Line to Harajuku Station or the Tokyo Metro Chiyoda Line to Meiji-Jingumae Station. After shopping, you can take a break by visiting the peaceful Meiji Shrine or strolling through Yoyogi Park, which is just around the corner from Harajuku.

For those who are passionate about vintage fashion, Shimokitazawa is a hidden gem that offers a more laid-back and bohemian shopping experience. Shimokitazawa is known for its narrow streets filled with vintage clothing stores, independent boutiques, and cozy cafes. It's a popular destination for those looking for unique, second-hand fashion pieces at affordable prices. Many of the vintage shops in Shimokitazawa sell retro clothing from the '60s, '70s, and

'80s, as well as accessories, shoes, and even vinyl records. The area has a relaxed, creative vibe, making it a great place to explore at your own pace and discover hidden treasures.

One of the best things about shopping in Shimokitazawa is the variety of stores, each offering something different. Some shops specialize in American vintage clothing, while others focus on Japanese and European styles. The sense of community and individuality is strong here, with many store owners curating their collections with great care. In addition to clothing, you'll also find small artisan shops selling handmade goods, accessories, and homeware.

Shimokitazawa is located just a few stops from Shibuya on the Keio Inokashira Line or Odakyu Line. Once you arrive, you can spend hours wandering through the charming streets, browsing the eclectic mix of shops, and enjoying the laid-back atmosphere. Shimokitazawa is also known for its live music venues and theaters, so after a day of shopping, you can check out a local performance or relax at one of the many indie cafes.

Another district worth exploring for fashion is Daikanyama, an upscale neighborhood known for its stylish boutiques and trendy atmosphere. Daikanyama has a reputation for being one of Tokyo's most fashionable areas, attracting a chic and fashionable crowd. The streets here are lined with boutique shops offering carefully curated collections of clothing, accessories, and home goods, many of which are from Japanese designers. The area's mix of modern architecture and lush greenery gives it a relaxed, sophisticated feel, making it a favorite destination for those looking to shop in a more tranquil setting.

One of the highlights of Daikanyama is T-Site, a multi-building complex that includes the famous Tsutaya Bookstore, cafes, and select fashion boutiques. The fashion shops here focus on high-quality, minimalist designs, often featuring local designers who emphasize craftsmanship and timeless style. Daikanyama is also home to several stores that sell premium denim, which is a must-try for anyone interested in Japanese fashion. The area is often compared to New York's SoHo for its cool, understated luxury and its blend of fashion, art, and culture.

To get to Daikanyama, you can take the Tokyu Toyoko Line to Daikanyama Station. The neighborhood is also close to the Shibuya and Ebisu areas, so you can easily combine your visit with a trip to these nearby districts.

Tokyo's fashion scene wouldn't be complete without mentioning Aoyama, one of the city's most upscale and avant-garde neighborhoods. Aoyama is known for its high-end fashion boutiques, contemporary art galleries, and architecturally striking buildings. The area is home to flagship stores for some of the world's most prestigious fashion houses, including Comme des Garçons, Yohji Yamamoto, and Issey Miyake, who are some of Japan's most influential designers. Aoyama's emphasis on innovation and artistry makes it a key destination for anyone interested in avant-garde and conceptual fashion.

The streets of Aoyama are quiet and sophisticated, and the shopping experience here is much more about quality than quantity. The boutiques in Aoyama often showcase cutting-edge fashion collections, blending modern design with traditional craftsmanship. In addition to fashion, Aoyama is also a great place to explore contemporary art galleries, design stores, and stylish cafes, making it a hub for creative inspiration.

Aoyama is located just a short walk from Omotesando, and you can reach the area by taking the Tokyo Metro Ginza Line, Hanzomon Line, or Chiyoda Line to Omotesando Station. After shopping in Aoyama, you can visit the nearby Nezu Museum, which is known for its collection of Japanese and East Asian art, as well as its beautiful traditional garden.

Tokyo's Quirky Shops: Anime, Gadgets, and More

Tokyo is a city where traditional culture meets modern innovation, and nowhere is this more evident than in its many quirky shops. From anime and manga to high-tech gadgets and uniquely themed stores, Tokyo offers shopping experiences unlike anywhere else in the world. For those who love pop culture, anime, electronics, and offbeat novelty items, exploring these quirky shops is a must. Not only do these shops offer products you won't find anywhere else, but they also reflect the creativity and individuality that make Tokyo such a vibrant city.

One of the best places to start your adventure is Akihabara, often referred to as "Electric Town." Akihabara is famous for its electronics shops, but it's also the center of Tokyo's otaku (geek) culture, particularly for anime, manga, and gaming enthusiasts. If you're a fan of Japanese pop culture, Akihabara is a paradise filled with stores dedicated to anime merchandise, figurines, video games, and everything in between. One of the most famous shops in Akihabara is Mandarake, a massive store that sells second-hand manga, anime DVDs, collectible figurines, and rare memorabilia. The Akihabara branch of Mandarake is spread across multiple floors, each dedicated to different categories, making it the perfect place to hunt for that elusive limited-edition figure or manga volume.

In addition to Mandarake, Animate is another must-visit for anime and manga lovers. Animate is one of Japan's largest chains of anime-related merchandise stores, and the Akihabara location is its flagship store. Here, you'll find everything from posters and keychains to exclusive anime-themed apparel and stationery. The store also hosts events and meet-and-greets with anime voice actors, making it a popular spot for fans. Whether you're looking to buy a gift for an anime enthusiast or simply want to browse the latest trends in Japanese pop culture, Animate is the place to go.

Beyond the realm of anime, Akihabara is also known for its electronic gadgets and novelty items. Yodobashi Camera, one of the largest electronics stores in Japan, offers a staggering range of products, from the latest smartphones and cameras to quirky household gadgets. The store is massive, with multiple floors dedicated to different categories, including computers, gaming consoles, and even musical instruments. If you're looking for high-tech gadgets or accessories, Yodobashi Camera is the best place to explore. You'll find everything from cutting-edge technology to fun, offbeat devices that can only be found in Japan.

Akihabara is easily accessible via Akihabara Station, which is served by the JR Yamanote Line, the Tokyo Metro Hibiya Line, and the Tsukuba Express. The area's bright neon signs and bustling streets make it an exciting place to visit, even if you're not a huge anime or tech fan. Just wandering through the maze of shops, arcades, and themed cafes is an experience in itself. Speaking of themed cafes, Akihabara is also home to numerous maid cafes, where waitresses dressed in maid costumes serve food and drinks in a playful, anime-inspired atmosphere. These cafes are a unique part of Akihabara's quirky charm and are popular among tourists looking for a fun and unusual dining experience.

For those interested in kawaii (cute) culture, Harajuku is another fantastic neighborhood to explore. Harajuku is famous for its bold and colorful fashion, but it's also home to a number of quirky shops that specialize in all things cute. Takeshita Street, the heart of Harajuku's shopping district, is lined with stores selling everything from neon-colored accessories to adorable plush toys. One of the most iconic shops in Harajuku is Kiddy Land, a multi-story store dedicated to all things cute. Kiddy Land is packed with character merchandise from popular Japanese and international franchises like Hello Kitty,

Rilakkuma, and Snoopy. The shop is a wonderland for anyone who loves cute and whimsical items, and it's the perfect place to find gifts for children or fans of Japanese kawaii culture.

Takeshita Street is also known for its many novelty stores, such as the famous Daiso 100-yen shop, where you can find an incredible variety of affordable goods, from quirky kitchen gadgets to fun stationery and accessories. Shopping at Daiso is a great way to pick up unique souvenirs without spending a lot of money, and the store's playful, colorful atmosphere makes browsing a fun experience.

If you're interested in exploring Harajuku's quirky offerings, you can take the JR Yamanote Line to Harajuku Station or the Tokyo Metro Chiyoda Line to Meiji-Jingumae Station. After shopping, you can also visit the nearby Meiji Shrine, one of Tokyo's most important Shinto shrines, or take a stroll through the peaceful Yoyogi Park, which offers a quiet escape from the busy streets of Harajuku.

For something truly unique and unusual, Tokyo's Don Quijote stores offer an unforgettable shopping experience. Don Quijote, also known as "Donki," is a discount store chain that sells a little bit of everything, from household items and cosmetics to quirky costumes and novelty goods. Each store is a labyrinth of narrow aisles packed with items, and you never know what you'll find around the next corner. One of the most popular Don Quijote locations is in Shibuya, just a short walk from the famous Shibuya Crossing. This particular store is open 24 hours a day, making it a great spot for late-night shopping.

Don Quijote is known for its wide selection of novelty goods, including unusual snacks, funny costumes, and bizarre gadgets that you didn't know you needed. The store is also famous for its tax-free shopping, which is a big draw for tourists looking to bring home unique Japanese products. Whether you're searching for a quirky souvenir or just want to explore the seemingly endless selection of items, Don Quijote is an essential stop on any shopping tour of Tokyo.

Shibuya itself is a dynamic and lively area, and it's well-known for its street fashion and trendy boutiques. In addition to Don Quijote, the neighborhood is home to many other unique shops, including Tower Records, which is one of the largest music stores in the world. If you're a fan of music, Tower Records is a must-visit, with its impressive selection of CDs, vinyl records, and music merchandise. The store also frequently hosts live performances and events, making it a cultural hub for music lovers.

Shibuya is easily accessible via Shibuya Station, which is served by the JR Yamanote Line, Tokyo Metro Ginza Line, and several other train lines. After shopping, you can also visit the iconic Hachiko Statue, a popular meeting point, or check out the nearby Shibuya 109, a multi-level shopping mall that caters to young women's fashion.

For a truly futuristic shopping experience, head to Odaiba, a man-made island in Tokyo Bay known for its entertainment and shopping complexes. Odaiba is home to several quirky and high-tech shops, including the Toyota Mega Web, an interactive showroom where you can see the latest Toyota cars and even test drive some of them on a special course. The futuristic theme continues at VenusFort, a shopping mall that is designed to resemble a European city, complete with artificial skies that change color throughout the day. VenusFort is filled with fashion stores, cafes, and novelty shops, making it a great place to spend an afternoon exploring.

One of the highlights of Odaiba is the giant life-size Gundam statue located outside DiverCity Tokyo Plaza. Gundam is one of Japan's most iconic anime franchises, and the massive statue is a popular attraction for fans. Inside DiverCity, you'll also find Gundam Base Tokyo, a shop dedicated to Gundam model kits and merchandise. The shop features an extensive collection of kits, including limited-edition items that can only be found in Japan.

Odaiba is easily accessible via the Yurikamome Line or Rinkai Line, both of which offer scenic views as they cross the Rainbow Bridge to the island. In addition to shopping, Odaiba offers plenty of other attractions, including teamLab Borderless, an interactive digital art museum, and Oedo Onsen Monogatari, a hot spring theme park where you can relax after a day of exploring.

For those looking for even more quirky shopping experiences, Nakano Broadway is a hidden gem that offers an alternative to the more famous Akihabara. Located in the Nakano district, Nakano Broadway is a multi-level shopping complex filled with stores specializing in anime, manga, and retro collectibles. The atmosphere here is more laid-back than Akihabara, but the selection of rare and vintage items is just as impressive. From old-school video games to hard-to-find anime merchandise, Nakano Broadway is a treasure trove for collectors and fans of Japanese pop culture.

Nakano Broadway is also home to Mandarake, which has several branches inside the complex. Each store focuses on different categories, such as toys, posters, and trading cards, allowing visitors to dive deep into the world of Japanese pop culture. The surrounding Nakano neighborhood is also known for its cozy izakayas (Japanese pubs), making it a great place to grab a bite to eat after a day of shopping.

To reach Nakano Broadway, take the JR Chuo Line or Tokyo Metro Tozai Line to Nakano Station. From there, it's just a short walk to the shopping complex. The relaxed and nostalgic vibe of Nakano makes it a refreshing alternative to the more crowded areas of Tokyo, and it's a great place to explore at a slower pace.

CHAPTER 10

CULTURAL ETIQUETTE AND LOCAL CUSTOMS

When visiting Tokyo, it is important to be aware of the cultural etiquette and local customs that are a fundamental part of life in Japan. Understanding these practices will not only help you navigate the city more smoothly, but also show respect for the local culture and people. While Tokyo is a modern, cosmopolitan city, deeply rooted traditions and social norms are still highly valued and adhered to in everyday life. These customs might seem subtle at first, but they play a significant role in maintaining harmony, politeness, and respect in Japanese society.

One of the first things to keep in mind when visiting Tokyo is the importance of manners and politeness. The Japanese place a strong emphasis on showing respect to others, and this is reflected in the way people interact in both formal and informal settings. Bowing, for example, is a common gesture of respect and is used in a variety of situations, from greetings to expressing thanks or apologies. While it is not necessary for tourists to bow frequently, being aware of when it is appropriate can be helpful. For instance, when meeting someone for the first time or when thanking someone for their help, a small bow is appreciated. It is also customary to bow slightly when entering or leaving a shop, restaurant, or someone's home, as a sign of respect.

Another key aspect of etiquette in Japan is the way people speak and behave in public spaces. Japanese people generally speak in soft tones, especially in crowded or enclosed spaces like trains, buses, and elevators. Speaking loudly or drawing attention to oneself is considered rude, as it disrupts the peace and quiet that is valued in public settings. When using public transportation, it is common to see passengers remain quiet, avoiding phone calls and speaking only when necessary. Even during rush hour, when the trains are packed with people, there is often a sense of calm and orderliness. As a visitor, it's important to follow this example by keeping your voice low and being mindful of others around you.

In addition to speaking quietly, it's also important to be aware of how you use your phone in public spaces. Using your phone to talk in crowded places, such as trains or buses, is considered impolite in Japan. If you need to take a call, it's best to step outside or find a more private area. Many locals will text or message quietly rather than speaking on the phone, and some trains even have designated "priority seats" where passengers are asked to turn off their phones entirely out of respect for those with medical devices. Paying attention to these rules shows that you are considerate of those around you.

When it comes to personal space, Japan is known for its emphasis on maintaining distance, even in busy places like Tokyo. While the city can be crowded, especially in areas like Shibuya and Shinjuku, there is still an unspoken understanding that people should avoid unnecessary physical contact. Standing too close to someone in line or bumping into people in crowded areas is best avoided. In elevators, trains, and buses, it's common to see people standing or sitting with their hands folded or in their laps, making as little contact with others as possible. This personal space etiquette extends to both public and private settings, and respecting it is a sign of politeness.

Another important custom to be aware of in Tokyo is the practice of removing your shoes before entering certain places. In Japanese homes, as well as in some traditional restaurants, temples, and ryokan (Japanese inns), you are expected to remove your shoes before entering. This custom is rooted in the belief that shoes carry dirt from the outside and should not be brought into clean indoor spaces. When visiting someone's home or entering a traditional establishment, you will usually find a small area called a genkan, where you can take off your shoes and store them on a rack or in a designated space. In some places, you may be given indoor slippers to wear instead. If slippers are provided, be sure to use them and avoid walking barefoot indoors.

It's also important to note that certain areas within a home or establishment may require further etiquette regarding footwear. For example, when entering a tatami room (a room with straw mat flooring), it is customary to remove even the indoor slippers and go barefoot or wear socks. This level of attention to cleanliness and tradition is something to keep in mind, especially if you plan to visit traditional tea houses, temples, or other cultural sites.

When dining in Tokyo, there are several key customs and manners to observe. In Japan, meals are seen as a time to enjoy food quietly and respectfully. Before eating, it is common to say itadakimasu, which is a way of expressing gratitude for the meal. At the end of the meal, people often say gochisousama deshita to thank the cook or host for the food. While eating, it's considered bad manners to talk with your mouth full or to point your chopsticks at someone. Chopsticks should be used carefully, and there are specific etiquette rules regarding their use. For example, it is considered impolite to pass food from chopstick to chopstick, as this resembles a funerary practice. Instead, if you need to pass food to someone, place it on a shared plate, and they can pick it up from there.

In addition, when using chopsticks, avoid sticking them upright into a bowl of rice, as this is associated with funerals and offerings to the deceased. When you are not using your chopsticks, it's polite to rest them on a chopstick holder or across the edge of a bowl, rather than placing them directly on the table. Following these simple chopstick etiquette guidelines will help you enjoy your meal in Tokyo without unintentionally offending anyone.

Another dining custom to be aware of is the practice of pouring drinks for others. In Japan, it is common for people to pour drinks for one another rather than pouring their own. If you are dining with others, it is polite to offer to pour your companion's drink, whether it's tea, beer, or sake, and they will likely do the same for you. When someone offers to pour your drink, it's customary to hold your glass or cup with both hands as they pour. If you're dining with a group, it's also common to wait until everyone has their drink before taking the first sip, and many people will say kanpai (cheers) before beginning to drink.

Tipping is another important topic to understand when visiting Tokyo. Unlike in many Western countries, tipping is not a common practice in Japan, and in fact, it can be considered rude. Whether you're dining at a restaurant, taking a taxi, or staying at a hotel, tipping is not expected. The Japanese take pride in providing excellent service as part of their job, and receiving a tip may be seen as unnecessary or even offensive. Instead of tipping, simply express your gratitude with a polite "thank you" and follow the customs of paying the bill promptly and respectfully.

One of the more surprising aspects of cultural etiquette in Tokyo is the importance of proper behavior in public baths, or onsen. If you visit an onsen or a sento (public bathhouse), there are several key rules to follow to ensure that you respect the traditions surrounding bathing. Before entering the communal baths, you must thoroughly wash and rinse your body at the shower stations provided. These stations are equipped with stools, soap, and water, and you are expected to clean yourself completely before soaking in the bath. The baths themselves are for relaxing, not for cleaning, so maintaining proper hygiene before entering is essential.

Another point to remember in the bathhouse is that towels should not be brought into the bathing area. Most people will place their small towel on the edge of the bath or keep it on their head while soaking. It's also important to remain quiet and respectful while in the communal baths, as these spaces are meant for relaxation and reflection. Many bathhouses also have separate areas for men and women, so be mindful of the signs indicating which section you should enter.

When exploring Tokyo, it's also worth noting the importance of cleanliness and waste disposal. Japan places a strong emphasis on keeping public spaces clean, and you'll notice that despite the lack of public trash cans, the streets are remarkably tidy. It's customary for people to take their trash with them and dispose of it properly at home or in designated areas. If you buy food from a convenience store or vending machine, you may need to hold onto your trash until you find an appropriate place to dispose of it. In train stations, you'll often find recycling bins, and it's important to sort your trash correctly, separating burnable items from recyclables like plastic bottles.

Lastly, Tokyo is a city where punctuality is highly valued, and being on time is a reflection of respect for others. Whether you're meeting someone for dinner, catching a train, or attending an event, arriving on time is an important aspect of Japanese culture. Trains in Tokyo are famously punctual, and the city's public transportation system runs like clockwork. If you're late, it's considered polite to apologize, even if it's just by a few minutes.

CHAPTER 11

DAY TRIPS AND EXCURSIONS FROM TOKYO

Mount Fuji: How to Get There and What to Do

Mount Fuji is one of Japan's most iconic landmarks and a popular destination for both locals and tourists. Located about 100 kilometers southwest of Tokyo, it stands majestically at 3,776 meters, making it Japan's tallest peak. Recognized as a UNESCO World Heritage Site, Mount Fuji is not just a stunning natural wonder but also holds significant cultural and spiritual importance in Japan. Many travelers visiting Tokyo make a day trip or an extended excursion to Mount Fuji to take in its beauty, experience its natural surroundings, or even challenge themselves to climb it.

Getting to Mount Fuji from Tokyo is relatively straightforward, and there are several options depending on your budget and preferences. One of the most common ways to reach the area is by taking a train. The most convenient train route is via the JR Tokaido Shinkansen (bullet train), which runs from Tokyo Station to Shin-Fuji Station. The ride takes about one hour, and from Shin-Fuji Station, you can catch a bus that will take you closer to the base of the mountain. Another option is to take the JR Chuo Line from Shinjuku Station to Otsuki Station, and then transfer to the Fujikyu Railway, which will take you to Kawaguchiko Station, a town located at the base of Mount Fuji. Kawaguchiko is a popular starting point for tourists as it offers stunning views of the mountain and serves as a gateway to many attractions in the area.

For those looking for a more budget-friendly option, buses are available from several locations in Tokyo, including Shinjuku and Tokyo Station, directly to the Fuji Five Lakes region or the Fuji Subaru Line 5th Station, which is the most popular starting point for those who plan to climb the mountain. The bus ride takes around two hours, and many buses offer comfortable seats and direct service, making it an easy and efficient way to reach Mount Fuji without the need for multiple transfers. If you plan to travel by bus, it's recommended to book your tickets in advance, especially during peak seasons, as buses can fill up quickly.

Once you arrive at Mount Fuji, there are a variety of activities and experiences to enjoy depending on the time of year and your interests. One of the most popular activities, especially during the climbing season, is hiking to the summit. Climbing Mount Fuji is a challenging but rewarding experience, and thousands of people attempt the ascent every year. The official climbing season is from early July to early September, when the weather is most favorable, and the mountain huts along the trail are open. There are several routes to the summit, but the most popular is the Yoshida Trail, which starts from the Fuji Subaru Line 5th Station. From here, the hike to the summit takes around six to eight hours, depending on your pace and the conditions.

For those who may not be interested in climbing all the way to the top, the Fuji Subaru Line 5th Station itself offers beautiful panoramic views and a chance to experience the mountain without the need for extensive hiking. The 5th Station is located at an elevation of about 2,300 meters and features a visitor center, shops, restaurants, and even a small post office where you can send postcards stamped with the official Mount Fuji postmark. From the 5th Station, there are shorter hiking trails that provide scenic views of the surrounding landscape and the opportunity to take in the natural beauty of the area without the rigors of a full ascent.

For a more leisurely experience, many visitors choose to explore the Fuji Five Lakes region, located at the northern base of Mount Fuji. The five lakes—Kawaguchiko, Saiko, Yamanakako, Shojiko, and Motosuko—offer some of the best views of the mountain and are surrounded by picturesque landscapes that are perfect for hiking, picnicking, and enjoying water activities. Lake Kawaguchiko, the most accessible of the five lakes, is a popular destination for sightseeing and offers boat rides, rental bikes, and opportunities for fishing. The area around Lake Kawaguchiko is also home to several hot spring resorts, known as onsen, where you can relax in a traditional Japanese bath while gazing at Mount Fuji.

If you visit during the spring or autumn months, the Fuji Five Lakes region is especially beautiful. In the spring, the cherry blossoms frame Mount Fuji, creating an iconic and unforgettable sight. Many photographers and travelers visit the area during cherry blossom season to capture this stunning view. In the autumn, the vibrant fall colors around the lakes add a dramatic contrast to the mountain's snow-capped peak, making it a favorite time of year for nature lovers.

Another must-visit attraction near Mount Fuji is the Chureito Pagoda, located in Arakurayama Sengen Park. This five-story pagoda offers one of the most famous postcard-perfect views of Mount Fuji, especially when surrounded by cherry blossoms in the spring. To reach the pagoda, you'll need to climb a series of steps, but the view from the top is well worth the effort. The pagoda, with Mount Fuji in the background, is one of the most photographed spots in Japan and offers a serene and spiritual atmosphere.

For those interested in the cultural and spiritual significance of Mount Fuji, a visit to the Fujisan Sengen Shrine is highly recommended. This Shinto shrine is dedicated to the goddess of Mount Fuji and has been an important site of worship for centuries. The shrine is located in the forested foothills of the mountain, and it's the starting point for the traditional pilgrimage route to the summit. Even if you're not climbing the mountain, a visit to the shrine provides a deeper understanding of the spiritual importance of Mount Fuji in Japanese culture. The peaceful surroundings of the shrine, with its towering cedar trees and tranquil atmosphere, make it a great place to reflect and connect with nature.

For thrill-seekers and families, the Fuji-Q Highland amusement park offers a different kind of adventure near Mount Fuji. This popular theme park is known for its record-breaking roller coasters, including some of the fastest and steepest in the world. In addition to the adrenaline-pumping rides, the park offers attractions based on popular anime series and has a variety of family-friendly rides and entertainment. Fuji-Q Highland is located near Lake Kawaguchiko and provides views of Mount Fuji while you enjoy the rides, adding an extra layer of excitement to the experience.

If you prefer a more educational experience, the Mount Fuji World Heritage Centre, located in Fujinomiya, is worth a visit. This modern museum offers interactive exhibits that explore the history, geology, and cultural significance of Mount Fuji. The center provides insights into the mountain's role in Japanese art, religion, and literature, as well as information about the flora and fauna that thrive in the region. The architecture of the building itself is impressive, with a design inspired by Mount Fuji, and it offers an observation deck with views of the mountain on clear days.

Visiting Mount Fuji is not just about the destination; it's about the journey and the many experiences you can enjoy along the way. Whether you're hiking to the summit, exploring the lakes, soaking in a hot spring, or learning about the mountain's cultural significance, a trip to Mount Fuji is a memorable and enriching experience. The mountain's changing appearance throughout the seasons—whether capped with snow in winter, surrounded by cherry blossoms in spring, or framed by fiery autumn leaves—makes it a destination that offers something new no matter when you visit.

In terms of logistics, it's important to plan your trip carefully, especially if you intend to climb the mountain or visit during peak tourist seasons. If you're climbing Mount Fuji, make sure to check the weather conditions, pack appropriate gear, and be aware of the altitude and physical demands of the hike. It's also a good idea to book accommodation in advance if you plan to stay overnight at one of the mountain huts during the climb, as these can fill up quickly during the official climbing season. Even if you're not climbing, it's best to arrive early in the day to avoid crowds and enjoy the peaceful beauty of the mountain.

Hakone: Hot Springs and Nature Retreat

Hakone is one of the most popular and scenic destinations for a day trip or a short excursion from Tokyo, offering a perfect retreat into nature, hot springs, and cultural exploration. Located about 100 kilometers southwest of Tokyo, Hakone is part of the Fuji-Hakone-Izu National Park and is renowned for its relaxing hot springs, or onsen, breathtaking views of Mount Fuji, and serene natural landscapes. For anyone seeking a peaceful escape from the hustle and bustle of Tokyo, Hakone is an ideal destination that combines relaxation, nature, and rich cultural experiences, making it a perfect getaway for travelers looking to unwind.

Getting to Hakone from Tokyo is convenient and relatively quick. One of the easiest ways to travel to Hakone is by using the Odakyu Railway from Shinjuku Station. The Odakyu Line offers direct trains, including the "Romancecar," a limited express train that takes you from Shinjuku to Hakone-Yumoto

Station in about 85 minutes. The Romancecar is a comfortable and scenic way to reach Hakone, offering panoramic windows that allow you to enjoy the changing landscapes as you leave the city behind and enter the lush, mountainous region of Hakone. If you prefer a more budget-friendly option, you can take the regular Odakyu Express train, which takes around two hours and requires a transfer at Odawara Station. Another option is to take the JR Tokaido Shinkansen from Tokyo Station or Shinagawa Station to Odawara Station, and from there, transfer to the Hakone Tozan Railway for the final leg of the journey.

Once you arrive in Hakone, there are many ways to explore the area, and one of the best options is to use the Hakone Free Pass, which allows unlimited access to buses, trains, cable cars, and boats within Hakone for a set number of days. This pass is not only cost-effective but also convenient, as it covers most of the transportation options you'll need to fully experience Hakone's highlights. You can purchase the Hakone Free Pass at Shinjuku Station or at Odawara Station if you're coming via the shinkansen.

One of the key draws to Hakone is its famous hot springs, which have been attracting visitors for centuries. The area is home to a variety of hot spring resorts and public baths, many of which offer stunning views of the surrounding mountains and forests. Onsen culture is deeply rooted in Japanese tradition, and Hakone provides one of the best opportunities to experience this in a tranquil and natural setting. Whether you're staying overnight at a traditional Japanese inn (ryokan) or visiting a public bath for a few hours, soaking in the mineral-rich waters of Hakone's onsen is both a relaxing and rejuvenating experience. The mineral content of the hot springs is said to have therapeutic benefits for the skin, muscles, and overall well-being, making it a perfect way to unwind after exploring the area.

If you're looking for a luxury hot spring experience, many ryokan in Hakone offer private onsen baths attached to their rooms, where you can enjoy the hot springs in privacy while overlooking beautiful natural scenery. Some of the most famous ryokan in Hakone include Gora Kadan and Hakone Kowakien Tenyu, both of which provide exceptional service, traditional Japanese meals, and private outdoor baths with stunning views. However, you don't need to stay overnight to enjoy the hot springs in Hakone, as there are many onsen facilities that are open to day visitors. Tenzan Onsen, located near Hakone-Yumoto, is one of the most popular public baths, featuring a serene outdoor bathing area surrounded by nature. The rustic atmosphere, coupled with the soothing hot spring waters, makes Tenzan Onsen a great place to experience the traditional onsen culture without an overnight stay.

Beyond the hot springs, Hakone offers a wealth of natural beauty and attractions that can be explored throughout the year. One of the best ways to take in the scenic landscapes of Hakone is by riding the Hakone Tozan Railway, which is Japan's oldest mountain railway. This charming train winds its way up the mountains, passing through forests, valleys, and hydrangea-covered hillsides. During the summer, the hydrangeas bloom along the railway tracks, creating a colorful and picturesque backdrop. In autumn, the foliage transforms the area into a stunning tapestry of reds and oranges, making the train ride one of the most popular ways to enjoy the seasonal beauty of Hakone.

At the top of the railway line is Gora, a quaint town known for its art museums and gardens. The Hakone Open-Air Museum is one of the top attractions in Gora, offering a unique blend of art and nature. The museum's vast outdoor spaces feature modern sculptures and installations set against the backdrop of the mountains and trees. In addition to its outdoor exhibits, the museum houses a large collection of works by Picasso, making it a must-visit for art lovers. The museum also has foot baths where visitors can soak their feet in hot spring water while enjoying the art and scenery, adding an extra layer of relaxation to the experience.

From Gora, you can continue your journey by taking the Hakone Ropeway, a cable car that offers breathtaking panoramic views of the surrounding mountains and, on clear days, stunning vistas of Mount Fuji. The ropeway takes you to Owakudani, a volcanic valley known for its active sulfur vents and hot springs. Owakudani is one of Hakone's most iconic spots, offering visitors a chance to see the steam rising from the ground and the distinctive smell of sulfur in the air. The area is famous for its "black eggs," which are eggs boiled in the sulfur-rich waters, turning their shells black. It's said that eating one of these eggs can add seven years to your life, making them a popular souvenir and snack for visitors.

From Owakudani, the ropeway descends to Lake Ashi, one of the most scenic areas in Hakone. Lake Ashi, also known as Ashinoko, is a beautiful crater lake formed after a volcanic eruption thousands of years ago. The lake is surrounded by forested hills, and on clear days, you can see Mount Fuji reflected in the calm waters of the lake, creating one of the most iconic views in Japan. One of the best ways to experience Lake Ashi is by taking a sightseeing cruise on one of the pirate-themed boats that operate across the lake. These boats offer a fun and scenic way to explore the lake while enjoying views of Mount Fuji, the surrounding mountains, and the picturesque Hakone Shrine.

Hakone Shrine is another must-visit spot near Lake Ashi, known for its peaceful atmosphere and striking torii gate that stands in the water along the lake's shore. The shrine itself is nestled within a forest at the foot of Mount Hakone and has long been a place of worship for those seeking blessings for safe travels and good fortune. Walking through the forested paths to the shrine offers a sense of serenity and connection with nature, and the sight of the red torii gate rising from the lake's waters is one of the most iconic and photogenic views in Hakone.

For those interested in hiking, Hakone offers several trails that take you through its stunning natural landscapes. One of the most popular hikes is the Old Tokaido Road, a historic route that once connected Tokyo and Kyoto. Parts of the ancient stone-paved road still remain, and walking along this trail provides a glimpse into Japan's feudal past. The trail passes through scenic forests and tea houses where travelers can stop for a rest and enjoy traditional Japanese sweets and tea. Along the way, you'll also encounter beautiful views of Mount Fuji, making this hike a rewarding experience for those who enjoy both history and nature.

If you're visiting Hakone during the autumn months, the area is especially beautiful with its vibrant fall colors. The trees surrounding Lake Ashi, the mountains, and the valleys burst into shades of red, orange, and yellow, creating a stunning contrast against the deep blue of the lake and the towering presence of Mount Fuji in the distance. Many visitors plan their trips to Hakone during this season to take in the breathtaking autumn foliage, which is particularly stunning around the Hakone Tozan Railway, Owakudani, and the Hakone Shrine area.

In addition to its natural beauty, Hakone is also known for its cultural attractions, such as the Pola Museum of Art, which is located in a lush forested area. This museum houses an impressive collection of European and Japanese art, including works by Monet, Renoir, and Picasso, as well as traditional Japanese paintings and ceramics. The museum's architecture is designed to blend harmoniously with the surrounding nature, making it a tranquil and aesthetically pleasing place to explore.

Nikko: Temples, Waterfalls, and Hiking

Nikko is one of Japan's most beautiful and culturally significant destinations, offering a rich blend of history, nature, and outdoor adventure. Located about 125 kilometers north of Tokyo, it's a perfect spot for a day trip or a longer excursion for those looking to experience Japan's stunning temples, waterfalls, and hiking trails. Nikko is renowned for its UNESCO World Heritage temples and shrines, scenic waterfalls, and its role as a gateway to some of Japan's most beautiful natural landscapes.

Getting to Nikko from Tokyo is quite easy, and there are a few different transportation options. One of the most convenient ways to reach Nikko is by taking the Tobu Railway from Asakusa Station in Tokyo. The Tobu Nikko Line offers direct limited express trains, such as the Tobu Limited Express SPACIA, which takes about two hours to reach Tobu-Nikko Station. This train is comfortable and offers scenic views along the way. Another option is to take the JR Tohoku Shinkansen from Tokyo Station or Ueno Station to Utsunomiya Station, where you can transfer to the JR Nikko Line, which will take you to JR Nikko Station. This route is covered by the JR Pass, making it a good option for travelers using the pass. Both stations, Tobu-Nikko and JR Nikko, are located near the main attractions, and once you arrive, you can explore the area on foot, by bus, or using a rental bike.

One of the primary reasons people visit Nikko is to explore its historical and cultural treasures, particularly the famous Toshogu Shrine. Toshogu is the most famous shrine in Nikko and is dedicated to Tokugawa Ieyasu, the founder of the Tokugawa Shogunate, which ruled Japan for over 250 years. The shrine complex is a masterpiece of architecture, featuring lavishly decorated buildings adorned with intricate carvings and vibrant colors. The Yomeimon Gate, in particular, is considered one of the most beautiful and elaborately decorated gates in Japan. It is often called the "Gate of the Setting Sun" because visitors can spend so long admiring its detailed carvings that the sun sets before they know it.

As you explore the Toshogu Shrine, you'll come across many famous symbols and carvings that carry deep cultural significance. One of the most well-known carvings is the "Three Wise Monkeys," which depict the saying "see no evil, hear no evil, speak no evil." These three monkeys are carved into the stable of sacred horses and have become a symbol of wisdom and restraint. Another famous carving is the "Sleeping Cat" (Nemuri-neko), which is located above a gate leading to Tokugawa Ieyasu's mausoleum. This small yet beautifully crafted cat is believed to symbolize peace and tranquility.
The Toshogu Shrine complex is expansive, and it's easy to spend several hours wandering through the various buildings and pathways. In addition to the shrine itself, the complex includes a five-story pagoda, treasure halls, and scenic forested areas. The surrounding cedar trees, some of which are over 400 years old, add to the sense of serenity and history that permeates the area. For those interested in learning more about the history of the Tokugawa Shogunate and the significance of the shrine, guided tours are available, and there are informative signs in English throughout the complex.

Adjacent to Toshogu Shrine is Rinnoji Temple, another important religious site in Nikko. Rinnoji was founded by the Buddhist monk Shodo Shonin, who is credited with introducing Buddhism to the Nikko region in the 8th century. The temple's main hall, the Sanbutsudo, houses large golden statues of the Amida Buddha and two bodhisattvas, Kannon and Bato Kannon, which are the principal deities of the temple. Rinnoji is closely associated with both Buddhist and Shinto traditions, reflecting the historical blending of these two religions in Japan. The temple's Shoyoen Garden, located behind the main hall, is a beautiful traditional Japanese garden featuring a pond, bridges, and seasonal flowers, making it a peaceful place to stroll and reflect.

Another must-visit site in Nikko is Futarasan Shrine, which is dedicated to the deities of the nearby sacred mountains: Mount Nantai, Mount Nyohō, and Mount Taro. Futarasan Shrine is considered one of the oldest shrines in Nikko, and its rustic, understated architecture contrasts with the opulence of Toshogu Shrine. The shrine is a popular spot for those seeking blessings for protection, good fortune, and relationships. It's also the starting point for pilgrimages to Mount Nantai, a sacred mountain that can be hiked by those seeking a more spiritual and challenging experience.

After exploring the historical and cultural treasures of central Nikko, many visitors choose to venture further into the surrounding natural landscapes, where they can experience the beauty of Nikko National Park. One of the highlights of this area is the stunning Kegon Falls (Kegon no Taki), one of

Japan's most famous waterfalls. Located near Lake Chuzenji, Kegon Falls cascades 97 meters down a rocky cliff and is surrounded by lush greenery in the summer and vibrant autumn colors in the fall. In winter, the falls can even freeze into a striking ice formation, making it a year-round attraction. There's an observation platform near the top of the falls that offers a fantastic view, and for a closer look, you can take an elevator down to a lower platform that provides a different perspective of the waterfall's power and beauty.

Lake Chuzenji, located at the base of Mount Nantai, is another natural gem in Nikko and a perfect place to relax and enjoy the scenery. The lake was formed over 20,000 years ago after a volcanic eruption, and its pristine waters are surrounded by mountains and forests, offering a serene escape from the city. You can rent a boat and take a leisurely ride on the lake, or simply walk along the lakeside trails to enjoy the fresh mountain air. In the autumn, the area around Lake Chuzenji is particularly beautiful, as the leaves turn brilliant shades of red, orange, and yellow, creating a picturesque landscape that draws photographers and nature lovers alike.

For those who enjoy hiking, Nikko offers a variety of trails that cater to different levels of experience. One of the most popular hikes is the Senjogahara Plateau, which is located in the Okunikko region, about 20 kilometers from central Nikko. The Senjogahara Plateau is a vast marshland that sits at an elevation of about 1,400 meters and offers stunning views of Mount Nantai and the surrounding mountains. The hiking trail through the plateau is relatively easy and takes about two to three hours to complete, making it accessible for most visitors. Along the way, you'll pass through scenic wetlands, forests, and rivers, and the trail is especially beautiful in the fall when the marsh grasses turn golden and the surrounding trees are ablaze with autumn colors.

Another great hiking option is the trail to Ryuzu Falls, which is located along the Yukawa River that flows into Lake Chuzenji. Ryuzu Falls, meaning "Dragon Head Falls," gets its name from the shape of the rock formations that resemble a dragon's head. The falls are surrounded by maple trees that make the area particularly beautiful during the fall foliage season. The hike to Ryuzu Falls is relatively short, but it's a great way to experience the natural beauty of Nikko's forests and rivers.

For those looking for a more challenging hike, climbing Mount Nantai is a rewarding experience. Mount Nantai is considered a sacred mountain and is one of the most important peaks in the Nikko region. The hike to the summit starts at Futarasan Shrine near Lake Chuzenji and takes about five to six hours round-trip. The trail is steep and can be difficult in some sections, but the views from the summit are breathtaking, especially on clear days when you can see Lake Chuzenji below and the surrounding mountains stretching into the distance. Climbing Mount Nantai is not only a physically rewarding challenge but also a spiritually significant journey, as the mountain has been a site of worship for centuries.

In addition to its temples, shrines, and natural beauty, Nikko is also known for its hot springs, or onsen. The area around Lake Chuzenji and Okunikko is home to several hot spring resorts where you can relax in the healing waters while enjoying views of the mountains and forests. Yumoto Onsen, located in Okunikko, is a small hot spring village with a long history of welcoming visitors seeking the therapeutic benefits of its sulfur-rich waters. Many ryokan in the area offer onsen baths, both indoor and outdoor, where you can soak and unwind after a day of sightseeing or hiking.

Nikko is also a great place to sample local cuisine, with many restaurants offering traditional Japanese dishes made from fresh, locally sourced ingredients. One of the region's specialties is yuba, which is made from the skin that forms on the surface of soy milk during the tofu-making process. Yuba is considered a delicacy in Nikko and can be enjoyed in a variety of dishes, including soups, sushi, and tempura. You'll find many restaurants in the area serving yuba dishes, making it a must-try for visitors interested in experiencing the local flavors.

Kamakura: Coastal Town and Buddhist Temples

Kamakura is a charming coastal town located about an hour south of Tokyo, and it makes for a perfect day trip or excursion for those seeking a combination of history, culture, and natural beauty. Known for its rich history, Kamakura was once the political capital of Japan during the Kamakura Shogunate from 1192 to 1333, and today it's famous for its impressive collection of Buddhist temples, Shinto shrines, and beautiful coastal views. The town is often referred to as the "Kyoto of Eastern Japan" due to its historical and cultural significance, as well as its peaceful atmosphere, which provides a serene escape from the busy streets of Tokyo. Whether you're interested in exploring centuries-old temples, enjoying a peaceful hike through the forested hills, or simply relaxing by the sea, Kamakura offers something for everyone.

Getting to Kamakura from Tokyo is easy, and there are several transportation options. One of the most convenient ways to travel is by taking the JR Yokosuka Line from Tokyo Station or Shinagawa Station, which takes about an hour to reach Kamakura Station. Another option is to take the JR Shonan-Shinjuku Line from Shinjuku Station, which also provides direct access to Kamakura. If you're staying near Shibuya, the JR Shonan-Shinjuku Line from Shibuya Station is another good option, offering a scenic and comfortable ride to the coastal town. Once you arrive at Kamakura Station, the town's major attractions are easily accessible by foot, bus, or a short train ride.

Kamakura is most famous for its iconic Great Buddha, known as the Daibutsu, which is one of the most visited attractions in the area. The Great Buddha is a massive bronze statue that stands at 13.35 meters tall, making it the second-largest Buddha statue in Japan, after the one in Nara. The statue was originally housed inside a temple hall, but the building was destroyed by typhoons and earthquakes in the 14th and 15th centuries, leaving the Buddha exposed to the elements. Today, the statue stands outdoors in the open air, creating a striking and serene sight against the backdrop of blue skies and green hills. The statue is located at Kotoku-in Temple, and visitors can even enter the interior of the Buddha for a small fee to get a closer look at how this impressive work of art was constructed. The Great Buddha is one of Kamakura's most iconic symbols and a must-see for anyone visiting the town.

Just a short distance from the Great Buddha is Hasedera Temple, another one of Kamakura's most beautiful and significant Buddhist temples. Hasedera is famous for its stunning gardens, peaceful atmosphere, and the eleven-headed statue of Kannon, the goddess of mercy, which stands over nine meters tall and is one of the largest wooden statues in Japan. The temple is situated on a hillside, and from the upper levels, you can enjoy panoramic views of Kamakura's coastline and the surrounding area. The temple's grounds are home to beautiful ponds, seasonal flowers, and tranquil walking paths that wind through the gardens, making it a peaceful retreat for visitors. In particular, the hydrangeas that bloom in June attract many visitors, as the temple's hillside is covered in thousands of vibrant hydrangea flowers. Hasedera Temple also has a cave called Benten-kutsu, which contains carved statues and is dedicated to Benzaiten, the goddess of the arts and wisdom.

Another important and historically significant site in Kamakura is Tsurugaoka Hachimangu Shrine, the most important Shinto shrine in the area. Founded in 1063 by Minamoto no Yoriyoshi, Tsurugaoka Hachimangu is dedicated to Hachiman, the god of war and the protector of the

Minamoto clan, who played a crucial role in establishing the Kamakura Shogunate. The shrine is located at the heart of Kamakura, and its approach is lined with cherry trees that bloom beautifully in the spring. The shrine itself sits at the top of a large flight of stone steps, offering views of the surrounding area. The grounds of Tsurugaoka Hachimangu also include tranquil ponds, gardens, and a museum that displays artifacts related to the history of the Kamakura Shogunate. The shrine is a popular place for traditional Shinto weddings, and it's also a hub for many of Kamakura's seasonal festivals and events, making it a lively and culturally rich place to visit.

For those interested in exploring more of Kamakura's temples, Kenchoji Temple is another must-see. Kenchoji is the oldest Zen temple in Kamakura and one of the most important Zen temples in all of Japan. Founded in 1253 by the ruling Hojo clan, Kenchoji is the first of Kamakura's five great Zen temples, known as the Kamakura Gozan. The temple complex is large and includes several impressive buildings, including the main hall (Butsuden), the Dharma Hall (Hatto), and the Sanmon Gate, which is one of the largest temple gates in Japan. Visitors can also explore the temple's Zen garden, which provides a peaceful and meditative atmosphere, and climb up to the Hansobo Shrine, which is located on the hillside behind the temple and offers beautiful views of Kamakura and the surrounding mountains.

Kamakura is also known for its natural beauty, and one of the best ways to experience this is by taking one of the many hiking trails that wind through the hills and forests surrounding the town. The Daibutsu Hiking Course is a popular trail that connects the Great Buddha with several temples and scenic viewpoints. This trail takes you through a peaceful forested area and offers a refreshing escape from the more crowded parts of Kamakura. Along the way, you'll pass small shrines, quiet bamboo groves, and scenic overlooks where you can enjoy views of the town and coastline. The trail is relatively easy and can be completed in about 1.5 to 2 hours, making it a great option for those who want to combine sightseeing with outdoor exploration.

For those who enjoy being by the sea, Kamakura's coastal location offers beautiful beaches where you can relax and enjoy the ocean. Yuigahama Beach, located just a short walk from Kamakura Station, is one of the most popular beaches in the area and is a great place to unwind, especially during the summer months. The beach is ideal for swimming, sunbathing, and even surfing, and it's lined with beachside cafes and restaurants where you can enjoy a meal or drink with a view of the ocean. Zaimokuza Beach, located nearby, is another option for beachgoers, offering a quieter and more laid-back atmosphere. Both beaches are popular spots for watching the sunset, with the ocean reflecting the warm colors of the sky as the sun sets over the horizon.

In addition to its temples, shrines, and beaches, Kamakura is also a great place to explore traditional Japanese crafts and culture. Komachi-dori, a lively shopping street located near Kamakura Station, is lined with shops selling local goods, souvenirs, and traditional handicrafts. This pedestrian-friendly street is a great place to sample local snacks, such as senbei (rice crackers) and taiyaki (fish-shaped pastries filled with sweet red bean paste), as well as pick up unique gifts to bring home. Many of the shops along Komachi-dori sell traditional Kamakura-bori lacquerware, a local craft that has been practiced in the region for centuries. You can also find shops selling handmade pottery, textiles, and other artisanal goods that reflect Kamakura's rich cultural heritage.

Kamakura's proximity to Tokyo makes it an easy and rewarding day trip, but for those who wish to spend more time exploring the town and its surroundings, there are several traditional inns (ryokan) and guesthouses where you can stay overnight. Staying in a ryokan allows you to experience traditional Japanese hospitality and enjoy a relaxing stay in a peaceful environment. Many ryokan in Kamakura offer hot spring baths (onsen) and traditional Japanese meals, providing a full cultural experience that complements the town's historical and natural attractions.

Throughout the year, Kamakura hosts various festivals and events that showcase its rich cultural traditions. One of the most famous festivals is the Kamakura Matsuri, held in April, which features traditional music, dance performances, and parades. During the festival, Tsurugaoka Hachimangu Shrine becomes the center of the celebrations, and visitors can watch performances of yabusame (Japanese horseback archery) and other traditional ceremonies. In the summer, the Kamakura Fireworks Festival is another popular event, drawing large crowds to the beaches to watch a spectacular fireworks display over the ocean.

Enoshima: Beaches and Island Getaway

Enoshima is a small island off the coast of Kanagawa Prefecture, located just an hour or so from Tokyo. It's a popular day trip destination, especially during the warmer months, offering a perfect blend of beaches, nature, history, and a laid-back island atmosphere. Connected to the mainland by a bridge, Enoshima serves as an island getaway that is easily accessible, making it a favorite spot for both locals and tourists looking to escape the fast pace of city life. With its scenic beauty, coastal attractions, and spiritual significance, Enoshima offers a peaceful retreat where you can enjoy the sea, explore historical sites, and immerse yourself in nature.

Getting to Enoshima from Tokyo is simple, and there are several transportation options. One of the most convenient ways to reach the island is by taking the Odakyu Line from Shinjuku Station to Katase-Enoshima Station, which takes about an hour and 15 minutes. The Enoshima-Kamakura Free Pass offered by the Odakyu Railway provides unlimited rides in the Enoshima and Kamakura area for one day and includes the round-trip fare from Shinjuku. This is a cost-effective option if you plan to explore both Enoshima and Kamakura. Another option is to take the JR Shonan Shinjuku Line from Shinjuku Station or the JR Tokaido Line from Tokyo Station to Fujisawa Station, where you can transfer to the Enoden (Enoshima Electric Railway) for a scenic ride along the coast to Enoshima Station.

As you approach Enoshima, one of the first things you'll notice is the long bridge that connects the island to the mainland. The Enoshima Benten Bridge offers a scenic walkway that leads to the island, and many visitors enjoy taking a leisurely stroll across the bridge while admiring the views of the ocean and the distant coastline. On clear days, you may even catch a glimpse of Mount Fuji in the distance, making the view even more breathtaking. The walk across the bridge sets the tone for your visit, providing a sense of calm as you leave the bustling mainland behind and enter the tranquil island environment.

Once on Enoshima, you'll find plenty to see and do. One of the island's main attractions is the Enoshima Shrine, which consists of three separate shrines: Hetsunomiya, Nakatsunomiya, and Okutsunomiya. The shrines are dedicated to Benzaiten, the goddess of music, art, and wealth, and they hold deep spiritual significance for the island. According to legend, Benzaiten created Enoshima Island in a single day to subdue a five-headed dragon that was terrorizing the area. Visitors can explore the shrine grounds, which are beautifully set among lush greenery and offer views of the surrounding landscape. Hetsunomiya Shrine is the most easily accessible, located near the base of the island's slopes, while Nakatsunomiya and Okutsunomiya require a bit more walking uphill, but the effort is rewarded with peaceful surroundings and fewer crowds.

For those who enjoy panoramic views, a visit to the Enoshima Sea Candle is a must. The Sea Candle is a lighthouse and observation deck that stands at the top of the island, offering sweeping 360-degree views of the coastline, Sagami Bay, and, on clear days, Mount Fuji. You can either climb the steps to the top or take an escalator known as the "Enoshima Escar," which makes the ascent to the island's peak easier. From the top of the Sea Candle, you'll be able to see the entire island as well as the mainland stretching out in all directions. It's particularly beautiful at sunset, when the sky turns shades of pink and orange over the water.

Enoshima is also known for its beautiful coastal scenery, and there are several walking paths around the island that allow visitors to take in the natural beauty of the area. One of the most popular spots is the Iwaya Caves, which are located on the southern side of the island. These sea caves have been carved out by centuries of wave action and were once considered sacred by locals. The caves are accessible via a coastal path that leads down to the water's edge, and inside, you'll find a series of narrow passages, small shrines, and statues of Buddhist figures. The caves are lit by lanterns, creating a mystical atmosphere as you explore their depths. The coastal path leading to the caves also offers fantastic views of the rocky shorelines and the Pacific Ocean.

For those looking to relax and enjoy the seaside, Enoshima's beaches are a major draw. The island is surrounded by several sandy beaches, with Katase Beach being one of the most popular. Katase Beach is located just across the bridge from Enoshima and offers a wide stretch of sand where visitors can swim, sunbathe, or enjoy water sports like surfing and paddleboarding. The beach is lined with seasonal beach huts and restaurants that offer food, drinks, and equipment rentals, making it an ideal spot for a leisurely beach day. During the summer months, the beach can get quite lively, with beachgoers enjoying the sun and sea, but it's also a great place to visit in the off-season if you prefer a quieter experience.

Enoshima also has several unique attractions that highlight its connection to the sea. The Enoshima Aquarium, located near the entrance to the island, is one of the best aquariums in the region and showcases a wide variety of marine life from Sagami Bay and beyond. The aquarium features exhibits on local marine ecosystems, jellyfish, sea turtles, and even penguins, making it a popular spot for families and marine enthusiasts. The highlight of the aquarium is its massive tank, which houses schools of fish, rays, and sharks, giving visitors a close-up view of the underwater world.

Another unique experience on Enoshima is trying the local seafood. Being an island, Enoshima is famous for its fresh seafood, and many restaurants specialize in serving local delicacies such as shirasu (whitebait). Shirasu can be eaten raw, boiled, or as part of a donburi (rice bowl) dish, and it's a must-try when visiting the island. Many of the restaurants near the island's entrance and along the main walking paths offer shirasu dishes, and you'll often see signs promoting these local specialties. In addition to shirasu, you can also enjoy other seafood dishes like grilled shellfish, octopus, and fresh fish, all of which are caught locally and prepared in a variety of traditional and modern styles.

If you're looking for a more adventurous way to explore the island's coastline, Enoshima is also a great place for hiking. The island's walking paths take you through lush greenery, rocky coastlines, and hidden viewpoints where you can enjoy stunning views of the ocean. One popular hiking route takes you from the main shrine area to the southern tip of the island, passing by the Iwaya Caves and continuing along the rugged coastline. The hike is relatively easy and can be completed in a few hours, making it a great way to see the island's natural beauty while getting some exercise.

In addition to its natural and cultural attractions, Enoshima is known for its unique festivals and events, which add to the island's charm and character. One of the most famous events is the Enoshima Lantern Festival, held in the summer months. During this festival, thousands of lanterns are lit up along the island's pathways and shrine grounds, creating a magical atmosphere as the island is illuminated at night. Visitors can walk through the island's lantern-lit paths, enjoy live performances, and take in the stunning nighttime views of the island and the sea.

Another seasonal highlight is the Enoshima Fireworks Festival, held in the summer and drawing large crowds to the beaches to watch a spectacular display of fireworks over the ocean. The fireworks reflect off the water and light up the night sky, making it one of the most anticipated events in the area. Watching the fireworks from the beach or the Sea Candle observation deck is a memorable experience that captures the beauty and festive spirit of Enoshima.

Enoshima is also known for its spiritual significance, and many visitors come to the island to seek blessings for love and romance. The island's shrines, particularly Okutsunomiya Shrine, are believed to be connected to Benzaiten, the goddess of love and beauty. Many couples visit the shrine to pray for happiness in their relationships, and there are even heart-shaped ema (wooden prayer plaques) where visitors can write their wishes for love and good fortune. The romantic atmosphere of the island, combined with its beautiful scenery and spiritual energy, makes it a popular destination for couples.

For those interested in shopping, Enoshima offers a variety of souvenir shops and boutiques that sell local goods, traditional crafts, and unique island-themed products. You'll find shops selling everything from shirasu-flavored snacks to handmade pottery, and many of the items are inspired by the island's coastal and spiritual heritage. Strolling through the island's narrow streets and browsing the shops is a great way to pick up souvenirs and support local artisans.

Disneyland and DisneySea: Theme Park Adventures

Tokyo Disneyland and Tokyo DisneySea are two of the most exciting and magical theme park experiences in Japan, offering an incredible range of attractions, entertainment, and immersive environments for visitors of all ages. Located just outside of Tokyo in Urayasu, Chiba Prefecture, these parks are a must-visit for anyone seeking a day of adventure and fun. As part of the larger Tokyo Disney Resort, both parks are designed to bring iconic Disney characters, stories, and fantasy worlds to life in a way that creates unforgettable memories for those who visit. Tokyo Disneyland and DisneySea offer distinct experiences, with Disneyland capturing the classic Disney magic and DisneySea providing a more unique, sea-inspired adventure that is not found in any other Disney Park in the world.

Getting to Tokyo Disneyland and DisneySea from central Tokyo is relatively easy and straightforward. The parks are accessible by train, with the most common route being via the JR Keiyo Line or JR Musashino Line from Tokyo Station to Maihama Station. Maihama Station is just a short walk from both Disneyland and DisneySea, making it convenient for visitors to reach the parks quickly. The journey from Tokyo Station to Maihama Station takes around 15 minutes, making the parks an ideal option for a day trip or even a multi-day excursion if you want to explore both parks fully. Once you arrive at Maihama Station, you can take the Disney Resort Line monorail, which circles the entire Tokyo Disney Resort and offers stops at both parks as well as at the resort hotels and Ikspiari, the shopping and entertainment district of the resort.

Tokyo Disneyland is the more traditional of the two parks, modeled closely after the original Disneyland in California and the Magic Kingdom in Florida. It is divided into seven themed lands, each with its own unique atmosphere and attractions. These include World Bazaar, Adventureland, Westernland, Critter Country, Fantasyland, Toontown, and

Tomorrowland. Each land offers a different experience, from thrilling rides and entertaining shows to meeting your favorite Disney characters and enjoying themed dining experiences.

One of the standout attractions in Tokyo Disneyland is "Pirates of the Caribbean" in Adventureland, a classic boat ride that takes you through scenes inspired by the famous pirate lore. This attraction, which inspired the popular film franchise, is an immersive experience with detailed sets, lifelike animatronics, and atmospheric lighting that bring the swashbuckling world of pirates to life. Another must-see attraction in Adventureland is the "Jungle Cruise," a boat ride that takes you on an adventurous journey through a lush jungle filled with exotic animals, ancient ruins, and humorous skippers who narrate the ride with witty commentary.

In Westernland, you can experience the Wild West with attractions like "Big Thunder Mountain," a thrilling runaway mine train roller coaster that races through a desert landscape of red rocks and abandoned mines. This ride is particularly popular with those seeking a bit of excitement, as it offers twists, turns, and drops that make it one of the park's most thrilling attractions. For a more relaxed experience, you can also hop aboard the "Western River Railroad" for a scenic train ride that offers great views of the park and takes you through the Westernland and Adventureland areas.

Fantasyland is the heart of Tokyo Disneyland, where classic Disney fairy tales come to life. This is where you'll find "Peter Pan's Flight," a beloved dark ride that takes you over the rooftops of London and into Neverland aboard a flying pirate ship. Another iconic attraction in Fantasyland is "It's a Small World," a charming boat ride that celebrates the unity of cultures around the world with its catchy theme song and colorful dolls representing children from various countries. Fantasyland is also home to Cinderella Castle, the iconic centerpiece of Tokyo Disneyland, where visitors can explore the beautiful interiors and enjoy stunning views from the top.

For younger visitors, Toontown is a delightful area where they can meet Mickey, Minnie, and other Disney characters in their homes. The whimsical design of Toontown, with its colorful buildings and cartoonish architecture, makes it a favorite spot for families. Here, you can take a ride on "Roger Rabbit's Car Toon Spin," a spinning dark ride that takes you through the zany world of Roger Rabbit, or visit Mickey's House and Minnie's House, where you can meet the famous mice in person.

Tomorrowland, on the other hand, is all about futuristic adventures and cutting-edge technology. One of the most popular attractions in this area is "Space Mountain," a high-speed indoor roller coaster that takes you on a thrilling journey through outer space. The park also offers "Buzz Lightyear's Astro Blasters," an interactive ride where you can help Buzz Lightyear defeat the evil Emperor Zurg by shooting laser targets as you move through the ride. Tomorrowland offers a mix of fast-paced thrills and fun, family-friendly attractions that appeal to visitors of all ages.

Tokyo DisneySea, which opened in 2001, is the second park in the Tokyo Disney Resort and is widely regarded as one of the most beautifully designed theme parks in the world. Unlike any other Disney park, DisneySea is based on exploration and adventure, with a focus on nautical themes and stories inspired by the sea. The park is divided into seven themed ports of call: Mediterranean Harbor, American Waterfront, Lost River Delta, Port Discovery, Mermaid Lagoon, Arabian Coast, and Mysterious Island.

One of the most impressive features of DisneySea is its attention to detail and the immersive environments created in each of the ports. Mediterranean Harbor, for example, is designed to resemble an Italian seaside town, complete with gondolas, cobblestone streets, and romantic architecture. Visitors can take a leisurely ride on the Venetian Gondolas, where gondoliers serenade guests as they glide through the canals. In the evening, the harbor comes alive with nighttime shows, including "Fantasmic!" which uses water, fire, and projections to tell a magical Disney story on the water.

In American Waterfront, visitors are transported to early 20th-century New York, with towering skyscrapers, a grand ocean liner, and vintage cars lining the streets. One of the top attractions in this area is the "Tower of Terror," a thrilling free-fall ride set in an abandoned hotel. The ride's spooky storyline, combined with its dramatic drops, makes it a favorite for thrill-seekers. Another notable attraction is "Toy Story Mania!," a 3D interactive shooting game that takes you through scenes inspired by the Toy Story films.

Mysterious Island is one of the most visually striking areas of DisneySea, located at the base of Mount Prometheus, the park's central volcano. This area is home to two of DisneySea's most iconic rides: "Journey to the Center of the Earth," a thrilling adventure that takes you deep into the volcanic caverns of Mount Prometheus, and "20,000 Leagues Under the Sea," an underwater exploration ride inspired by Jules Verne's classic novel.

For younger visitors, Mermaid Lagoon is a magical underwater kingdom where they can meet Ariel and explore the colorful world of The Little Mermaid. The indoor area is designed to look like an underwater wonderland, with gentle rides and playgrounds that are perfect for children. Visitors can enjoy attractions like "Flounder's Flying Fish Coaster" or watch live performances in "King Triton's Concert."

Arabian Coast is inspired by the tales of Aladdin, with its intricate Middle Eastern architecture, marketplaces, and magic carpets. Here, you can take a magical journey on "Sindbad's Storybook Voyage," a boat ride that tells the adventures of Sindbad the Sailor through beautiful scenes filled with animatronics and music.

Port Discovery is the park's futuristic port, where visitors can embark on adventurous journeys in attractions like "Aquatopia," a unique water ride that uses trackless technology to spin and glide through a pool of water, or "Nemo & Friends SeaRider," where you shrink down to fish size and explore the ocean with Nemo and his friends.

DisneySea also offers a wide variety of dining options, ranging from quick snacks to elaborate themed restaurants. Each port of call features restaurants that match the theme of the area, offering both Japanese and international cuisine. Popular spots include Magellan's, a fine dining restaurant located in Mysterious Island, and Casbah Food Court in Arabian Coast, where you can enjoy Middle Eastern-inspired dishes. Street food is also a big part of the DisneySea experience, with unique treats like the park's famous popcorn in different flavors, steamed buns shaped like characters, and seasonal desserts that reflect the park's creativity.

Both Tokyo Disneyland and DisneySea offer seasonal events and themed decorations, particularly during holidays like Halloween and Christmas. During these times, the parks are transformed with special shows, parades, and decorations that add even more magic to the experience.

CHAPTER 12

TOKYO BY NIGHT: NIGHTLIFE AND ENTERTAINMENT

The Best Bars, Clubs, and Karaoke Spots

Tokyo's nightlife is as dynamic and diverse as the city itself, offering a wide variety of options for people looking to experience the city after dark. From trendy bars and buzzing nightclubs to the quintessential karaoke experiences, Tokyo has something for everyone. Whether you're in search of a sleek cocktail bar with a stunning city view, a lively club with top international DJs, or a private karaoke room where you can belt out your favorite songs, Tokyo's nightlife scene is full of opportunities for fun and memorable nights out. The city's various neighborhoods each offer a distinct flavor of nightlife, so no matter what your style is, you're sure to find a spot that suits your tastes.

One of the best places to start exploring Tokyo's bar scene is in Shibuya, a district known for its vibrant energy and youthful crowds. Shibuya is packed with bars, ranging from small, hole-in-the-wall establishments to more stylish venues. One of the standout bars in the area is "Nonbei Yokocho," a hidden alleyway located just behind the Shibuya Station. Nonbei Yokocho, which translates to "Drunkard's Alley," is a narrow, atmospheric street lined with tiny bars, many of which only accommodate a few customers at a time. The bars here are intimate and often offer a warm, welcoming vibe, making it easy to strike up a conversation with the bartender or fellow patrons. Each bar has its own unique style, from traditional sake spots to places that serve creative cocktails, giving visitors a chance to experience a variety of drinks and atmospheres within a small space.

In addition to the more casual bars in Shibuya, there are also several higher-end cocktail bars that offer a refined drinking experience. For example, "Bar Trench" is an elegant speakeasy-style bar located in Shibuya's quieter side streets. Known for its craft cocktails and expert bartenders, Bar Trench specializes in classic cocktails with a modern twist, often incorporating unique ingredients like absinthe or rare spirits. The dimly lit interior and vintage decor create a sophisticated atmosphere, perfect for enjoying a carefully crafted drink in a more relaxed setting.

If you're looking for a more vibrant and trendy bar scene, head to Roppongi, a district famous for its international atmosphere and lively nightlife. Roppongi is home to a wide range of bars that cater to both locals and expatriates, making it one of the most diverse areas to experience Tokyo's nightlife. Bars like "Agave" offer a large selection of tequila and mezcal, making it a popular spot for those looking to sample high-quality spirits in a stylish environment. Agave boasts an impressive collection of over 400 varieties of tequila, and the knowledgeable staff are always happy to help guide you through their extensive menu.

Another popular bar in Roppongi is "Geronimo Shot Bar," a high-energy venue known for its party atmosphere and, as the name suggests, its focus on shots. This bar is particularly popular with tourists and expats looking for a lively night out, and the bar staff often encourage guests to participate in drinking games and challenges, adding to the festive atmosphere. The bar can get crowded, especially on weekends, but it's a great place to let loose and meet new people.

For those who prefer a more relaxed and upscale environment, Tokyo's Ginza district offers a more refined bar scene. Ginza is known for its luxury shopping and fine dining, and its bars are no exception when it comes to quality and sophistication. "Bar High Five" is one of the most famous cocktail bars in Ginza, regularly ranked as one of the top bars in the world. Located in a basement, Bar High Five offers an intimate and elegant setting, with bartenders who specialize in making personalized cocktails based on your preferences. There is no set menu, which allows the bartenders to create unique drinks tailored to your tastes, using high-quality ingredients and precise techniques. The attention to detail at Bar High Five makes it a must-visit for anyone who appreciates fine cocktails and a sophisticated atmosphere.

For a truly unforgettable bar experience, Tokyo is also home to some incredible rooftop bars that offer breathtaking views of the city skyline. "Two Rooms Grill & Bar," located in the Omotesando/Aoyama area, is a sleek and modern venue that features a spacious outdoor terrace with stunning views of Tokyo's skyline. The bar offers a wide range of drinks, including classic cocktails, wine, and champagne, making it a great spot to enjoy a drink while taking in the city lights. Whether you're visiting in the daytime or at night, the views from the terrace are spectacular, and the atmosphere is both relaxed and chic.

When it comes to clubbing, Tokyo is home to some of the best nightclubs in Asia, attracting world-class DJs and offering incredible sound systems, impressive light shows, and a wide variety of music genres. In the Shibuya and Shinjuku areas, you'll find some of the city's biggest and most popular clubs. "WOMB" in Shibuya is one of the most famous clubs in Tokyo and is known for its cutting-edge electronic music and top-tier DJ lineups. With a massive dance floor, an excellent sound system, and an energetic crowd, WOMB is a great spot for fans of techno, house, and electronic dance music. The club also hosts themed nights and international DJs, making it a popular destination for both locals and tourists.

Another well-known club in Tokyo is "ageHa," located a bit further from the city center in Shin-Kiba. AgeHa is Tokyo's largest nightclub, featuring multiple dance floors, outdoor spaces, and a pool, giving it a festival-like atmosphere. The club is known for its diverse music offerings, from EDM and house to hip hop and live performances. AgeHa's large outdoor area is particularly popular during the summer months, where you can dance under the stars or relax by the pool. Due to its size and high-energy atmosphere, ageHa is a favorite destination for those looking to experience Tokyo's nightlife on a grander scale.

For those who prefer a more intimate club experience, "VENT" in Omotesando is a smaller venue that focuses on underground electronic music. The club's minimalist design and high-quality sound system make it a favorite among serious music lovers who come to enjoy sets by both local and international DJs. VENT's crowd is often more laid-back compared to the larger clubs, making it a great spot for those who want to enjoy a night of music without the overwhelming size of a mega-club.

Karaoke is another essential part of Tokyo's nightlife culture and is a must-try experience for visitors. Unlike Western-style karaoke bars, where you might sing in front of a large audience, karaoke in Japan is typically done in private rooms that you can rent by the hour. This makes the experience much more intimate and allows you to sing your heart out with just your friends. One of the best places to try karaoke is in the Shibuya or Shinjuku districts, where you'll find a wide range of karaoke establishments.

"Karaoke Kan" is one of the most well-known karaoke chains in Tokyo, with locations all over the city. The Shibuya branch, in particular, is famous for its large selection of songs in multiple languages, as well as its iconic appearance in the movie Lost in Translation. Karaoke Kan offers a variety of room types, from simple rooms with basic amenities to more luxurious rooms with big screens, comfortable seating, and high-quality sound systems. You can order drinks and snacks to your room, making it easy to spend a few hours singing and relaxing with friends.

Another popular karaoke spot is "Big Echo," another major chain that offers a wide range of karaoke rooms and services. Big Echo is known for its extensive song selection, and many branches offer themed rooms with fun decor and lighting effects. Some locations also offer all-you-can-drink packages, making it an affordable and enjoyable option for groups looking to spend the evening singing and socializing.

For a more unique karaoke experience, "Lovenet" in Roppongi offers luxurious karaoke suites that are equipped with private Jacuzzis, large screens, and even massage chairs. Lovenet is a great option for those looking for a more upscale and indulgent karaoke experience, making it a popular choice for special occasions or parties.

Live Music, Jazz, and Performing Arts

Tokyo has a vibrant and diverse live music, jazz, and performing arts scene that draws both locals and visitors who appreciate a wide range of musical genres and artistic performances. As a cultural hub, the city offers numerous opportunities to enjoy everything from cutting-edge contemporary music to classic jazz, as well as traditional Japanese performing arts and modern theatrical productions. Whether you're a music lover, a jazz enthusiast, or someone interested in live performances, Tokyo has something to offer on any given night. The city's rich music culture and its long-standing appreciation for the performing arts make it a global destination for anyone wanting to experience world-class entertainment.

One of the best ways to experience live music in Tokyo is by visiting its many live houses, which are small to mid-sized venues that host performances by both local and international artists. These live houses are scattered throughout the city, especially in neighborhoods like Shibuya, Shimokitazawa, and Koenji, which are known for their indie music scenes. Shibuya, in particular, is a hotspot for live music, and you can find everything from rock and pop to electronic and experimental genres being performed here.

"Shibuya O-East" and "Shibuya O-West" are two of the most well-known live houses in the Shibuya area. These venues host a wide range of musical acts, from up-and-coming Japanese bands to established international artists. The intimate size of the venues means you can get up close to the performers, making for a more immersive concert experience. The atmosphere at these venues is lively and energetic, with dedicated music fans often filling the space. Another notable venue in Shibuya is "Club Quattro," which has a reputation for hosting some of the best live shows in the city. Known for its excellent acoustics and professional setup, Club Quattro attracts both local and international acts, with performances spanning a wide range of musical styles.

If you're interested in exploring Tokyo's indie music scene, Shimokitazawa is a neighborhood you won't want to miss. This area is known for its bohemian atmosphere, vintage shops, and thriving live music scene. Small live houses such as "Shelter" and "Club Que" are popular spots for indie rock, punk, and alternative music performances. The vibe in

Shimokitazawa is more laid-back compared to the bigger, glitzier venues in Shibuya, and it's a great place to discover new, up-and-coming artists in an intimate setting.

For those who prefer jazz, Tokyo has a long history of embracing the genre, and the city is home to some of the best jazz clubs in the world. Jazz was first introduced to Japan in the early 20th century, and since then, it has flourished, with Tokyo becoming a key destination for jazz lovers. The city offers a wide range of jazz venues, from small, smoky clubs where you can listen to traditional jazz standards to more upscale venues featuring renowned Japanese and international musicians.

One of the most famous jazz clubs in Tokyo is "Blue Note Tokyo," located in the Aoyama district. Blue Note Tokyo is part of the legendary Blue Note jazz club franchise, which originated in New York City. The Tokyo branch is known for its elegant atmosphere, world-class performances, and impeccable service. It regularly hosts top international jazz musicians, as well as Japanese jazz greats, making it a must-visit for anyone serious about jazz. The club's intimate setting allows for an up-close experience of the music, with the audience seated at tables while enjoying dinner or drinks. Blue Note Tokyo is the perfect venue for a sophisticated evening out, combining excellent live jazz with fine dining.

Another iconic jazz venue in Tokyo is "Cotton Club," located near Tokyo Station. Like Blue Note, Cotton Club offers an upscale experience with high-quality performances by both

Japanese and international jazz artists. The venue is modeled after the famous Cotton Club in Harlem, New York, and it has a classic, elegant feel with its dark wood interiors and candlelit tables. Cotton Club's lineup features a mix of jazz, soul, and funk, with performances that attract a diverse audience of music lovers.

For a more traditional jazz club experience, "The Pit Inn" in Shinjuku is one of Tokyo's oldest and most respected jazz venues. Opened in 1966, The Pit Inn has been a staple of the city's jazz scene for decades and is known for its focus on serious jazz performances. The club hosts both established and emerging jazz musicians, with performances that often include improvisational sets and experimental jazz. The Pit Inn has a no-frills atmosphere, with the focus entirely on the music, making it a favorite among jazz purists.

In addition to live music venues and jazz clubs, Tokyo also has a rich tradition of performing arts, with many theaters offering everything from classical Noh and Kabuki performances to modern theater and dance productions. Kabuki, a traditional form of Japanese theater known for its elaborate costumes and stylized performances, can be experienced at venues such as the Kabukiza Theatre in Ginza. Kabuki performances are a visually stunning spectacle, with actors portraying historical and mythical characters in a highly expressive and theatrical style. The Kabukiza Theatre is the most famous Kabuki theater in Tokyo, offering regular performances that provide an authentic cultural experience for visitors. English audio guides are available for those unfamiliar with the art form, allowing international audiences to fully appreciate the performances.

Noh is another traditional form of Japanese theater that has been performed for centuries. Known for its slow, meditative pace and minimalistic staging, Noh focuses on conveying deep emotions and spiritual themes through the use of masks, music, and movement. The National Noh Theatre in Tokyo offers regular performances, and like Kabuki, it provides English guides to help foreign audiences understand the complex stories and symbolism behind the performances.

For fans of modern theater, Tokyo also has a thriving contemporary performing arts scene. Venues like "The New National Theatre Tokyo" in Shibuya regularly host performances of contemporary drama, ballet, and opera. The theater is known for its avant-garde productions and international collaborations, making it a key player in Tokyo's performing arts landscape. Whether you're interested in watching a new Japanese play, a classic Western opera, or a modern dance performance, the New National Theatre Tokyo offers a diverse lineup of shows throughout the year.

Dance is another important part of Tokyo's performing arts scene, with venues like "SuperDeluxe" and "WWW" offering experimental performances that blur the lines between music, theater, and dance. These venues are known for their cutting-edge programming, featuring contemporary dance companies and performance artists who push the boundaries of traditional forms. The performances at these venues are often innovative and thought-provoking, attracting an audience that appreciates bold and experimental art.

In addition to these formal venues, Tokyo's streets and parks also come alive with performances throughout the year. Street performers, known as "buskers," can often be found entertaining crowds in areas like Yoyogi Park, Ueno Park, and along the bustling streets of Shibuya. These performers showcase a wide range of talents, from musicians and dancers to acrobats and magicians, providing a lively and spontaneous form of entertainment for passersby.

Night Tours and Scenic Views After Dark

Tokyo is a city that comes alive at night, offering a whole new perspective when the sun sets and the city's neon lights begin to glow. The city's blend of modern skyscrapers, historic landmarks, and vibrant nightlife districts makes it a fascinating place to explore after the day has ended. Tokyo's night tours and scenic views offer an opportunity to see a different side of the city, and there are plenty of ways to experience the magic of Tokyo under the stars.

One of the best ways to start your evening is by heading to one of Tokyo's many observation decks that provide panoramic views of the city's skyline. Tokyo Skytree, the tallest structure in Japan, is a must-visit for those looking for breathtaking views. Standing at 634 meters, Skytree offers two observation decks—one at 350 meters and another at 450 meters. At night, the view from these decks is stunning, as the city below transforms into a sea of twinkling lights. The sprawling urban landscape of Tokyo stretches out in all directions, and on clear nights, you can even see the faint outline of Mount Fuji in the distance. Skytree also lights up at night, making it a beautiful sight from the outside as well. Inside, the elevators to the observation deck are illuminated with soft colors, adding to the experience of rising above the city for a bird's-eye view.

Another fantastic spot for night views is Tokyo Tower, an iconic symbol of the city that resembles the Eiffel Tower. At 333 meters, Tokyo Tower offers observation decks at 150 meters and 250 meters, both of which provide spectacular views of the city. From here, you can admire the bright lights of central Tokyo, including famous districts like Roppongi and Shibuya. Tokyo Tower itself is illuminated at night, glowing with a warm orange light that contrasts beautifully with the dark sky. The tower also changes its lighting scheme for special occasions and events, so you might catch a unique light display depending on the time of your visit.

For a more elevated and luxurious experience, head to one of Tokyo's skyscraper hotels or rooftop bars. The Park Hyatt Tokyo in Shinjuku, made famous by the movie Lost in Translation, offers incredible views from its New York Grill & Bar on the 52nd floor. From here, you can enjoy a cocktail or a fine dining experience while gazing out at the glittering lights of the city below. The combination of the sleek, modern interior with the expansive night views creates a sophisticated atmosphere that makes for an unforgettable evening. Similarly, the Andaz Tokyo Toranomon Hills offers a rooftop bar with stunning night views, where you can sip drinks while overlooking the city from high above.

For those who prefer to explore the city streets, there are several neighborhoods in Tokyo that are particularly captivating at night. Shibuya, with its famous Scramble Crossing, is one of the most dynamic spots to visit after dark. The massive video screens and neon lights that surround the crossing create a dazzling spectacle as thousands of people move through the intersection at once. The energy of Shibuya is palpable, and it's a great place to wander around, visit bars, or take in the vibrant nightlife. You can also head to the nearby Shibuya Sky, an open-air observation deck located at the top of the Shibuya Scramble Square building. From here, you can take in panoramic views of the city while feeling the cool night breeze.

Shinjuku is another district that is particularly lively at night, known for its bustling nightlife, entertainment, and glowing skyscrapers. The Kabukicho area in Shinjuku, often referred to as Tokyo's red-light district, is famous for its neon signs, restaurants, and entertainment venues. Although it can get a bit chaotic, Kabukicho is a fascinating place to explore for those interested in Tokyo's nightlife. If you prefer something more relaxed, Omoide Yokocho, a narrow alleyway in Shinjuku, offers a nostalgic experience with its small, traditional izakayas (Japanese pubs) where you can enjoy yakitori (grilled chicken skewers) and a drink in a cozy, dimly lit setting.

For those who prefer a more organized way of exploring the city at night, several night tours offer guided experiences that showcase Tokyo's highlights after dark. One popular option is the Tokyo Bay Night Cruise, which offers a scenic boat ride around Tokyo Bay while taking in views of the city's waterfront skyline. The cruise passes by landmarks such as Rainbow Bridge, Odaiba, and Tokyo Tower, all illuminated and reflecting off the water. Some cruises also offer dinner or drinks onboard, allowing you to enjoy a meal while taking in the views. A night cruise on Tokyo Bay is a relaxing and romantic way to see the city from a different perspective, with the calm waters providing a beautiful contrast to the bright lights of the city.

Another popular night tour option is a guided walking tour of Tokyo's historic Asakusa district. While Asakusa is best known for its traditional charm and the famous Senso-ji Temple, visiting this area at night offers a completely different experience. Senso-ji Temple, with its iconic red lanterns, is beautifully illuminated after dark, creating a serene and almost mystical atmosphere. The streets around the temple are much quieter at night, allowing you to explore the area without the usual crowds of tourists. Many tours also include a visit to the nearby Tokyo Skytree for views from above, making it a great way to experience both the old and new sides of Tokyo in one evening.

For a more offbeat night tour experience, you can also join one of Tokyo's famous "ghost tours." These tours take you through some of Tokyo's most haunted spots, sharing eerie stories of the city's supernatural history. The tour guides often dress in traditional Japanese ghost costumes, adding to the spooky atmosphere as you explore temples, shrines, and hidden corners of the city after dark. While this may not be for everyone, it's a unique way to experience a different side of Tokyo's history and folklore.

Odaiba, a futuristic island located in Tokyo Bay, is another great spot for scenic night views. Odaiba is home to several attractions that are beautifully lit up after dark, including the Rainbow Bridge, the futuristic buildings of the Telecom Center, and the giant Ferris wheel known as the Daikanransha. The view of Rainbow Bridge from Odaiba is particularly striking, as the bridge is illuminated with colorful lights that change throughout the evening. You can stroll along Odaiba's waterfront, visit the various shopping malls and entertainment centers, or take a ride on the Ferris wheel for a panoramic view of Tokyo Bay at night.

In addition to the man-made lights of Tokyo, you can also enjoy some of the city's natural beauty after dark. Yoyogi Park, for example, offers a peaceful retreat in the middle of the city, and walking through the park at night can be a calming experience. During certain times of the year, Tokyo's parks are illuminated with seasonal light displays, known as illuminations. These light displays are especially popular during the winter months and Christmas season, with areas like Shibuya, Roppongi, and Tokyo Midtown transformed into magical wonderlands filled with millions of sparkling lights. The illuminations often feature elaborate themes, and they attract both locals and tourists who come to enjoy the festive atmosphere.

Another natural spot to visit at night is the Sumida River, where you can take a leisurely stroll along the riverside promenade. The Sumida River is particularly beautiful at night when the lights from nearby buildings and bridges reflect off the water. You can walk along the river from Asakusa to Tokyo Skytree, taking in the peaceful ambiance and scenic views along the way. In the summer months, the Sumida River is also the site of the Sumida River Fireworks Festival, one of the largest and most famous fireworks displays in Japan.

No visit to Tokyo at night would be complete without experiencing the city's vibrant entertainment districts, which offer a variety of options for dining, drinking, and socializing. Roppongi, in particular, is known for its international nightlife scene, with bars, clubs, and restaurants that cater to both locals and expatriates. Roppongi Hills, a large shopping and entertainment complex, is beautifully illuminated at night, offering great views of Tokyo Tower and the city skyline from its outdoor terraces. The area is also home to several high-end restaurants and rooftop bars, where you can enjoy a meal or a drink with stunning views of the city below.

Tokyo's Best Theaters, Movies, and Kabuki Shows

Tokyo is a city where tradition and modernity blend seamlessly, and this is reflected in its rich and diverse theater, movie, and performance scene. The city is home to some of Japan's most famous theaters, each with its own unique offerings, making it an ideal destination for anyone who loves performing arts or cinema.

Kabuki is one of Japan's oldest and most celebrated forms of traditional theater, and Tokyo is home to Kabukiza Theatre, the most famous venue for Kabuki performances in the country. Located in the upscale Ginza district, Kabukiza Theatre has been a cultural landmark for centuries and continues to be a hub for those interested in this highly stylized form of Japanese drama. Kabuki is known for its elaborate costumes, exaggerated gestures, and dramatic storytelling, often based on historical events, legends, and traditional folklore. The performances are rich with symbolism and often feature a combination of acting, music, and dance, making it a unique experience for anyone unfamiliar with this type of theater.

Visiting Kabukiza Theatre is a wonderful way to immerse yourself in Japan's traditional performing arts. The theater itself is an architectural marvel, blending traditional Japanese design with modern elements. Inside, the theater features tiered seating, with box seats and a mezzanine level, allowing for an unobstructed view of the stage. Kabuki performances are typically divided into multiple acts, and each act can last anywhere from 30 minutes to several hours. For those who are new to Kabuki, the theater offers an option to purchase tickets for individual acts, allowing you to experience a portion of the show without committing to a full performance, which can sometimes last all day. English audio guides are available, providing translations and explanations of the plot, making it accessible even for those unfamiliar with the language or the cultural context.

In addition to Kabuki, Tokyo also offers Noh and Bunraku, two other traditional forms of Japanese theater. Noh, which is the oldest form of Japanese theater, is a highly ritualistic performance art that incorporates music, dance, and drama. Noh performances are slow-paced and meditative, with actors wearing elaborate masks that represent different characters. The National Noh Theatre in Sendagaya, Shibuya, is the best place to watch these performances in Tokyo. The theater is known for its serene atmosphere and the skillful performances of its actors, who convey deep emotions through minimalist movements and gestures. Like Kabuki, Noh performances also provide English translations to help international visitors understand the complex narratives.

Bunraku, or traditional Japanese puppet theater, is another fascinating art form that can be experienced in Tokyo. The National Theatre, located near Hanzomon, is the premier venue for Bunraku performances. In Bunraku, large, lifelike puppets are manipulated by skilled puppeteers, while a narrator and musicians provide the dialogue and musical accompaniment. The puppeteers are visible on stage but dressed in black to blend into the background. Bunraku performances are highly intricate and require years of training to master, making them a mesmerizing spectacle for the audience.

For those who prefer contemporary theater, Tokyo has a thriving modern theater scene, with a variety of venues offering everything from traditional plays to experimental performances. The New National Theatre Tokyo in Shibuya is one of the city's premier venues for contemporary performing arts, hosting a wide range of productions including drama, opera, ballet, and modern dance. The theater is known for its cutting-edge productions and international collaborations, bringing together artists from Japan and abroad. The building itself is a modern architectural masterpiece, with spacious performance halls and state-of-the-art facilities that make it a top destination for anyone interested in modern theater or performing arts.

Another notable venue for contemporary theater is the Setagaya Public Theatre, located in the hip district of Sangenjaya. This theater focuses on contemporary drama and dance, often featuring bold and experimental productions that push the boundaries of traditional performance art. The intimate size of the theater allows for a close connection between the performers and the audience, creating an engaging and immersive experience. The Setagaya Public Theatre is particularly known for its emphasis on fostering new talent and supporting emerging artists, making it a great place to see innovative performances by up-and-coming creators.

Tokyo is also home to a number of smaller, independent theaters that offer a more intimate and alternative theater experience. Shimokitazawa, a trendy neighborhood known for its bohemian atmosphere, is a hotspot for independent theater productions. The area is filled with small, experimental theaters and performance spaces where you can catch a wide variety of shows, from fringe theater to contemporary dance. Many of these performances are in Japanese, but the artistic expression and creativity often transcend language barriers, making them enjoyable for an international audience.

In addition to live theater, Tokyo boasts an impressive array of movie theaters, ranging from small, independent cinemas to massive multiplexes showing the latest Hollywood blockbusters and Japanese films. For movie lovers, visiting a cinema in Tokyo is an experience in itself. The city's cinemas are known for their comfortable seating, advanced sound systems, and impeccably clean facilities. Many theaters also offer 4D screenings, where you can experience films with moving seats, wind, scents, and water effects, adding an extra layer of immersion to the movie-watching experience.

One of the most famous movie theaters in Tokyo is the TOHO Cinemas in Shinjuku, which is recognizable by the giant Godzilla statue perched on top of the building. TOHO Cinemas is part of a nationwide chain, and its Shinjuku location is one of the largest and most popular in the city. The theater screens both Japanese and international films, and many movies are shown with English subtitles, making it accessible to non-Japanese speakers. The IMAX screen at TOHO Cinemas is particularly impressive, offering an unparalleled viewing experience for action-packed films and major releases.

Another unique cinema experience can be found at the Shin-Bungeiza theater in Ikebukuro, which specializes in screening classic films, independent movies, and retrospectives. If you're a fan of Japanese cinema, Shin-Bungeiza is the place to go to catch older films by renowned directors like Akira Kurosawa or Yasujirō Ozu. The theater often hosts special events and all-night screenings, where you can watch a series of films in one sitting, complete with vintage film posters and an old-school cinema vibe.

For those who enjoy independent and arthouse films, the Uplink cinema in Shibuya offers an eclectic mix of independent Japanese and international films. Uplink is a small, cozy cinema with a focus on experimental and avant-garde films, as well as documentaries and art films that you might not find in larger, mainstream cinemas. In addition to its film screenings, Uplink also has an attached gallery space and café, making it a great spot for a more relaxed and artsy movie experience.

For a more luxurious cinema experience, Tokyo also offers premium cinemas like the "TOHO Cinemas Premium" in Roppongi Hills, where you can enjoy reclining seats, gourmet food options, and private viewing boxes. These premium cinemas are perfect for those looking to elevate their movie-going experience and enjoy a night of indulgence. The screens at these theaters are large, and the sound systems are state-of-the-art, making them ideal for watching high-budget films with stunning visuals and sound effects.

CHAPTER 13

NATURE AND OUTDOOR ACTIVITIES IN TOKYO

Parks and Gardens: Peaceful Retreats in the City

Tokyo may be known for its skyscrapers, bustling streets, and fast-paced lifestyle, but the city is also a gateway to some incredible hiking trails and outdoor adventures. Just beyond the urban sprawl, nature lovers will find a variety of landscapes, from towering mountains and lush forests to rivers and serene lakes, all offering a peaceful escape from city life.

One of the most popular hiking destinations near Tokyo is Mount Takao, located just an hour from the city by train. Mount Takao is a great option for both beginner hikers and those looking for a quick outdoor getaway. The mountain offers a variety of trails, with the most popular being Trail 1, which leads to the summit in about 90 minutes. This trail is well-maintained and relatively easy, making it accessible to hikers of all levels. Along the way, you'll pass through beautiful forests and encounter various points of interest, such as Yakuoin Temple, a Buddhist temple located halfway up the mountain. The temple is a serene place to stop, explore, and appreciate the spiritual atmosphere of the area.

As you continue your ascent, you'll reach the summit of Mount Takao, which stands at 599 meters. From the top, you'll be rewarded with breathtaking views of Tokyo on clear days, and if the weather is especially good, you may even catch a glimpse of Mount Fuji in the distance. Mount Takao is particularly beautiful in the autumn when the leaves turn shades of red, orange, and yellow, creating a stunning backdrop for hikers. In addition to the hiking trails, Mount Takao also has a cable car and chair lift for those who prefer a more relaxed journey to the top, making it a versatile destination for families or casual visitors.

For more experienced hikers looking for a challenging adventure, Mount Mitake offers a more rugged and scenic hiking experience. Located in the Okutama region, about two hours from central Tokyo, Mount Mitake is part of Chichibu-Tama-Kai National Park, an area known for its mountainous terrain and unspoiled nature. To reach the summit, hikers can take a cable car from the base of the mountain, followed by a moderate hike through dense forests and ancient cedar trees. Along the way, you'll encounter the Musashi Mitake Shrine, a centuries-old Shinto shrine perched near the summit. The shrine is a popular destination for spiritual pilgrims and offers stunning views of the surrounding mountains.

From Mount Mitake, hikers can continue on to the Rock Garden, a picturesque area with moss-covered rocks, flowing streams, and small waterfalls. The trail through the Rock Garden is particularly peaceful, and the sound of the water creates a calming atmosphere as you make your way through the lush greenery. For those seeking an even greater challenge, there are connecting trails from Mount Mitake to Mount

Odake, which is another nearby peak offering panoramic views of the Okutama region. The entire hike can take several hours, but the reward is a deep sense of connection to nature and the opportunity to explore some of Tokyo's most beautiful and remote landscapes.

Another popular hiking destination near Tokyo is Mount Tsukuba, located about 90 minutes from the city. Mount Tsukuba is unique because it consists of two peaks: Nantai and Nyotai, which are often referred to as the "male" and "female" peaks. The mountain is considered sacred in Japanese mythology and is known for its stunning views of the Kanto Plain and the city of Tsukuba below. There are several hiking trails to choose from, with varying degrees of difficulty. The trail to the summit is relatively steep in some areas, but hikers are rewarded with breathtaking views at the top. For those who want to take it easy, a cable car and a ropeway are available, offering scenic rides up the mountain.

Mount Tsukuba is particularly famous for its seasonal beauty, especially during the spring when the azaleas bloom, covering the mountain in vibrant colors. In autumn, the changing leaves create a picturesque landscape that attracts hikers from all over. The mountain is also home to Tsukubasan Shrine, which is located at the foot of the mountain and is dedicated to the mountain's deities. Visiting the shrine before or after your hike adds a cultural and spiritual element to your outdoor adventure, making it a well-rounded experience.

For those looking to venture a bit further from Tokyo, the Tanzawa-Oyama Quasi-National Park offers a more remote and challenging hiking experience. The park is located in the western part of Kanagawa Prefecture, about two hours from Tokyo, and is known for its rugged mountains, deep forests, and clear rivers. Mount Oyama is one of the park's most popular hiking destinations and offers several trails that range in difficulty. The trail to the summit is steep and demanding, but the views from the top are spectacular, with sweeping vistas of the surrounding mountains and, on clear days, views of Mount Fuji.

In addition to the natural beauty, Mount Oyama is home to Oyama Afuri Shrine, a historic Shinto shrine that has been a place of pilgrimage for centuries. The shrine is divided into two parts: the lower shrine, which is easily accessible by cable car, and the upper shrine, which is located near the summit and can only be reached by hiking. The shrine is said to offer protection from natural disasters, and the area has a deeply spiritual atmosphere. After your hike, you can relax and unwind in one of the nearby hot spring resorts, which offer a perfect way to soothe tired muscles after a day on the trails.

The Okutama region, located on the western outskirts of Tokyo, is another fantastic destination for outdoor enthusiasts. Okutama is part of Chichibu-Tama-Kai National Park and offers a wide range of hiking trails, waterfalls, and rivers. One of the most popular hikes in the area is the trail to Mount Kumotori, which is the highest peak in Tokyo at 2,017 meters. The hike to the summit of Mount Kumotori is challenging and usually requires an overnight stay in a mountain hut, but the panoramic views from the top make it well worth the effort. From the summit, you can see not only Tokyo but also Mount Fuji and the surrounding mountains, providing a truly awe-inspiring experience.

In addition to hiking, Okutama is a great place for outdoor activities such as camping, fishing, and kayaking. The Tama River, which runs through the region, is a popular spot for white-water rafting and canoeing, offering a more adventurous way to enjoy the natural beauty of the area. There are also several campgrounds in Okutama, where visitors can stay overnight and experience the peacefulness of the Japanese countryside.

For those who enjoy exploring lakes and waterfalls, Lake Okutama is a serene and beautiful destination within the Okutama region. The lake is surrounded by forested mountains and offers a tranquil setting for hiking, boating, and picnicking. The area around Lake Okutama is crisscrossed with hiking trails, some of which lead to hidden waterfalls and secluded spots where you can enjoy the natural beauty in peace. One of the most popular trails in the area is the hike to Mito Falls, a stunning waterfall that cascades down into a clear pool. The trail to the falls is relatively easy and is perfect for families or those looking for a more relaxed hike.

In addition to these destinations, there are many other hiking and outdoor adventure opportunities near Tokyo. Whether you're looking to climb mountains, explore forests, or simply take a peaceful walk in nature, Tokyo's surrounding regions offer endless possibilities. The ease of access to these outdoor areas from the city makes it possible to enjoy a day trip or a weekend getaway without having to travel far. Hiking and outdoor activities near Tokyo provide a perfect way to escape the city and connect with Japan's incredible natural beauty. From the well-trodden paths of Mount Takao to the remote and challenging trails of the Okutama region, there is something for everyone, no matter your experience level or interests.

Hiking and Outdoor Adventures Near Tokyo

For those looking to escape the fast-paced life of Tokyo, the surrounding areas offer some of the most beautiful and accessible hiking trails and outdoor adventures in Japan. Within a short train or bus ride from the heart of the city, you can find yourself surrounded by forests, rivers, lakes, and mountain peaks that provide the perfect setting for reconnecting with nature. These outdoor activities near Tokyo not only offer physical exercise and fresh air but also provide a much-needed break from urban life. Whether you are an experienced hiker or someone just looking for a leisurely day out in nature, there are a variety of hiking spots and outdoor adventures that cater to all skill levels and interests.

One of the most popular hiking destinations near Tokyo is Mount Takao, located just about an hour from the city center. With its well-maintained trails, ease of access, and beautiful views, it's no wonder that Mount Takao is a favorite for both locals and tourists alike. At 599 meters high, it's not the tallest mountain in the region, but it provides a rewarding hike that can be completed in a few hours. There are several different trails to the top, with Trail 1 being the most popular. It's paved for much of the way, and along the route, you'll find small shrines, statues, and resting areas. As you ascend, you'll come across the Yakuoin Temple, a Buddhist temple that has been an important spiritual site for over 1,200 years. Many hikers stop here to pay their respects and enjoy the peaceful atmosphere.

The summit of Mount Takao offers sweeping views of Tokyo and, on a clear day, Mount Fuji in the distance. One of the highlights of visiting Mount Takao is the changing scenery throughout the seasons. In the spring, cherry blossoms dot the trails, while in the autumn, the vibrant colors of the leaves draw large crowds. In addition to hiking, Mount Takao has a cable car and a chair lift for those who prefer a less strenuous route to the summit. Once at the top, there are several spots where you can sit, enjoy a packed lunch, or grab a bite from one of the small eateries serving local dishes like soba noodles and mitarashi dango (rice dumplings in a sweet soy sauce glaze).

For those seeking more challenging hikes, Mount Mitake in the Okutama region offers a more rugged and less crowded alternative. Mount Mitake stands at 929 meters and is part of the Chichibu-Tama-Kai National Park, an area known for its scenic beauty and varied terrain. The hike begins with a cable car ride up to the base of the mountain, followed by a hike through ancient forests and rocky paths. Along the way, you'll pass through the Musashi Mitake Shrine, which has a history dating back nearly 2,000 years. The shrine is dedicated to the mountain's protective spirits and sits at the top of the mountain, offering hikers both cultural and spiritual experiences.

From Mount Mitake, adventurous hikers can continue to the Rock Garden, a tranquil area with moss-covered rocks, waterfalls, and clear streams. This part of the trail is particularly scenic, with the sounds of flowing water creating a peaceful backdrop to the hike. For those looking for an extended adventure, it's possible to combine the Mount Mitake hike with neighboring Mount Odake, which offers even more stunning views of the Okutama region.

The Okutama area, located on the western edge of Tokyo, is a nature lover's paradise and offers many other outdoor activities beyond hiking. Okutama Lake, surrounded by forested hills, provides a peaceful setting for a day trip. The area is ideal for leisurely walks, cycling, and fishing, with plenty of opportunities to stop and take in the scenery. There are also several well-marked hiking trails around the lake, leading to waterfalls and scenic viewpoints. One popular trail in the area is the hike to Mito Falls, a serene waterfall nestled deep within the forest. The hike is relatively easy and suitable for all skill levels, making it a great option for families or those looking for a more relaxed outdoor experience.

For hikers looking to conquer Tokyo's highest peak, Mount Kumotori offers a more challenging adventure. At 2,017 meters, Mount Kumotori is part of the Okutama mountain range and is the highest point in the Tokyo metropolitan area.

The hike to the summit is long and requires a good level of fitness, but it rewards those who make the effort with panoramic views of Mount Fuji, the Kanto Plain, and surrounding mountains. Due to the length of the hike (which can take 6-8 hours one way), many hikers choose to stay overnight at one of the mountain huts located near the summit. These huts provide basic accommodations and allow hikers to break up the trek into two days, ensuring they have enough time to enjoy the stunning views and natural beauty.

For a hike that combines both nature and history, Mount Tsukuba, located in Ibaraki Prefecture, is an excellent choice. Known as one of Japan's "100 Famous Mountains," Mount Tsukuba offers a unique hiking experience. The mountain has two peaks—Nantai and Nyotai—which are often referred to as the "male" and "female" peaks. The trails leading to the top of each peak are well-maintained and provide stunning views of the Kanto Plain, Tokyo, and on clear days, Mount Fuji. The hike to the summit is moderately difficult, but there are also cable cars and ropeways for those who want to take a more relaxed approach.

Mount Tsukuba is famous not only for its hiking but also for its cultural significance. At the base of the mountain, you'll find Tsukubasan Shrine, which has been a place of worship for over 1,000 years. The shrine is dedicated to the deities of the mountain and is a popular spot for visitors seeking blessings and good fortune. In spring, the mountain is covered in beautiful pink azaleas, making it a particularly attractive time to visit.

For outdoor enthusiasts who enjoy water-based activities, the Tama River in the Okutama region is a popular spot for rafting, kayaking, and fishing. The river flows through scenic gorges and valleys, offering thrilling rapids for those seeking adventure. Several companies offer guided rafting and kayaking tours along the river, providing all the necessary equipment and safety briefings. For those who prefer a more relaxing day by the water, there are quieter sections of the river perfect for swimming or having a picnic along the banks.

Cycling is another great way to explore the areas surrounding Tokyo, and several regions offer scenic cycling routes. One of the most popular routes is the Arakawa Cycling Road, which runs along the Arakawa River and offers beautiful views of the river, bridges, and city skyline. The cycling path is well-maintained and mostly flat, making it suitable for cyclists of all levels. Along the route, you'll find plenty of spots to stop and rest, including parks and picnic areas. The ride is particularly enjoyable in spring when the cherry blossoms along the river are in full bloom.

Tokyo's proximity to the sea also means that beach lovers can enjoy coastal activities without having to travel far. Enoshima Island, located just an hour from Tokyo by train, is a popular destination for beachgoers and outdoor adventurers alike. The island is connected to the mainland by a bridge and offers a variety of activities, including hiking, surfing, and exploring caves and temples. Enoshima is famous for its beautiful coastal views and is a great place to watch the sunset. The island's beaches are popular in the summer months, and there are plenty of cafes and restaurants where you can relax after a day of outdoor activities.

Another coastal destination worth exploring is Kamakura, a historic town known for its temples, shrines, and beautiful beaches. Kamakura offers several hiking trails that wind through the hills and forests surrounding the town, providing stunning views of the coastline and the Pacific Ocean. One of the most popular trails is the Daibutsu Hiking Trail, which connects the famous Great Buddha (Daibutsu) statue to several other historical sites, including Jochiji Temple and Zeniarai Benten Shrine. The trail is relatively easy and provides a mix of cultural and natural experiences, making it a great option for those looking to combine hiking with sightseeing.

Cherry Blossoms and Fall Foliage: Nature's Beauty

Tokyo, Japan, offers a unique blend of natural beauty and cultural experiences that captivate tourists from around the world. Among its most mesmerizing natural events are the cherry blossom season in spring and the vivid fall foliage in autumn. These two periods of the year transform Tokyo's landscape into breathtaking scenes that draw visitors to parks, gardens, and temples throughout the city. Experiencing these phenomena firsthand provides tourists with not only beautiful sights but also an opportunity to engage in Japan's deep-rooted appreciation for nature.

Cherry blossoms, or "sakura," are an iconic symbol of Japan. Each spring, cherry trees bloom across Tokyo, covering the city in delicate shades of pink and white. This short-lived display, lasting only a week or two, has become one of Japan's most cherished traditions. Cherry blossom season typically occurs from late March to early April in Tokyo, though the exact timing depends on the weather each year. The arrival of cherry blossoms is widely anticipated, and many locals and visitors engage in "hanami," which means "flower viewing." Hanami is more than just admiring flowers; it's a social activity where people gather under cherry trees to enjoy picnics with family and friends, taking in the scenery while appreciating each other's company. The custom has been practiced for centuries, embodying the Japanese belief in the beauty of fleeting moments. Spots like Ueno Park, Shinjuku Gyoen, and the Chidorigafuchi Moat are particularly popular for hanami gatherings. Ueno Park, for example, has over 1,000 cherry trees lining its paths, creating an enchanting tunnel of blooms. Shinjuku Gyoen offers a more serene experience, with spacious lawns and various cherry blossom varieties that showcase different shades of pink. The Chidorigafuchi Moat, near the Imperial Palace, allows visitors to rent boats and enjoy the blossoms from the water, offering a picturesque view as petals gently fall onto the surface.

The appeal of cherry blossoms goes beyond their visual beauty; they represent the impermanence of life. In Japanese culture, the brief blooming period is a reminder to appreciate life's transient nature, encouraging people to value each moment. This concept, known as "mono no aware," resonates deeply in Japanese society and is a significant reason why cherry blossoms are so revered. During sakura season, Tokyo also holds numerous festivals, food stalls emerge in parks, and stores sell cherry blossom-themed items, from sweets to souvenirs, making the season a multi-sensory experience for all who visit.

In contrast to spring's pastel blossoms, autumn in Tokyo presents a stunning display of fall foliage, known as "koyo." From late November to early December, the city's trees turn vibrant shades of red, orange, and yellow, offering a completely different but equally captivating view of nature. The arrival of koyo signals a time for reflection and appreciation of the changing seasons, which is another deep-rooted aspect of Japanese culture. Gardens and parks throughout Tokyo become vibrant with the colors of maple trees, gingko trees, and other seasonal foliage. Rikugien Garden, Koishikawa Korakuen Garden, and the Meiji Shrine's Inner Garden are particularly famous for fall foliage viewing. Rikugien Garden, known for its traditional Japanese landscape design, is especially beautiful in autumn, with carefully placed maple trees that light up in shades of crimson and gold. Koishikawa Korakuen Garden offers a mix of both historical architecture and natural beauty, with red maples contrasting against the stone bridges and ponds. The Meiji Shrine's Inner Garden, tucked away from the city's hustle and bustle, provides a tranquil setting for visitors to experience the beauty of autumn leaves without the usual crowds.

Unlike the bustling atmosphere of hanami, koyo viewing tends to be a more contemplative experience. Many people take slow walks through gardens and parks, appreciating the quiet beauty of autumn leaves and the peaceful surroundings. The tradition of koyo viewing has long been linked with Japanese poetry, literature, and art, reflecting a cultural appreciation for nature's cycles. During this season, some gardens and temples offer night illuminations, where the autumn leaves are lit up after sunset, creating an enchanting atmosphere. Rikugien Garden's night illumination is especially famous, with paths that guide visitors through a magical display of colors reflected on ponds and carefully designed landscapes.

For tourists, experiencing both cherry blossoms and fall foliage in Tokyo offers insight into the Japanese way of connecting with nature. These seasonal changes are more than just visually striking; they are an essential part of Japanese cultural identity. Both cherry blossoms and autumn leaves are celebrated with practices that encourage mindfulness and gratitude for nature's beauty. While the cherry blossoms embody the joy and fleeting nature of life, the autumn foliage represents reflection and change. Tourists can immerse themselves in these traditions and gain a deeper appreciation for Japan's respect for nature and the seasons.

Beyond the visual experience, both seasons offer a variety of seasonal foods that tourists can enjoy. In spring, sakura-flavored treats are widely available, such as sakura mochi (a rice cake filled with sweet red bean paste and wrapped in a salted cherry blossom leaf) and sakura-flavored ice cream.

During autumn, sweet potatoes, chestnuts, and mushrooms are in season, and food stalls often sell roasted sweet potatoes, which are a popular snack. These seasonal foods add an extra layer to the experience, giving tourists a taste of Japan's culinary connection to the seasons.

Tokyo's cherry blossom and fall foliage seasons provide visitors with a perfect blend of beauty, tradition, and culture. From the bustling atmosphere of hanami picnics under cherry blossoms to the quiet contemplation of autumn leaves, each season brings its unique charm. For those who visit, these natural spectacles are more than just sights to see; they are experiences that offer a glimpse into the heart of Japanese culture and an opportunity to appreciate nature's changing beauty.

River Cruises and Boat Rides Around Tokyo Bay

Tokyo Bay offers a range of boat rides and river cruises that allow tourists to experience the beauty of the city from the water. These boat rides are a relaxing way to take in Tokyo's skyline, appreciate the mix of modern and traditional architecture, and observe local life along the water's edge. River cruises around Tokyo Bay provide a fresh perspective on the city, different from exploring its busy streets or visiting landmarks on land. With Tokyo's unique waterways, a river cruise is an immersive experience that combines scenic views with Tokyo's cultural and historical landmarks.

One of the most popular ways to explore Tokyo Bay is by taking a boat ride along the Sumida River. The Sumida River, which flows through central Tokyo, is lined with parks, bridges, and important sites that tourists can view comfortably from a boat. The river offers routes that pass by famous landmarks such as the Asakusa district, known for the Senso-ji Temple, one of Tokyo's oldest and most famous temples. These river cruises also pass by the Tokyo Skytree, Japan's tallest structure, offering tourists a remarkable view of the tower against the cityscape. As the boat travels along the river, passengers can enjoy an uninterrupted view of the Tokyo skyline and observe daily life along the riverbanks. The relaxed pace of the boat makes it easy for tourists to take photographs and enjoy the scenery without the crowds commonly found in the city's busy districts.

For a more leisurely experience, tourists can take one of Tokyo's traditional yakatabune, or Japanese houseboats. These boats have been used for centuries as pleasure boats and provide an authentic way to explore Tokyo's waterways. Yakatabune are typically designed with tatami mats, low tables, and large windows, creating a comfortable and traditional environment for guests. Most yakatabune cruises offer meal services, where tourists can enjoy Japanese cuisine while taking in views of the Tokyo Bay. The meals often include tempura, sashimi, and other Japanese dishes that reflect the country's culinary culture. In the evening, yakatabune cruises provide stunning views of Tokyo's illuminated skyline, including views of the Rainbow Bridge and Odaiba's futuristic buildings. The combination of traditional Japanese dining and scenic views creates a memorable experience that allows tourists to connect with Japan's cultural heritage while enjoying the modern cityscape.

Tokyo Bay also offers more modern cruise options, such as the futuristic water buses known as Himiko and Hotaluna. These boats were designed by Leiji Matsumoto, a well-known Japanese manga artist, and feature unique, spaceship-like designs with large panoramic windows. These futuristic boats travel between Asakusa, Odaiba, and Toyosu, providing a comfortable and scenic ride with excellent views of Tokyo's waterfront. The Himiko and Hotaluna boats are popular choices for tourists who want to travel between different districts of Tokyo Bay while enjoying a pleasant, scenic journey. These water buses allow tourists to travel between popular destinations without the need for public transportation, making it a convenient and enjoyable option for sightseeing.

One of the highlights of taking a boat ride around Tokyo Bay is the view of the Rainbow Bridge, a suspension bridge that connects the Shibaura Pier with the Odaiba waterfront. The Rainbow Bridge is especially beautiful in the evening when it is illuminated with colorful lights that reflect off the water, creating a vibrant scene. Many river cruises and boat rides pass directly under the Rainbow Bridge, providing a unique view of this iconic Tokyo landmark. The area around the bridge is lively, with Odaiba's futuristic buildings and entertainment complexes, adding to the visual appeal of the cruise. Passengers can see the contrast between Tokyo's modern architecture and the natural beauty of the bay, making for a well-rounded experience.

The Odaiba district, located on an artificial island in Tokyo Bay, is another popular destination for boat tours. Odaiba offers a variety of attractions, including shopping malls, entertainment centers, and unique landmarks like the replica of the Statue of Liberty and the giant Gundam statue. Boat rides that travel to Odaiba give tourists a chance to view these attractions from the water, adding a different perspective to their experience. Odaiba is also home to Tokyo's largest Ferris wheel, which is visible from many of the boats and provides an eye-catching sight, especially in the evening when the wheel is illuminated. A boat ride around Tokyo Bay allows tourists to enjoy Odaiba's lively waterfront area, capturing views of its attractions from a comfortable vantage point on the water.

For those interested in a more natural view, boat rides around Tokyo Bay can also provide glimpses of marine life and natural landscapes. The bay is home to various species of fish and birds, and some cruises are designed to highlight the natural beauty of the area. There are eco-friendly boat tours that focus on environmental conservation and provide information about Tokyo Bay's ecosystem. These tours are an excellent choice for nature enthusiasts who want to learn about the bay's marine life and the efforts to protect the environment. These eco-tours give tourists a deeper appreciation for the balance between Tokyo's urban development and its natural surroundings.

Another option for tourists looking to experience Tokyo Bay is the Tokyo Bay Dinner Cruise, which offers a more luxurious experience with gourmet dining on board. These cruises typically feature multi-course meals with fresh seafood and other Japanese specialties, allowing tourists to enjoy high-quality cuisine while admiring the night views of Tokyo's skyline. Tokyo Bay Dinner Cruises often include live music or other entertainment, creating a pleasant and sophisticated atmosphere. The views from these cruises are especially impressive at night, as tourists can see the city's illuminated buildings, the Rainbow Bridge, and the reflections on the water, creating a memorable evening.

CHAPTER 14

SAFETY AND HEALTH TIPS FOR TOURISTS

Staying Safe in Tokyo: Crime and Precautions

Tokyo is widely known as one of the safest large cities in the world, offering an environment where visitors generally feel secure and can enjoy their travel experience without constant concerns about crime. However, like any major city, Tokyo is not entirely free of crime, and there are basic precautions that tourists should take to ensure their safety while traveling.

Crime rates in Tokyo are remarkably low compared to other major cities. Violent crime, such as assault or mugging, is rare, and Tokyo residents are known for their respectful and considerate behavior. Visitors will often notice that people leave their belongings unattended in cafes or on park benches, which might be surprising to those from places where petty theft is common. However, even though Tokyo has a low crime rate, tourists should remain aware of their surroundings, as petty crimes like pickpocketing can still occur in busy areas. Crowded places, such as train stations, tourist hotspots, and shopping districts, are usually where pickpocketing incidents are most likely to happen. It is advisable to keep wallets, phones, and other valuables in a secure place, such as a front pocket or a bag that closes tightly, to prevent any accidental loss or theft.

Another aspect of staying safe in Tokyo involves understanding cultural etiquette. Japanese society values politeness, and there are unspoken social rules that contribute to a peaceful and orderly environment. For instance, it's common for people to speak quietly on public transportation and avoid phone conversations. Tourists should aim to follow these norms, as respectful behavior helps maintain harmony and reduces the chance of misunderstandings or conflicts. Additionally, it's considered rude to point or gesture aggressively, as these actions may be seen as confrontational. While misunderstandings are generally resolved calmly, being mindful of local customs can help visitors feel more comfortable and respected by locals.

Tokyo's nightlife is vibrant and generally safe, but there are certain areas where tourists should be more cautious. Districts like Shinjuku's Kabukicho and Roppongi are popular for their nightlife, featuring numerous bars, clubs, and entertainment venues. While these areas are mostly safe, they do have a reputation for occasional scams, particularly targeting tourists. Some establishments in these areas may charge unexpected fees, and there have been reports of tourists being overcharged for drinks. It is wise to research reputable bars and clubs in advance, avoid going to unfamiliar establishments, and be cautious if approached by individuals offering free drinks or entry to a specific location. Additionally, staying in a group and not accepting drinks from strangers can help ensure a safe and enjoyable night out.

In Tokyo, it's common to see police boxes, known as "koban," located throughout the city. These small police stations are staffed with officers who can assist with various issues, such as giving directions, helping with lost items, or reporting a crime. If tourists ever find themselves in need of assistance, approaching a koban is a reliable option. Japanese police are generally friendly and helpful, even if there may be a language barrier. Many officers speak at least basic English, and they are accustomed to helping tourists navigate the city. In cases where language becomes a barrier, translation apps can be helpful for effective communication.

Lost items are handled with a high level of honesty in Tokyo, reflecting the strong cultural emphasis on respect for other people's belongings. If a tourist loses an item, there is a good chance it will be turned in to a lost and found location, such as a koban or the lost and found department of a train station. Tokyo has an efficient lost property system, and it's not uncommon for people to recover their belongings even days after losing them. Visitors who lose something should report it as soon as possible, providing a description of the item and the location where it was lost. The detailed system in place for lost items is an example of the respect and trust that is deeply ingrained in Japanese culture.

Tokyo's transportation system is not only efficient but also one of the safest ways to travel around the city. However, tourists should be aware of the crowded conditions, especially during rush hours in the morning and evening. During these times, the trains can become extremely packed, which may feel overwhelming for those not used to crowded environments. It's important to remain calm and avoid pushing, as everyone tries to be considerate of others even in crowded spaces. In recent years, there have been measures to prevent incidents such as inappropriate behavior, with increased surveillance and station staff monitoring the platforms. Many trains also have "women-only" cars during rush hours, designated by pink signs, which are intended to provide a safe space for female passengers. Women travelers may choose these cars to feel more comfortable, especially when traveling alone.

Tokyo's clean and organized streets contribute to its safe atmosphere, but there are still a few precautions to keep in mind when exploring the city. While traffic rules are generally followed strictly, it's essential to remain alert when crossing streets, as bicycles are commonly used and sometimes share sidewalks with pedestrians. Bicycles in Tokyo are often quiet, making it easy to overlook them, so paying attention to one's surroundings is always recommended. Tourists should also be cautious when exploring unfamiliar neighborhoods, especially at night, though Tokyo's streets are well-lit and safe for evening strolls. In some quieter areas, especially away from main streets, it may be a good idea to travel with a companion if possible.

Japan occasionally experiences natural events such as earthquakes and typhoons, which may be unfamiliar to some tourists. Earthquakes are a natural part of life in Japan, and buildings are designed to withstand tremors, so visitors should not feel alarmed if they experience a small earthquake during their stay. In the event of a more significant earthquake, hotels and public places usually have safety instructions, and staff are trained to assist. Tourists should familiarize themselves with basic earthquake safety tips, such as staying away from windows and finding shelter under a sturdy table if indoors. Typhoon season in Tokyo typically occurs from late summer to early autumn, and it's best to check weather updates, as some outdoor activities or transportation may be temporarily affected. In general, Tokyo's infrastructure is well-prepared to handle such events, but tourists should follow any advisories and remain indoors if a strong typhoon is forecasted.

Health and emergency services in Tokyo are highly reliable, and visitors can feel reassured knowing that they will receive prompt assistance if needed. Japan has an advanced healthcare system, and many hospitals have English-speaking staff or translation services for foreign visitors. Tourists should consider purchasing travel insurance that covers medical expenses in case of illness or injury. In case of an emergency, Japan's emergency contact numbers are 110 for police and 119 for medical or fire services. While calling these numbers is not common for most tourists, knowing them can be useful in unexpected situations. Japan's emergency response teams are efficient and professional, and they strive to provide assistance promptly, ensuring that visitors are well cared for.

Tokyo's reputation for safety is well-deserved, but a cautious approach is always wise. By being mindful of their surroundings, respecting local customs, and following simple precautions, tourists can enjoy a pleasant and trouble-free visit to one of the world's most exciting and secure cities. This sense of safety, combined with Tokyo's rich culture and hospitality, makes it a top destination for travelers worldwide.

Emergency Numbers and Help for Tourists

In Tokyo, Japan, tourists can rely on a well-organized system of emergency numbers and services designed to ensure safety and assistance during their visit. Knowing these emergency contacts is essential for travelers, as being able to reach help quickly can make a significant difference in urgent situations. Japan is known for its efficient emergency services, which include police, fire services, and medical assistance. Each service has its own contact number, which is simple to remember and easy to use. For tourists who may not speak Japanese, there are also support systems in place to help bridge language barriers, making these services accessible to everyone, regardless of language proficiency.

In any emergency situation in Tokyo, dialing the number 110 connects you directly to the police. The police in Tokyo are highly trained and are prepared to respond swiftly to a variety of incidents, including accidents, theft, lost items, or any situations where personal safety is at risk. Tokyo's police force is known for its professionalism, and officers are accustomed to assisting tourists. Many police stations, particularly in areas frequented by visitors, have staff who can communicate in basic English, and in some cases, other foreign languages. The police can also assist with directions or provide help if tourists feel lost or uncomfortable in a certain area. Additionally, Tokyo has numerous police boxes, called "koban," stationed throughout the city. These koban serve as small police outposts where officers can offer support to those in need. If a tourist requires non-urgent assistance, such as directions or help with minor concerns, approaching a koban is often the most convenient option. Officers in these police boxes are approachable, and tourists should not hesitate to seek help from them if needed.

In cases where medical assistance or fire services are needed, dialing the number 119 will connect tourists with emergency medical responders and fire services. This number is crucial for any health-related emergencies, accidents, or fires. When calling 119, tourists will initially be asked if they require an ambulance or fire service, as the same number serves both needs. Ambulance services in Tokyo are highly reliable and are dispatched promptly to assist those in need of medical care. Tokyo's ambulances are equipped to provide immediate first aid and transport patients to nearby hospitals for further treatment. It's important to note that Japanese hospitals may require patients to present proof of insurance or payment options, so tourists are encouraged to have travel insurance that covers medical expenses while in Japan. Language barriers can sometimes be an issue, but many hospitals have staff or interpreters who can assist non-Japanese speakers. In addition, some translation apps are useful in emergencies and can help tourists communicate essential information to medical staff.

For tourists who may feel intimidated by the language difference, Tokyo has several helplines that offer support in multiple languages. The Tokyo Metropolitan Government operates a service called the "Tokyo Multilingual Call Center," which provides assistance to tourists over the phone. This service can answer questions in several languages, including English, Chinese, Korean, and others, and is available 24 hours a day. Tourists can call this center for guidance on various topics, including emergencies, transportation, medical facilities, and even local customs. By offering multilingual support, the Tokyo Multilingual Call Center helps bridge the language gap, ensuring that tourists can receive help quickly and effectively. This service is particularly useful for tourists who may find themselves in unfamiliar situations and need advice on what steps to take.

Tokyo also has specific hotlines for tourist information that provide advice on common issues visitors may face. The Japan National Tourism Organization (JNTO) operates a "Japan Visitor Hotline" that assists tourists in need of guidance on safety, health, or general travel concerns. This hotline is available 24/7 and offers assistance in English, Chinese, Korean, and Japanese. The JNTO Japan Visitor Hotline can be an invaluable resource for tourists who encounter unexpected problems, such as lost items, illness, or general questions about their travel plans. Operators at this hotline are familiar with common tourist concerns and can provide information on topics ranging from where to find the nearest pharmacy to how to navigate transportation systems during holidays or busy periods.

Tourists who lose personal belongings, such as passports, phones, or wallets, can also receive assistance in recovering these items. Lost items in Tokyo are often turned in to local police stations or public lost-and-found centers, as Japan has a reputation for its honest and respectful citizens who frequently turn in found items. Visitors who lose an item should report it as soon as possible, providing a detailed description and the approximate location where it was lost. In most cases, contacting the nearest koban or visiting the lost-and-found department of major train stations can help tourists recover their belongings. Tokyo's train stations, airports, and shopping centers all have designated lost-and-found services, and items left on public transportation are often turned over to these centers for safekeeping.

Another important aspect of staying safe in Tokyo involves natural disasters, as Japan is prone to earthquakes, typhoons, and occasional volcanic activity. The Japanese government has implemented comprehensive systems to inform and protect residents and visitors during these events. In the event of an earthquake, tourists will often receive emergency alerts on their mobile phones, as Japan has a sophisticated earthquake warning system. Hotels and public buildings in Tokyo are well-prepared for earthquakes, with clear instructions posted in multiple languages about what to do in case of a tremor. Many hotels also provide information on emergency exits, evacuation procedures, and emergency supplies. During typhoon season, which typically occurs from late summer to early autumn, tourists should check weather updates frequently and follow any advisories from local authorities. For those staying in hotels, staff are usually trained to assist guests in case of severe weather and can provide updates on transportation or any changes to planned activities.

In more serious cases, tourists may need assistance from their embassy or consulate, especially if they experience legal issues, lose important documents, or require other urgent help. Tokyo hosts a wide range of embassies and consulates for countries around the world, providing support and services to their citizens. These diplomatic missions can assist with replacing lost passports, offering legal guidance, and arranging transportation back to a tourist's home country in emergencies. It is advisable for tourists to keep their embassy's contact information on hand during their stay in Tokyo. Knowing the location of the nearest embassy or consulate can be a helpful resource, as embassy staff are dedicated to assisting citizens in need and can provide valuable support in various situations.

Travel insurance is also an essential consideration for tourists visiting Tokyo, as it can cover medical expenses, lost items, or unexpected changes to travel plans. Many hospitals and clinics in Tokyo provide high-quality care, but medical services can be costly without insurance. Additionally, having travel insurance can give tourists peace of mind, knowing that they have financial protection in case of unexpected events. It's a good idea to keep a copy of insurance documents, as well as emergency contact numbers, easily accessible in case of an emergency.

Tokyo's reputation for safety and preparedness is well-deserved, and the city's extensive emergency services reflect Japan's commitment to protecting both residents and visitors. By being familiar with these emergency numbers and services, tourists can feel confident that help is readily available if needed. Japan's dedication to safety, hospitality, and organized assistance ensures that tourists can explore Tokyo knowing they have support systems in place for any situation.

CHAPTER 15

INSIDER TIPS AND HIDDEN GEMS

Off-the-Beaten-Path Places to Visit

Tokyo is known worldwide for its bustling city life, vibrant neon-lit districts, and iconic landmarks like Shibuya Crossing and Tokyo Tower. However, beyond these well-known sites, there are countless hidden gems throughout the city that provide a different perspective on Tokyo's rich culture, history, and daily life. These lesser-known spots offer a chance to experience a quieter, often more authentic side of Tokyo, where tourists can explore the city away from the usual crowds and uncover unique attractions that might not appear on typical travel guides.

One such place is the neighborhood of Yanaka, located near Ueno. Yanaka is one of Tokyo's few areas that survived the bombings of World War II, preserving its old-fashioned charm and traditional wooden houses. Walking through Yanaka feels like stepping back in time, as the streets are lined with traditional shops, artisan stores, and family-owned cafes. Yanaka Cemetery, one of Tokyo's largest and oldest cemeteries, is a peaceful area with cherry trees that create a beautiful scene during sakura season. Many locals enjoy taking quiet walks here, making it a relaxing spot for visitors looking to experience Tokyo's historical atmosphere. The area is also known for its temples, with some dating back centuries, and is home to a community of artists whose studios are open for visitors. Exploring Yanaka provides a glimpse into Tokyo's past and a slower pace of life rarely seen in other parts of the city.

Further south, the neighborhood of Kagurazaka is another hidden gem that offers a blend of traditional and modern influences. Kagurazaka was once a prominent geisha district, and today, its narrow streets are lined with both French-inspired cafes and traditional Japanese restaurants. The neighborhood's unique charm comes from its stone-paved alleys, which give it a timeless feel. Walking through Kagurazaka, visitors may find small shrines, hidden tea houses, and stores selling kimono or artisanal crafts. The area's historic connection to Japanese arts is evident in its architecture and the subtle, refined ambiance of its streets. Kagurazaka is also known for its annual festival, held in July, where geisha perform traditional dances, creating an atmosphere that captures the essence of old Tokyo. The district's blend of old and new, along with its tranquil setting, makes it a perfect place for tourists seeking an off-the-beaten-path experience.

In the heart of Tokyo, Kiyosumi Garden offers a peaceful escape from the city's busy streets. Located in Koto City, this Japanese-style garden is known for its serene ponds, carefully designed landscapes, and traditional bridges. Unlike Tokyo's more famous gardens, Kiyosumi Garden is rarely crowded, allowing visitors to enjoy its beauty in a quiet setting. The garden is especially lovely during the autumn season, when the trees change colors, reflecting shades of red and orange on the water. Many people come here to stroll along the stone paths or relax on benches while taking in the garden's scenic views. Kiyosumi Garden is a perfect example of Tokyo's hidden nature spots, where the beauty of traditional Japanese landscaping can be appreciated without the usual tourist crowds.

For those interested in Japanese folklore, the Toden Arakawa Line offers a unique way to see Tokyo from a different perspective. This tram line, one of the last in Tokyo, runs through quiet neighborhoods that feel worlds away from the city center. The Arakawa Line passes by various points of interest, including Asukayama Park and Oji Shrine. Taking this tram is like experiencing a slower, more relaxed side of Tokyo, where the journey itself becomes the main attraction. Passengers can observe local life as the tram moves through small streets, passing by local shops, residential areas, and parks. The Toden Arakawa Line is a rare opportunity to experience Tokyo's vintage charm, as most of the city's tram lines were replaced by subways and buses decades ago. Riding this line allows visitors to see a side of Tokyo that remains largely untouched by modern development.

On Tokyo's outskirts, the area of Todoroki Valley provides an unexpected escape into nature. Located in Setagaya Ward, this lush, green valley follows the course of the Yazawa River and is lined with trees, bamboo, and small waterfalls. Walking through Todoroki Valley feels like stepping into a forest, as the narrow trails wind through a cool, shaded environment far removed from the city's noise. The valley is a favorite among locals who come here for short hikes, picnics, or simply to relax by the river. Visitors will find Todoroki Fudoson, a small temple nestled among the trees, where they can explore the traditional architecture and enjoy a quiet retreat. Todoroki Valley is a true hidden gem, offering a natural escape that contrasts sharply with the city's urban landscape.

In the eastern part of Tokyo, the Fukagawa Fudo Temple stands out for its vibrant atmosphere and unique ceremonies. This temple, located in the Fukagawa neighborhood, is known for its "goma" fire ritual, performed several times a day. During this ceremony, Buddhist priests chant and burn wooden sticks as an offering, creating an intense and mesmerizing atmosphere filled with the sound of drums and chanting. Watching this ritual is a memorable experience, as it showcases a more spiritual and mystical side of Japanese culture. Fukagawa Fudo Temple is also home to several smaller shrines and statues, providing visitors with an interesting look at Japanese religious practices. Unlike some of Tokyo's more tourist-heavy temples, Fukagawa Fudo Temple has a local feel, allowing visitors to observe rituals that are deeply rooted in tradition.

Another fascinating spot to explore is the Gotokuji Temple, known as the birthplace of the "maneki-neko" or "beckoning cat" figurine. Located in Setagaya Ward, Gotokuji Temple is famous for its large collection of white cat statues, believed to bring good luck. Rows upon rows of these cats fill the temple grounds, creating a whimsical and unique sight. The temple itself is peaceful and quiet, and visitors often leave small cat figurines as offerings, contributing to the temple's collection. Gotokuji Temple's connection to the iconic maneki-neko makes it an intriguing place for tourists who are interested in Japanese folklore and lucky symbols.

The Koishikawa Korakuen Garden, though not completely unknown, is often less visited than other famous gardens in Tokyo. This traditional landscape garden, located near the Tokyo Dome, dates back to the Edo period and is one of Tokyo's oldest gardens. Designed to reflect both Chinese and Japanese landscaping styles, Koishikawa Korakuen features ponds, bridges, and carefully placed stones that create a tranquil atmosphere. The garden's layout was inspired by famous landscapes, and visitors will notice elements that represent mountains, rivers, and lakes. Koishikawa Korakuen is especially beautiful during autumn and spring, when the trees change colors and flowers bloom. This garden provides a quiet place for reflection and is a wonderful example of traditional Japanese garden design.

Tokyo's hidden treasures reveal a side of the city that is often missed by tourists focused on major attractions. Exploring these off-the-beaten-path places allows visitors to discover Tokyo's quieter, more traditional side, where the pace of life slows down and the city's cultural depth becomes more evident. These unique places not only offer stunning views and memorable experiences but also provide a deeper understanding of Tokyo's history, customs, and daily life. For tourists who wish to go beyond the usual spots and explore

Tokyo in a more personal and intimate way, these lesser-known areas present a rewarding adventure that captures the essence of Japan's enduring charm.

Lesser-Known Attractions and Local Secrets

Tokyo is a city where modern skyscrapers stand side by side with traditional temples, and crowded shopping districts give way to quiet, hidden corners. While many visitors flock to popular attractions such as the Tokyo Skytree, Shibuya Crossing, and Senso-ji Temple, there are lesser-known sites and local secrets tucked away across the city. These places offer unique insights into Tokyo's local culture, history, and everyday life, allowing tourists to experience the city in a more personal way.

One of these lesser-known attractions is Shibamata, a charming neighborhood located on the eastern edge of Tokyo. Shibamata feels as if it has been preserved in time, with its traditional wooden shops, narrow streets, and old-fashioned atmosphere. The area is famous for Taishakuten Temple, a Buddhist temple known for its intricate wooden carvings that depict scenes from Buddhist scriptures. Visitors to Shibamata can walk along Taishakuten Sando, a lively street leading up to the temple, lined with small shops selling sweets, souvenirs, and handmade goods. The street offers a nostalgic look at Tokyo's past, as vendors display their goods in a way that hasn't changed much in decades. Shibamata is also home to the Yamamoto-tei, a beautifully preserved Japanese-style residence with a serene garden that overlooks a koi pond. This peaceful setting offers visitors a quiet space to relax and appreciate traditional Japanese architecture, far from the city's usual crowds.

Another hidden gem is Kyu-Iwasaki-tei Gardens, a historical residence and garden in the Ueno area. Built in the late 19th century for the Iwasaki family, founders of the Mitsubishi conglomerate, this Western-style mansion is a unique example of Meiji-era architecture. The residence combines Western and Japanese design elements, with rooms decorated in European styles and traditional Japanese tatami rooms. The garden surrounding the mansion is meticulously maintained and provides a beautiful setting for a stroll, especially in spring and autumn when the seasonal colors are most vibrant. Unlike other popular gardens, Kyu-Iwasaki-tei remains relatively quiet, making it an ideal spot for visitors who want to experience historical architecture in a peaceful environment.

For those interested in Tokyo's artistic side, the 3331 Arts Chiyoda is a lesser-known but highly creative space that should not be missed. Located in a repurposed junior high school building in the Akihabara district, 3331 Arts Chiyoda is an independent arts center that showcases contemporary Japanese art, photography, and experimental projects. The center features exhibition rooms, artist studios, and spaces for community events, allowing visitors to see Tokyo's modern art scene in an informal and interactive setting. Each floor of the building offers different experiences, with installations and exhibits that change regularly, providing something new with each visit. The relaxed and inviting atmosphere makes it easy to explore, and tourists can often meet and talk with artists who work within the building. This creative hub is a true hidden gem, offering a glimpse into Tokyo's vibrant art community away from the mainstream museums.

Another intriguing location that most tourists overlook is Shimokitazawa, a neighborhood known for its bohemian atmosphere, independent shops, and vintage clothing stores. Shimokitazawa has a relaxed vibe that attracts young people and artists, and its narrow streets are filled with small cafes, record shops, and quirky boutiques. Visitors can find unique items here, from second-hand clothes to handmade jewelry, giving the area a distinctive charm that feels worlds away from Tokyo's more commercial districts. Shimokitazawa is also known for its small theaters and live music venues, where tourists can experience Tokyo's indie music scene up close. This neighborhood is ideal for those who enjoy exploring offbeat places, as it offers a sense of community and creativity that is hard to find in larger shopping districts.

For travelers interested in Tokyo's spiritual side, the Oiwa Inari Shrine in Yotsuya is a little-known shrine with a fascinating story. Dedicated to Oiwa, a figure from Japanese folklore who is believed to be a spirit of revenge, this shrine has a somewhat eerie reputation. According to legend, Oiwa was wronged and her spirit has been worshiped for centuries to avoid misfortune. The shrine itself is peaceful, with stone statues and a shaded pathway leading to the main altar. People come here to pray for protection and to pay their respects, making it a meaningful place for those interested in Japanese myths and legends. Unlike larger shrines, Oiwa Inari is seldom crowded, allowing visitors to take their time and experience the quiet, slightly mysterious atmosphere.

The Nihon Minka-en (Japan Open-Air Folk House Museum) offers another unique experience, allowing visitors to explore traditional Japanese houses from various regions of Japan. Located in the suburban city of Kawasaki, this open-air museum showcases a collection of historical houses, farm buildings, and tea houses that have been relocated and preserved. Each building reflects the traditional architectural styles of different regions, with thatched roofs, wooden beams, and tatami floors. Walking through the museum feels like stepping into Japan's rural past, and visitors can learn about the lifestyle and craftsmanship of previous generations. This museum is a hidden treasure for anyone interested in Japan's architectural heritage and provides a glimpse into the country's diverse cultural history.

Tokyo also has a thriving café culture that extends beyond the usual chain coffee shops. Places like the Mori Ogai Memorial Museum Café, located in the former residence of a famous Japanese writer, offer a unique blend of history and relaxation. Visitors can enjoy a quiet cup of coffee while surrounded by historical artifacts and literary displays, making it a perfect stop for book lovers and those who enjoy peaceful environments. The café's connection to literature and its tranquil setting give it a special appeal that is rarely found in typical tourist locations.

One more local secret is the Golden Gai area in Shinjuku, a maze of narrow alleys packed with tiny bars and eateries.

Golden Gai is famous among Tokyo locals for its unique charm, as each establishment has its own theme, from jazz bars to retro-style pubs. Many of the bars are small, seating only a handful of people, which gives the area an intimate and welcoming feel. Although Golden Gai is gradually becoming more popular with tourists, it still retains a local atmosphere where people come to relax, enjoy drinks, and socialize. For tourists looking to experience Tokyo's nightlife in a cozy, authentic setting, Golden Gai offers an unforgettable experience.

Tokyo's lesser-known attractions provide an opportunity to experience the city's authentic side, where history, art, spirituality, and modern culture blend seamlessly. These hidden spots not only offer unique sights and experiences but also allow visitors to connect with Tokyo on a more personal level. Exploring these local secrets reveals the quieter, more intricate side of Tokyo, offering tourists a chance to go beyond the city's famous landmarks and discover its hidden depths.

CONCLUSION

Tokyo is a city that offers an extraordinary blend of modern wonders and ancient traditions, bustling attractions and hidden treasures. This travel guide has taken you through both iconic landmarks and lesser-known spots, providing insights into the many layers that make Tokyo a captivating destination for every kind of traveler.

As you venture into Tokyo, remember that the true essence of this city often lies beyond the major tourist sites, in the quiet streets of neighborhoods like Yanaka, the artistic vibes of Shimokitazawa, and the unassuming beauty of places like Kiyosumi Garden or the serene paths of Todoroki Valley. Tokyo's character is woven from a tapestry of experiences, and its people and places warmly welcome those who take the time to understand its unique blend of past and present.

Whether you are here to witness the spring cherry blossoms, enjoy the city's vibrant food scene, or simply wander through Tokyo's rich history and culture, this city has something for everyone. Embrace the chance to discover new sights, engage with local customs, and perhaps find a few favorite spots that you can carry home as cherished memories. May this guide help you uncover the heart of Tokyo and inspire you to experience the city with curiosity, respect, and wonder. Safe travels, and enjoy every moment of your Tokyo journey.

EVELYN BLAIR.

27810801R10219